Truth and Interpretation

SUNY series in Contemporary Italian Philosophy

Silvia Benso and Brian Schroeder, editors

Truth and Interpretation

Luigi Pareyson

Translated and with an Introduction by
Robert T. Valgenti

Revised and Edited by
Silvia Benso

Foreword by
Gianni Vattimo

SUNY PRESS

Published by State University of New York Press, Albany

Printed in the United States of America

For information, contact State University of New York Press, Albany, NY
www.sunypress.edu

Production by Eileen Nizer
Marketing by Fran Keneston

Library of Congress Cataloging-in-Publication Data

Pareyson, Luigi.
[Verità e interpretazione. English]
Truth and interpretation / Luigi Pareyson ; translated and with an introduction by Robert T. Valgenti ; revised and edited by Silvia Benso; foreword by Gianni Vattimo.
pages cm — (Suny series in contemporary Italian philosophy)
Includes bibliographical references and index.
ISBN 978-1-4384-4749-0 (hardcover) ISBN 978-1-4384-4750-6 (paperback)
1. Truth. 2. Ideology. I. Valgenti, Robert T. II. Title.

BD171.P3713 2013
121—dc23 2012037054

10 9 8 7 6 5 4 3 2 1

Contents

Acknowledgments vii

Translator's Note ix

Foreword xi
Gianni Vattimo

Translator's Introduction: Luigi Pareyson's Vindication of Philosophy xvii
Robert T. Valgenti

TRUTH AND INTERPRETATION

Preface 3

Introduction: Expressive Thought and Revelatory Thought 13

PART I: TRUTH AND HISTORY

1. Permanent Values and Historical Process 31

2. The Originarity of Interpretation 47

PART II: TRUTH AND IDEOLOGY

3. Philosophy and Ideology 81

4. The Destiny of Ideology 113

Part III: Truth and Philosophy

5. The Necessity of Philosophy 167

6. Philosophy and Common Sense 185

Bibliography 205

Index 207

Acknowledgments

There are many who have been instrumental to the idea and execution of this long-overdue translation. In particular I would like to thank Claudio Ciancio, Marco Ravera, Maurizio Pagano, Francesco Tomatis, Gianluca Cuozzo, Ezio Gamba, and all those at the Centro Studi Filosofico-Religiosi "Luigi Pareyson" in Turin, whose generosity, time, and resources in 2001 and again in 2005 helped to initiate this project; the Department of Philosophy at DePaul University, and the Office of Academic Affairs at Lebanon Valley College, who in varying stages of this project provided the time and financial support necessary for this work; my colleagues in the Department of Religion and Philosophy at Lebanon Valley College—Noel Hubler, Jeffrey W. Robbins, Noëlle Vahanian, and Matthew Sayers—who deserve special recognition for creating and supporting an environment where such work can thrive; Anthony Feudale, for his careful and timely work on the index; and Gaetano Chiurazzi and Santiago Zabala, who have served as trustworthy guides and colleagues in this long process. Of course, I am indebted to Gianni Vattimo, who many years ago first suggested I study his teacher Pareyson and undertake this translation, and whose mentorship over the years has been invaluable and inspiring. I especially want to thank Silvia Benso for her expert and patient editing of this text, which was absolutely essential to the successful translation of Pareyson's profound and often difficult thinking.

Translator's Note

In the following translation I have tried to remain true to the language and intent of Pareyson's original. When appropriate, I have provided the original Italian word in brackets to indicate a particularly difficult and/or important term in the work. I have retained Pareyson's original notes, placing them at the end of each of the work's sections. When possible, I have provided the English-language references and translation of quotations, placing those in brackets in his notes. Where Pareyson's original included non-Italian words or quotations, I have retained the original Greek, Latin, German, or French but provided the appropriate translation: from extant English translations if available, or in certain cases, my own translation.

Foreword

Gianni Vattimo

Translated by Silvia Benso

"There are no facts but only interpretations. And this too is an interpretation." Most likely, Luigi Pareyson would have never subscribed to this famous claim by Nietzsche although (considering myself loyal to his philosophy) I think that he should have at least confronted it.

We speak, however, from a place that is only partially still similar to the one from which Pareyson spoke, in the early seventies of the last century. What we share with the original situation of his *Truth and Interpretation* is what I consider to be the still unsurpassable timeliness of hermeneutics.

What we experience today, and was not equally present in the cultural climate of forty years ago, is probably a hardening of the realm of facts. This circumstance reduces some of the urgency of Pareyson's rejection of "praxis" and of the enslavement of philosophy to politics in order to defend instead the transcendence and eternity of truth.

We should not forget that *Truth and Interpretation* was originally published in Italian in 1970, that is, immediately after the protest movements that had occurred in universities (and later in factories) throughout the Western world starting in 1968. Not without some good reason, Pareyson suspected (and of a similar mind was also an intellectual such as Pier Paolo Pasolini) that the youth protest movement was merely a way of asserting one's right to a more consumerist society, more tolerant but certainly also more "American" and subjected to the rules of dominating monopolistic capitalism. The student movement's proposal of a reformation of the university system seemed to him (and to us) to be in the end inspired by an American, productivistic model that risked destroying, together with the "university chair barons" [*i baroni delle cattedre*], also the patrimony of typically European values. It is not by chance that, some years later, one of Bush's ministers would scornfully dismiss such values as things belonging to "old Europe," no longer fit for the modern world (of the Iraqi and Afghan wars).

Already at that time, Pareyson's position in those years (and on those issues) seemed to me to be the view of an enlightened conservative—whom I always respected since I knew of his anti-fascist involvement (he had been part of the Italian Resistance movement against Fascism and the Nazis when he was a high school teacher in Cuneo), but whose political convictions I could not share. In his insistence on the transcendence and eternity of truth, which he coupled with the great claim that "*of truth, there is only ever interpretation,* and . . . *there is no interpretation, lest it be of truth*" (*Truth and Interpretation*, p. 47), I forebode, and perceive even more clearly today, the persistence of a metaphysical residue that will be more frankly dissolved, I think, in his later "ontology of freedom."

When thinking of Pareyson's lesson today, the question I once again ask myself is this: Can we think of hermeneutics in such radical terms as his ("of truth, there is only ever interpretation, etc.") and not assert at the same time, as Pareyson conversely did, the transcendence and eternity of truth?

What I name, or what appears to me as a metaphysical residue in Pareyson's philosophy of those years is the fact of still thinking of truth as "substance," that is, in the end as a permanent "being," somewhat like the "existing" God of Christian dogmatics. A thesis that Pareyson probably never considered is the one expressed in Dietrich Bonhoeffer's famous claim that "*Einen Gott den es gibt, gibt es nicht* [a God that exists, does not exist]." The question that I still ask Pareyson, and that I ask myself as his reader and disciple, is: What do transcendence and eternity of truth mean if truth gives itself only in interpretation—that is, in interpretations that occur historically . . . ?

The answer remains the same as that which Pareyson offered ever since the time of his aesthetic theory as theory of formativity: In artistic making, and truly in all forms of human invention, something entirely new happens that, however, is neither arbitrariness nor subjective contingency, but rather implies the presence of something else that, like "the forming form," guides the act of concrete formation. Briefly, according to Pareyson we must acknowledge that when artists create, they also and always correct and change under the guidance of the law of the thing itself, as it were, which transcends the artist's arbitrariness and the contingency of the circumstances. In Heideggerian terms, we can speak of an event of being, which, as is well known, for Heidegger occurs eminently in the work of art (the putting to work of truth). That an event is an event of being, opening of a new way of being's self-giving (and thus happening of a new paradigm, of a new epoch) can be said only afterward. Likewise, a great "classic" artwork can be recognized only when it has become such, in a happening that is not contained in its origin or in the initiative of its author.

I propose that we should think of the relation between truth and interpretation in Pareyson along similar lines: There is no truth except than in the interpretative event, which is always historically situated; yet interpretation is such only if, as is the case for the artwork, it "succeeds." This is so first of all in the sense that interpretation is true only if it does not claim to replace truth, its unicity, and transcendence. Unicity and transcendence operate here not so much as positive, substantial features of a truth that gives itself (as in the "*es gibt*" that Bonhoeffer excludes) but rather as negative prescriptions: The one that claims to be unique and definitive is not true interpretation "because truth can assert its own unicity and atemporality only within each of the individual formulations that it obtains and collects, or better, provokes and demands" (*Truth and Interpretation*, p. 55). The analogy with the success of an artwork seems to me undeniable here. As for the artwork, here too the transcendent element, the law of the artwork that cannot be reduced to the artist's subjective will, is announced and can be perceived only in someone else's reception. The ontological rooting, that is, the meaning of the work or the interpretation within the history of being (to maintain the Heideggerian terminology), is all in the cogency that each interpreter perceives in the interpretative act (and, beforehand, that the artist perceives in the creation) and that holds true for any of the multiple formulations of such truth.

We are not that far here from a possible reading of the happening of truth of which Heidegger speaks, a happening that is possible "ever since we are a conversation": *seitdem wir ein Gespräch sind*, as Hölderlin says. We are not that far either from a very sensible resonance with the Christian doctrine of the Incarnation, both in terms of the sense of a purely negative proscription of the unicity and atemporality of the truth, and in terms of God's giving himself in his son who was concretely born and lived among us. What is here suggested, and even more than suggested, are reasons to think that the possible "metaphysical" reading of the concept of truth in Pareyson should be limited by or definitely replaced with an "event-like" conception of truth. If there is no truth except in its interpretations, truth is not something that stands somewhere on its own ever since the beginning and forever after; truth lives only in interpretations that are such only if they involve the interpreters through the cogency with which they demand that they are understood.

We can thus return to the different historical collocation of us interpreters in comparison with the situation in which Pareyson thought and acted forty years ago. The urgency he felt was one presented by a society seemingly threatened with chaos and the connected risk of losing the characteristic values of European, liberal, and Christian humanism. Today such values, and especially those of peace and solidarity, are equally threatened—no longer by the disorder of a very charged youth or workers' protest, but rather by the fact that some sort of a resigned acceptation of the status quo, no matter what it is, has been established; recurrent crises are matched with restorative adjustments that reestablish the same conditions that have provoked such crises. This is what Heidegger calls the absence of emergency. Nothing emerges, nothing truly happens at the level of the modes of collective existence, at least not in the late industrial world of the West, of the *Abenland*, the land of the sunset, as Heidegger calls it. Everyone is simply worried with preserving the actual conditions out of fear of an impending worse situation. I think that mainly out of these reasons today we are, we feel less sensitive toward the metaphysical temptation of identifying truth and what transcends and lasts for eternity, and are instead more worried about the concrete happening of truth in dialogue and in those few conflicts that still find a way within the overall silence.

The condition of absence of emergency, that is, absence of an event (in an ontological sense), is deeply determined by fear—fear of international terrorism, of the loss of one's job—and also by the multiculturalism of a globalized society that has been constructed mainly through the will of the great economic world powers. One of the elements in the fear that today dominates Western masses is "the others." To them, often usurping "Christian values," one opposes our own absolute truth, namely the great Western civilization that should be able to resist the new barbarism. It is increasingly evident that truth can happen only if and as long as "we are a conversation," as Hölderlin has already been mentioned to say.

I am simply trying to explain, first of all to myself, why today Pareyson should be read without all the "metaphysical" implications that, at the time of the book publication, were perhaps a temptation also for him. The book, as I think can be claimed also on the ground of the passages I have referred to, authorizes and demands, or at least suggests, my interpretative proposal. This is legitimated even more by taking into consideration the further development of Pareyson's thought, as is attested in the writings collected in the later volume *Ontologia della libertà* [*Ontology of Freedom*]. The act of freedom that we must acknowledge, or at least postulate, as origin of the freedom we experience within our own existence is precisely an event more than a substance (from which no freedom but merely a consequence obtained *more geometrico* could derive). This very event is the outcome of its own self-position as victory over nothingness, as Pareyson argues with reference to his beloved Schelling. Also and precisely when it is read in these terms, Pareyson's ontological hermeneutics reveals itself as an interpretation capable of being historically valid even for us, thereby asserting its very truth.

Translator's Introduction

Luigi Pareyson's Vindication of Philosophy

Robert T. Valgenti

> Scientific truth is impersonal and demonstrable: it would thus be absurd to want to die for it. . . . Philosophical truth, on the other hand, is personal and decisive: affirming it means that one is ready to die for it.[1]

This translation of Luigi Pareyson's *Truth and Interpretation,* now more than twenty years after his passing, is somewhat overdue but perhaps never more timely. *Truth and Interpretation* fulfills many roles: It sets forth a philosophical hermeneutics that stands shoulder to shoulder with, and in its origins predates, the well-known theories of Hans-Georg Gadamer and Paul Ricoeur; it marks the mature articulation of a theory of interpretation that has roots in existential personalism and draws its influence from figures as wide-ranging as Plotinus, Schelling, Vico and Heidegger; it expresses the theoretical struggles of post-war Italy (and in fact, the broader scope of Europe) by carving out a philosophical space

1. All quotations are from this translation of *Truth and Interpretation* unless otherwise noted.

between the dogmatic force of ideologies and the decentering vortices of the various species of relativism; and most importantly, in a way that is truly *attuale* and indicative of our concerns today, *Truth and Interpretation* stands as a resolute defense of philosophy, a claim for its relevance in human affairs and its ability to resist the destructive forces that beset it (and, in fact, humanity) from all sides. The goal of this introduction is to highlight the importance of this particular trajectory in Pareyson's thinking—his resolute vindication [*rivendicazione*] of truth and philosophy—in the face of the influences today that threaten to undermine its legitimacy or usurp its unique and powerful role.

If Pareyson's vindication of philosophy has a signature feature, a guiding thread from its existentialist beginnings in the 1940s to the emblematic "Ontology of Freedom" of his later years, it is the setting of incommensurable opposites into fertile dialogue. How is it that universality and particularity, unity and plurality, freedom and necessity, theory and practice, revelation and expression, truth and interpretation (to name only a few) are thought simultaneously and productively without lapsing into the spurious infinity of conflicting interpretations, or being resolved in a totalizing worldview? How can life be viewed as something other than a choice between such conceptual extremes, a perpetual dilemma whose successful resolution (or complete overcoming, violently or not) has been falsely set up as the criterion for its effectiveness? Pareyson's philosophy is a firm response to this sort of conceptual blackmail and in fact finds, in the face of these apparent impasses to thinking, the originary grounds for philosophical dialogue.

Although such an itinerary is certainly not the most common in the secondary literature dedicated to Pareyson, it nonetheless underscores what I believe to be the particular relevance of a work like *Truth and Interpretation* today: that in the face of radical skepticism and political dogmatism, of moral relativism and religious fanaticism, philosophy has the particular task of articulating why these forms of extremism taken on their own are neither viable nor desirable. Philosophy examines and celebrates truth as the measure for a *lived* life in all fields of human activity by offering an alternative to the measures that constrain and manipulate the positive possibilities of human existence. As is apparent in this book, the relation of "truth" and "interpretation" is neither one of simple opposition, nor one of equivalence. The relation is one of mutual dependence—necessity—and yet simultaneously one that is independent and freely chosen. As Pareyson most emblematically states it: "This means that *of truth, there is only ever interpretation,* and that *there is no interpretation, lest it be of truth. . . .* Interpretation is that form of knowledge that is *at one and the same time* and inseparably truth-bearing and historical, ontological and personal, revelatory and expressive" (47). It is the very nature of the person that ensures the formulation of truth never reaches a point of closure. Moreover, the stewardship of the relation between truth and interpretation falls into the critical yet caring hands of philosophy, which by its very nature encourages the open search for truth and the steadfast commitment to its necessarily multiple and personal formulations.

1. Origins of Interpretation

Luigi Pareyson was born in Piasco, Italy, a small town west of Torino in the province of Cuneo, in 1918. In 1935, he began his studies at the University of Turin, eventually working under the aegis of Augusto Guzzo, with whom he completed his *laurea* thesis in 1939 on the existential philosophy of Karl Jaspers. In the summers during his years of study in Torino he traveled to Germany, where he first read the works of Jaspers, Karl Barth, Martin Heidegger, Søren Kierkegaard, and Piero Martinetti. In Heidelberg he had frequent conversations with Jaspers, and in September 1937 he was even a guest at Heidegger's home in Freiburg. It was in 1938, however, that he was first noticed for his philosophical gifts by his teacher Guzzo, who suggested to Giovanni Gentile that he publish the young Pareyson's remarkably acute and profound analysis of Jaspers and Heidegger in his *Giornale critico della filosofia italiana*.[2]

From the very beginning of his career, Pareyson saw his philosophical work as necessarily intertwined with all human activities, including the political—a fact due as much to his philosophical views as to the onset of war in 1940.[3] During the war years, Pareyson was an active member of the Action Party [*Partito d'Azione*] and the broader anti-fascist resistance movement in the Piedmont region of Italy, where he crossed paths with notable philosophers of his generation and future colleagues

2. Pareyson's essay, "Note sulla filosofia dell'esistenza," *Giornale critico della filosofia italiana*, 1938, 6, 407–438, later becomes part of his *Studi sull'esistenzialismo* (1943), now published in the series of Pareyson's complete works: vol. 3 (Milan: Mursia, 2001).

3. For many of the details related to this period of Pareyson's life I am particularly indebted to the chronology of events assembled by Francesco Tomatis in *Pareyson: Vita, filosofia, bibliographia* (Brescia: Editrice Morcelliana, 2003).

at the University of Torino also engaged in the resistance: Enzo Paci and Pietro Chiodi, among others. From 1940 to 1944, he was the professor of philosophy, history, and political economy at the Liceo Classico Silvio Pellico in Cuneo. With many of his former students actively involved in the resistance, Pareyson conducted lessons on philosophy and politics with selected graduates, instructing them so that they could spread the anti-fascist doctrine through the Action Party's underground publications. Pareyson wrote philosophical, as well as political, essays and texts at this time, and in 1944 was taken into custody for his work against the fascists until a local priest vouched for his name and had him released. His teaching was, however, suspended until the war's end.

Although Pareyson managed to write and present a good deal of material on the various themes and figures of existentialism during this period, his anonymous publications[4] for the Action Party offered substantial insight into the various themes and itineraries that would guide him through the remainder of his career. In an early essay entitled "Angoscia o Rischio?" ["Anxiety or Risk?"], Pareyson set forth a picture of the philosophical life that not only distinguished the unique character of his (and perhaps all Italian) existential thinking, but more importantly brought the relevance and timeliness of true philosophical thinking to the fore. Philosophical investigation is more than concrete: It is "life itself," life that is truly lived in a manner that is "decisive" and fully aware of the degree to which each of us, as individuals invested in life, are always faced with possibilities: "Only through self-reflection can life truly take on its most profound meaning and assume its 'decisive' character for the one who lives it."[5] Although certainly in its most nascent form, Pareyson's understanding of the life lived in an ontologically profound manner embodied the union of incommensurable opposites in a fruitful and profound instance of reflection. For Pareyson, the task of philosophizing, in these early existential terms, was "the coincidence of theoretical speculation and practical action, as it neither grasps philosophy in the abstract nature of pure theory, nor does it assume life in the spontaneity of mere acting, but penetrates, uncovers and scrutinizes the *problematicity of existence*."[6] The philosopher faced a decisive confrontation with the gravity and risk of

4. These writings are now gathered in Luigi Pareyson, *Iniziativa e libertà*, (complete works vol. 3) edited by Francesco Tomatis, (Milan: Mursia, 2005).

5. Pareyson. "Angoscia o rischio" in *Iniziativa e libertà*, 18–19.

6. Ibid., 19.

life such that "by making the risk-filled decision of one's own destiny, one will know how to say astutely with Plato: *kalos gar ho kindunos* (*Phaedo*, 114d)."[7] That the key to a concrete, decisive, and ultimately "lived" life is profound self-reflection on the necessity and risk of human freedom presages the central role that philosophy, as a specific and essential mode of human being, will play across the broad spectrum of Pareyson's works.

If the predominant direction of Italian thinking before the war was embodied in the works of Benedetto Croce and Giovanni Gentile, who despite their varying agendas, attempted to eliminate any notion of transcendence from philosophy and to rescue an immanent conception of Spirit from the heritage of Hegelian thought, the philosophical conversation in Italy after the war split into a number of autonomous factions that embraced Catholic, Marxist, and secular (or "neo-enlightenment") agendas.[8] Pareyson's Italian influences can be traced back to the transcendent spiritualism of Martinetti, and more directly, the Christian thought of figures like Guzzo and Armando Carlini. This soon developed, however, into a critical and hermeneutic study of *Existenzphilosophie*[9] that not only widened the conversation to include the broader panorama of existentialism in both its religious and secular forms, but also sought to correct the shortcomings of thinkers who did not take the individuality of the person in its most radical sense.

For Pareyson, existentialism was the philosophy of *crisis* in the distinct sense that "Existentialism expresses that sense of depression, of prostration, of disorientation that seems to characterize contemporary consciousness."[10] The key figures of existentialism each recognized the crisis

7. Ibid., 21. The Socratic appeal to the "noble risk" of philosophy is invoked once again in Pareyson's preface to *Truth and Interpretation*.

8. For a thorough and insightful explanation of the philosophical climate in Italy in the decades after World War II, see Maurizio Pagano, "The Confrontation between Secular and Religious Thought" in *Contemporary Italian Philosophy*, eds. Silvia Benso and Brian Schroeder (Albany: State University of New York Press, 2007), 1–13. For the particular history of hermeneutic thought in Italy during the same period, see Franco Bianco, "L'ermeneutica in Italia dal 1945 ad oggi" in *Rivista di Filosofia*, vol LXXIX, no. 2–3, August–December, 1988, pp. 459–490.

9. Two main texts are of note during this stage: the recently expanded and republished *Studi sull'esistenzialismo* in *Opere Complete*, vol. 2, ed. Claudio Ciancio (Milan; Mursia, 2001), originally published in 1943; and, *Karl Jaspers* (Genoa: Marietti, 1997), originally published in 1940.

10. *Esistenza e persona*, 79.

(Heidegger's end of metaphysics; Jasper's understanding of faith and thinking that finds itself within humanity; Marcel's natural foundation for the sacred; and Sartre's heroic conception of life and human destiny), but each one failed to recognize a crucial point: Whereas existentialism is more than a mere expression of the crisis and offers a key to interpret the crisis, it is ultimately incapable of resolving it. In particular, Pareyson explained that the existential philosophies of both Heidegger and Jaspers fail to grant the person the freedom required to develop a full relation with Being: "In both, the person is negated by necessity: for Heidegger due to the necessity of structure, for Jaspers, through the necessity of fate."[11] Pareyson positioned himself between the two thinkers and contended that if existence is truly the coincidence of the relation to one's self [*autorelazione*] and the relation to the other [*eterorelazione*], the two relations are actually one and there should be no friction between relation to self and relation to Being.[12] Pareyson confronted this relation through his philosophy of the person, a theoretical itinerary that he described as "a passage from existentialism to ontological personalism" and that even at this early stage identified interpretation as the form of thinking that avoids the reductive tendencies of transcendental formalism and unavoidable fatalism.

2. Ontological Personalism

Pareyson's early critical and historiographic explorations of *Existenzphilosophie* developed throughout the 1940s into a distinct "ontology of the person" presented in his 1950 work, *Esistenza e persona* [*Existence and Person*]. Pareyson's reflection took as its starting point the Kierkegaardian problem of the person as the coincidence of the relation to one's self and to the other, particularly as it evolved out of the dissolution of Hegelianism and rational metaphysics.[13] The overarching theoretical concern is, once

11. Ibid., 167.

12. See Francesco Paolo Ciglia, *Ermeneutica e libertà: L'itinerario filosofico di Luigi Pareyson* (Rome: Bulzoni, 1995), 31–35.

13. The dissolution of Hegelian idealism—an act Pareyson most clearly associated with Ludwig Feuerbach and Søren Kierkegaard—is a powerful current within Pareyson's early thinking and places him well within the Italian milieu of post-World War II responses to the idealism of figures such as Gentile and Croce. On the dissolution of Hegelianism, see Pareyson, *Esistenza e persona*, 41–76; on the anti-Idealism of post-war Italian philosophy, see Luca Bagetto, *Il Pensiero della possibilità. La filosofia torinese come storia della filosofia*, 3–11 and F. Bianco, "L'ermeneutica in Italia dal 1945 ad oggi."

again, the seeming incommensurability of two opposites—the finite and the infinite, singularity and universality, particularity and totality, and so on—in which Pareyson found the origin for a philosophy of the person that embraces the infinite scope of possibilities, breathes new life into finite human experience, and defends the ability of philosophy to engage alterity.

"The person" [*la persona*] is the concept of the individual as the lived synthesis of singularity and universality, a universal *constituted through* the individual process of interpretation. The "personality" [*personalità*] of the person differs from the epistemic formality of the Kantian subject and the existential formality of Heidegger's *Dasein* through that person's recognition of its own historicity, its self-constitution as an ever-forming "work" [*opera*], and most importantly, its respect for and dependence on alterity as a source of self-knowledge. The person is a work that stands, at any moment, within its own completion while simultaneously finding continual development in a process of open-ended formation. The person, as a work in process, constitutes its existence historically ("historizes" or *geschieht*)[14] but is more than a mere expression of the limits of its own time. The person's "work," therefore, is unique and singular, yet also "universal" as the realization of a historical value. "Universal" does not signify "general" or "absolute," but a "universally recognizable validity" [*validità omniriconoscibile*][15] that places its shared traits, rather than the rupture of the heterogeneous encounter with the other, at the center of the act of interpretation. The universality of the work, constituted through the singularity of the person, is not an abstract and depersonalized project but something that is always already an "initiated initiative" within a temporal process of development. The truly philosophical character of this initiative emerges through a powerful "exercise of alterity" that resists, in the process of knowing, the complete subordination of the other to one's own understanding.

In "the uncertain adventure of the encounter," the knowledge of others thus has all the characteristics of *interpretation*, that is, of "a knowledge in which subject and object are individuals and in which the object reveals itself according to the degree that the subject expresses itself, and of a knowledge that attains its goal always with the risk of failure, and that, far from being unique and definitive, can only present itself as the result of a continual exercise of revision and deepening."[16]

14. Pareyson's analysis of Heidegger picks up on this very terminology. See Pareyson, *Studi sull'esistenzialismo*, 160.

15. Pareyson, *Esistenza e persona*, 176.

16. Ibid., 211.

This hermeneutic entails a *solidarity* that "contains together the *duty* of judging and being judged in the name of the universal, the *need* and the *right* of being understood by others, and a solicitation to modify itself according to a mutual *call* to the laws of universal reason. Knowledge of others implies an *exercise of freedom* as dialogue, conversation, interpretation, understanding, the exertion of placing oneself in the point of view of others."[17] Although self-knowledge looks more toward the openness of the future, the corresponding knowledge of others looks more toward the completed past; both exchange and prolong one another in a dialogue of freedom and historical substance. Knowledge of others is in this mode possible only due to the universality of human interpretation, which, in one way, relies on the individuality of the person's perspective, and in another way, relies on the other who demands our most attentive listening. Such interpretation is the discovery of our solidarity *as* humans in dialogue with other humans, as co-creators of knowledge rather than as its instruments.

As an exercise of finitude, interpretation is always an active and performative process because the individuality of the person makes its own historical situation[18] an instrument for indicating and revealing truth. This productivity, which invents and formulates plans, verifies their adequacy, and brings them to fruition in an organic and living form is a free and voluntary action defined primarily by a constant listening and attentiveness. The situation is therefore not a fixed closure (as historicism might interpret it), but a metaphysical positioning [*collocazione*] that interprets passivity as a horizon of existence and a relation with Being.

17. Ibid., 212.

18. By "situation," Pareyson has specifically in mind, ". . . *die Stellung des Menschen im Kosmos*, as Max Scheler says, the place of the human being in the cosmos; not only its historical position, but also its ontological position. In this sense, the human being is a relation: not that it is in relation, or that it has a relation, but is a relation, more precisely a relation with Being (an ontological relation), a relation with the other (intentionality, that is, Husserlian intentionality deepened through ontology). And in this relation, a relation that is the human being itself, one finds human beings' existentiality, individuality, and historicity. Thus situation has not only a historical aspect, but also an ontological one: it is not only the 'border' of existence, but an opening to Being; not a limitation, but a means for access; it has a personal-historical and ontological aspect, that is, it is 'expressive' and 'revelatory,' and represents the solidarity of the person and truth, of the person with truth." See Luigi Pareyson, *Ontologia della libertà: il male e la sofferenza* (Turin: Einaudi, 1995), 10.

In contrast to the history of metaphysical rationalism, most notably that of Hegel, Pareyson explained that finitude cannot be interpreted according to the category of totality, but only according to the "dialectic of positivity and insufficiency, in which the finitude of the human being manifests itself in the fact that it is positive, but not to the point of being sufficient; and insufficient, but not to the point of being negative."[19] There is no possibility for a direct relation with the infinite; there is rather the basis for a relation between finite and infinite based on the existential and hermeneutic character of the person. This claim rests on two ontological premises: The first, that Being is inexhaustible and allows for an infinite production of relationships or interpretations; and the second, that human reality can only ever be lived through a multiplicity of relations with Being: "the relation to Being is not a property or a faculty or a possibility of human beings, but it is their very *being*."[20] To affirm the ontological opening and the hermeneutic nature of all human existence signifies that for the person, "situation" is ultimately a *metaphysical* placement that demands the freedom (and thus responsibility) of the person to provide an individual perspective on truth and Being.[21] This relation to Being, defined paradoxically by its positivity *and* its insufficiency, characterizes the inexhaustibility of the ontological "opening" that rests at the core of Pareyson's hermeneutics. Although more thoroughly developed in *Truth and Interpretation*, this early formulation of the relation between the person's expression of history and revelation of Being underscores the careful path that Pareyson traced between the rich fore structures of hermeneutics and the revolutionary critiques of ideology, between the dogmatic absolutes of metaphysics and the reductive gestures of relativism.

3. The Art of Interpretation

The development of interpretation as the central feature of human existence also has deep roots in Pareyson's aesthetic theory. Pareyson's *Estetica*[22] argues that the study of aesthetics reveals a movement in thinking

19. *Esitenza e persona*, 242. Pareyson's critique of Hegelianism stretches throughout his corpus and reflects a persistent attention to the dangers of historicism and absolutizing thought.

20. Ibid., 243.

21. Ibid., 244.

22. Luigi Pareyson, *Estetica: teoria della formatività* (Florence: Bompiani, 1954).

that is constitutive of the very being of the human, one that is marked by the risk and responsibility of interpretation. The hermeneutic framework of dialogue between philosophy and experience, thought and deed, sets up the characteristic dialectic of two incommensurables: "In philosophy experience is at the same time the object of reflection and the verification of thought, and thought is at the same time the result and the guide of the interpretation of experience."[23] Interpretation as an active choice or "attempt" [*tentativo*] illustrates the tension between the particular and the universal as a hermeneutic "play" in the process of artistic formation and evaluation. It would be incorrect to claim that the growing ubiquity of interpretation in Pareyson's work suggests a general aestheticization of experience (in the manner theorized by his student Gianni Vattimo).[24] Yet, Pareyson argued that if all experience did not already have something of an aesthetic aspect to it, aesthetics would not be able to distinguish its unique character, one that in Pareyson's broader defense of philosophy involves its ability to reveal, in its unadulterated and shared aspect, the ontological bearing of all human activity.

This shared aspect is *formativity*—a type of doing that, in the course of doing, invents the way of doing. The completed work, as "formed form" [*la forma formata*], is the realization of the process of forming where the form itself accomplishes its intrinsic and self-imposed end. The work of art does not "work" if it is not completing [*compiendo*], executing [*eseguendo*], producing [*producendo*], and achieving [*realizzando*]: "In short, the working [*l'operare*], the activity that it specifies for itself, always involves that process of production and invention that constitutes the forming, and all works, as results, are forms endowed with independence and exemplarity."[25] The production of works is "personal," to build on the distinc-

---

23. Ibid., 15.

24. Vattimo presents the general aestheticization of experience that accompanies the arrival of "weak" thought as a primarily negative phenomenon, as if it were an unavoidable destiny with which the West must grapple; conversely, Pareyson's notion carries a much more positive connotation, as his concept does not contain Vattimo's reading of Heidegger and the end of metaphysics, but merely the possibility of a formative performance in every realm of human activity. For more on Vattimo's position, see his *The Transparent Society* (Baltimore, MD: John Hopkins University Press, 1992) and *The End of Modernity* (Baltimore, MD: John Hopkins University Press, 1989). Also see his chapter "Pareyson: From Aesthetics to Ontology" in *Art's Claim to Truth*, ed. Santiago Zabala (New York: Columbia University Press, 2008), 77–89.

25. *Estetica: teoria della formatività*, 19.

tions outlined above, and takes the person's inimitable perspective as a necessary condition for its development. Moreover, all human activity has a formative character to it: "In the capacity for human industriousness [*operosità*] there is an inventive and innovative side as the premise of every achievement; and so, exactly for this reason, there can be art *in* every human activity, indeed there is an art *to* every human activity."[26] All formative activity is "aesthetic," and therefore worthy of contemplation, whether art proper or performance in the realms of philosophy and morals. To say that all experience, and therefore all human activity has an aesthetic character to it means that all human activity is, at its root, formative, and therefore open to infinite interpretative possibilities while still bound to the finitude of individual commitment.

Estetica contains Pareyson's most direct explanation of interpretation prior to *Truth and Interpretation*. Knowledge [*la conoscenza*] is formative, and "sensible knowledge succeeds in catching the reality of things only as it represents them, and therefore it produces and forms the images of reality."[27] Human knowledge is productive and formative, and its actualization in a finite act of interpretation illustrates once again the productive tension of seeming incommensurables: "Interpreting is that form of knowledge in which, on the one hand, receptivity and activity are indistinguishable, and on the other hand, the known is a form and the knower is a person. . . . Interpreting is seizing, catching, grasping, getting to the heart of the matter."[28] As active and receptive, Pareyson understood that interpretation is not the willing of a vision or perspective on the world: The Pareysonian subject does not have the certainty of a Cartesian *cogito* that stands over and against objects as things-in-themselves, or merely receives their impressions as empirical data. To say that the interpreter forms knowledge is also to say that the knowledge is open to being formed. All human performance, which includes knowledge, arises from within a unique and irreplaceable situation, but produces an interpretation that nonetheless resists any reduction to that situation. Thus, although the act of interpreting is necessary, the form of that interpretation is the product of the interpreter's freedom. Interpretation always presupposes an occasion, event, initiation, or stimulus. It is not known, but rather an issue for the person because its "form" is "something yet to be interpreted."

26. Ibid.

27. Ibid., 179.

28. Ibid., 180.

One might say that human performance is always attuned toward its situation, or that it is active by always being open toward the given conditions of its existence. Receptivity is not passive, but reaches out to lengthen and develop itself. In the end, Pareyson claimed that "knowledge, regarded as the indistinguishable synthesis of receptivity and activity, is precisely, as one says, interpretation."[29] The activity of interpretation "adopts the rhythm of the object,"[30] and that receptivity, as the resonance of the object, prolongs itself in activity. The interpreter, as active, turns openly and outwardly toward the object, allowing the object to impress itself through an actualizing of the receptive potentiality of the subject.

If there is any unique aspect to the interpretative model put forth by Pareyson, it might be its particular ability to resolve the conceptual tension between the finite limits of the interpreter and the infinite possibilities of interpretation—the problem of relativism. It is not just that there is a play between interpreter and interpreted, nor that the prejudices of the interpreter shape the interpretation of the object, and vice versa. The final form, although completed [*compiuto*], is never closed, as within it stand all of the open possibilities and choices that brought it to form. The circle of interpretation is in fact never closed because the interpreter always stands within that very circle and is implicated in the very knowledge that results: It is infinite in the number of ways it can occur as well as in the variety of processes through which it arrives at knowledge. It has an infinity that is both quantitative and qualitative. By this, Pareyson meant that the determinate and unique natures of forms and individuals as things interpreted and things interpreting respectively are what ground the infinity of interpretation: "It is precisely the infinite inexhaustibility of the form and of the individual that grounds the quantitative infinity of interpretation, and it is exactly the fact that no one of the aspects of the individual and of the form is exhaustive that grounds the qualitative infinity of interpretation."[31] The sheer openness of possibility in the in the interpretative act is its quantitative infinity, and the inability of interpretation to exhaust all possibilities, its "infinite limit" in a sense, is its qualitative measure.

This infinite is not, however, an abstract construct or ideal; rather, this knowledge, as a finite grasping of the infinite aperture of interpreta-

29. Ibid., 182.

30. Ibid.

31. Ibid., 187.

tion, bears the marks of autonomous subjects and objects in relation to each other: "Interpretation is a knowledge in which the object reveals itself according to the measure by which the subject expresses it. The independence of the interpreted and the personality of the interpreter are not obstacles to interpretation, but are the only condition possible for it: this condition does not impede it, but rather constitutes it."[32] As infinite, and yet conditioned, any act of interpretation is constituted through the limits it inherits and in relation to the infinity that grants it transcendence. As freedom in a situation, as autonomy in the midst of other autonomous entities, the person must, in the act of interpretation, reveal its originary freedom through the expression of its unchosen and thus given inheritance. The interpreter chooses freely, but also finds that this responsibility is such that one *cannot not choose*. Pareyson concluded that any philosophy of the human being [*filosofia del'uomo*] must therefore be identical with the philosophy of formativity, a series of attempts that constitute and yet render forever open the human being as a formative self-work [*auto-opera*].

4. The Unity of Philosophy

Although Pareyson's treatment of aesthetics reveals the pure "form" of human activity as one of interpretation, "The Unity of Philosophy"[33] gives what are perhaps the clearest motivations behind his vindication of philosophy and truth. Although the essay itself was originally written as a methodological introduction to a course on the history of philosophy, its concerns place it within the broader intellectual and political considerations that faced Italian philosophy after World War II by asking whether there is nothing more than a plurality of philosophies and worldviews caught in an inevitable (and potentially interminable) conflict of interpretations, or whether there is a unity at the root of all philosophies, one true philosophy

---

32. Ibid., 189.

33. This essay, which appeared in the January 1952 issue of *Filosofia*, is the only substantial work of Pareyson's translated into English (*Cross Currents* IV, no. 1 [1953]: 57–69) before the collection of writings edited by Bubbio, in which this essay also appears. For the sake of consistency, I have freshly translated any quotations from "Unità della filosofia" in Luigi Pareyson, *Interpretazione e storia*. Opere Complete, vol. 14. Edited by Amalia de Maria (Milan: Mursia, 2007), 97–108.

toward which all historical philosophies strive? The first parts of the essay detail Pareyson's argument that both sides—those who claim there is one, definitive and unified philosophy, and the others who claim there is only an irreducible multiplicity of philosophies—are equally guilty of an uncritical and ultimately dogmatic view of philosophy. In both cases, the very idea of philosophy is lost because it is reduced to one idea—dogmatically universal or dogmatically singular—that restricts the mobility of the investigation, progress, and infinity of philosophical inquiry. Philosophy worthy of the name is capable of maintaining the two poles, since "a vigorous speculative thought freely poses its own problems, and demands an understanding that should rise from an unavoidably human beginning to a universal problem, which is precisely what makes thinking philosophical, namely, expressible in terms of a specifically speculative evaluation and critique."[34]

In order to conceive of philosophy that is at once personal and universal, tied to a particular situation and yet engaged in the search for truth, Pareyson pointed to a shared "respect [for] the laws of *universal* reason,"[35] which help to guide the free initiative of the philosopher and avoid relativism precisely because "every philosopher demands not only to be understood but judged, and if need be, contradicted."[36] Truth is not something to be grasped definitively once and for all; rather, "it is present as demand and norm: as the demand that compels the philosopher to search for *one* truth, and as the norm which judges *the* (*multiple*) truths [*i veri*] such inquiry attains. Precisely because truth is one, philosophy cannot be one. . . ."[37] It is the personality of philosophy that provides the point of equilibrium between the multiplicity of philosophies and the unity of philosophy, an equilibrium that functions to underscore the idea that any philosophy, however personalistic and individual, is always a philosophizing with others [*confilosofia*]. The "unity" of philosophy is therefore a common discussion, a dialogue that is forever open and that on the one hand resists the sublated resolution of dialectic into "one true philosophy," and on the other, the mindless conflict of interpretations: "I am moved by a necessity *common* to every thinking being, the need for truth. It is not to my philosophy that I am dedicated: It is *philosophy itself* that I serve, even if, in such service, I develop a philosophy of my own."[38]

34. "Unità della filosofia," 102.

35. Ibid., 103.

36. Ibid., 105–106.

37. Ibid., 106.

38. Ibid., 103.

The criterion for this defense of philosophy's unity is the demand of reason, whereas the impetus for the endeavor is the initiative of the philosopher who understands that although "truth is inexhaustibly infinite," the finite individual, who is "motivated by its demands, undertakes a search for it, is preeminently free."[39] Such a criterion is neither a circular appeal to the principles of reason, nor a validation of the particular historical circumstance of the philosopher, nor even a resignation to an unending dialectic of incommensurables, as none of these would provide a defense of philosophy that stretches beyond the already canonized methodologies of the worldviews under critique. Pareyson's notion of philosophy finds its proper vindication in its disciplined avoidance of any of the three aforementioned aporias, and the steadfast promotion of the idea that philosophy is profoundly and preeminently *dialogue*.

5. Truth and Interpretation

Luigi Pareyson described his 1971 work *Truth and Interpretation* as a "defense of philosophy" and a "vindication of truth" that has the task of "restoring thought's genuine principle." Interpretation, the form of thinking that is preeminently free and dialogical, is the centerpiece of this philosophy's charge to be sufficiently critical while avoiding the scourges of dogmatism and relativism. One should therefore read his text not merely as an investigation of hermeneutic theory, but properly as an answer to those forms of thinking today—in religion, politics, science, and the social sciences—that threaten to abandon reason in favor of empty speculation or to reduce reason to merely instrumental thinking.

One of Pareyson's explicit goals in the text is to restore a universal and speculative character to philosophy, two aspects he felt were under assault by those forms of thinking that either absolutize truth or reduce it to its historical expression. The book begins with an examination of two types of thought: revelatory [*pensiero rivelativo*] and expressive [*pensiero espressivo*]. Thought that is "expressive" does nothing but express its own age; "revelatory" thought, however, reveals Being while simultaneously expressing its own time through the free mediation of the individual person in a way that is never final or complete, but always open to the inexhaustible quality of Being. For Pareyson, revelatory thought marked the end of ontic and objective metaphysics and signalled a new ontological

39. Ibid., 108.

and indirect metaphysics that could preserve the uniquely universal and speculative character of philosophy—metaphysics properly conceived as an ongoing dialogue between the inexhaustible reserve of Being and its historical interpretations. The revelation of truth occurs in all aspects of human activity where the choice for Being and truth has been made, whether in philosophy, morality, art, or politics. Philosophy differs from other human endeavors only because it seeks to *articulate* this speculative aspect as the "truth" of human life. *Truth and Interpretation* is therefore a work of profound ontology that neither mystifies Being through enthusiastic claims about its ineffable or absolute nature nor reduces Being to its historical expression and ontic instrumentalization.

Pareyson claimed that "the protagonist in revelatory thought is certainly truth," the unobjectifiable and irreducible source of meaning in human life. As the particular focus of philosophy, the interpretation of truth assumes its proper role as a critical and problematizing engagement with the world, such that "human beings are confronted with their own responsibilities" and encounter it not as a discovery but as a witnessing that can "sharpen the problematicity of the human being" (25). Truth is an origin that stimulates and liberates, and any thinking that binds human thinking to an unchanging natural, divine, or human order rejects its power to inspire, stimulate, and support rather than dominate, impose, and subjugate. This attitude toward truth is at first glance quite distant from Gianni Vattimo's recent call to bid a farewell to truth and its dominion over the history of metaphysics. The patrimony of ideas shared by student and teacher is, however, much stronger than it first appears, as both answer the threat of dogmatic and ultimately violent forms of thinking with interpretation—that form of thinking that finds unity in dialogue, universality in plurality, and freedom in the very necessity of Being.

In the first section of *Truth and Interpretation*, Pareyson presented the relation between truth and history, the infinite and the finite, plurality and individuality, as one of interpretation. Taking his cue from Nietzsche's critique of historicism, Pareyson challenged the predisposition of modern society toward historicism and empiricism, found the ability to renounce these methods within history itself, and identified the inexhaustibility of Being as the source of truth within historical forms. Moving beyond the perspectivism of Nietzsche, however, Pareyson rejected any suspected relativism by emphasizing the relation between the personal formulation of truth and its inexhaustible reserve in Being (rather than a relation merely between formulations): In one way, an interpretation is the "*personal* possession of *the* truth," and in another way it is the "*possession* of an *infinite.*" It is at one and the same time necessary, as truth can only be revealed through a historical formulation; and yet, it is free, since such formulations are the interpretative work of unique individual perspectives. As such, interpretation gives "a personal and thus *plural* formulation of something that is *one* and indivisible without compromising or losing its unity" (70). Its truth is always something yet further or ulterior [*ulteriore*], offering itself only through one of its formulations and residing in each one as *inexhaustible* [*inesauribile*]. As a *relation* grounded in Being, there are an infinity of possible interpretations of truth, and each one is the truth, rather than a mere reflection or approximation of some truth that stands beyond or outside the formulations themselves.

At the other end of this relation, the freedom and historicity of interpretation are held together in the concept of the person. The freedom of the person is embodied in the risk associated with any interpretation, since the formulation of truth is never a complete unveiling of truth, but rather a revelation of truth obtained as a temporary (and temporal) victory over the ever-present menace of its concealment. The freedom of the person, who can err as well as succeed, makes any and every interpretation precarious and liable to obscurity. This freedom, although a source of risk and failure, is also what allows an interpretation to unite truth and history without reducing one to the other. Truth is neither reduced to history, nor exalted as something beyond all time. The person, who exists historically, formulates truth through this existence as a historical instantiation of truth. To depersonalize truth as something beyond time that is merely represented or approximated in a historical formulation, or that is grasped "objectively" or "neutrally," would be to forget history, namely, that interpretations are the production of a person living in history, a person who *has* history but is not reduced to it. So although an interpretation, as a formulation of truth, must necessarily occur in time, its temporality and personality is not a sufficient condition for its truth. The person approaches truth only as an organ of revelation, as an interpreter of the inexhaustible and unobjectifiable meaning of Being.

The person is not only the basis for each individual interpretation, but also for the communicability of various interpretations. That an interpretation has meaning, is coherent, and can be communicated—its "universally recognizable validity"—rests on the notion that each interpretation, in its uniqueness and inimitability, is also an interpretation among innumerable personal perspectives. Both the production and the understanding of an interpretation rely on the individuality of each personal perspective as "a" perspective on truth. Without the person at the root of interpretation, "not only is a personal formulation of truth compromising, but so is the communication between its various and diverse formulations . . . " because ". . . one needs to take or have taken a position in order to understand another position, and any interpretation can be understood solely from another interpretation" (74). Rather than rely on a presupposed universality or an empty abstraction, a formulation of truth can be shared precisely because of the kindredness [*congenialità*][40] among persons as interpreters of truth and the demand for dialogue and communication among free beings involved in the risk of interpretation: "It is thus not the case of a pre-existing universality but of a universality to be established. This can be accomplished only by instituting a community of kindred persons, brought together by a similar interpretation of truth, and precisely for that reason able to understand and communicate reciprocally" (74). This shared bond also avoids the dogmatism of shared opinion because each individual interpretation maintains its vital link to the inexhaustible reserve of possibility that can never be objectified. For this reason, truth cannot simply be held in contrast to the falsehood or error of any given interpretation. The ulteriority of truth is not an admission that each formulation is inadequate, such that it remains inaccessible and ineffable, hopelessly beyond the reach of our interpretations. Truth is fully present in each formulation, but as a unique and inimitable formulation. It has neither one proper formulation nor is it an abstraction from out of many possible or actual formulations; thus, one can say that "interpretation occurs only when truth actually *coincides* with its formulation without being *confused* with it, so that it maintains its *plurality*" (70). To err in interpretation does not signify "missing the truth" or "distorting reality" because both notions presuppose an object to be grasped, or an idea that conforms to some reality outside of our existing in it. Rather, error in interpretation reflects thinking that is, in Pareyson's terminology, merely "expressive" of its own time, thinking that does not entertain alternatives and forgets that it is only that—an interpretation.

The work's second part presents Pareyson's critique of ideology, which aims to undermine its tendency to reduce, totalize, and instrumentalize thinking in the service of a prevalent and noncritical worldview.

---

40. For more on Pareyson's understanding of tradition in hermeneutics, especially as compared with Gadamer's notion of tradition, I refer the reader to my essay "The Tradition of Tradition in Hermeneutics" in *Consequences of Hermeneutics*, eds. Jeff Malpas and Santiago Zabala (Evanston, IL: Northwestern University Press, 2010), 66–80.

Ideology is that form of thinking that has relevance only within its own situation and cannot survive but through an unbreakable connection with the conditions that produced it. Bound in this way, ideology merely serves the immediate demands of its age rather than the responsibility associated with the freedom and risk of interpretation. There can be a rehabilitation of metaphysics, and thus a revelation of Being as the original hermeneutic relation, only when philosophy avoids the pitfalls of ideology and historicism and becomes a truly *critical* philosophy of its own time.

Thinking is nonetheless unavoidably historicized and thus always in danger of merely expressing its age without the critical apparatus to transcend itself through ever-newer interpretations. On this model, Pareyson argued, ideologies often are treated not as historically conditioned thought, but as thought that is completely identified with its own historical situation. Ideology expresses the necessity of the given, but unlike philosophy, does not possess the critical freedom to interpret that given. As a result, these ideologies come to represent the technicization of reason through systems of thinking and meaning that are ultimately measured against the standards of pragmatic ends that merely appear as natural and immutable. The historicization of thought and the technicization of reason are thus the two traits of merely expressive thought that cannot carry the ontological weight and personal commitment demanded of interpretation. Thus, on the one hand, there is the dogmatism associated with forms of ideology that claim to know the objective truth and gear the various means within society toward the pragmatic achievement of that end. On the other hand, this dogmatism is in fact the product of a radical skepticism towards the very nature of truth itself, a skepticism that responds to the potential plurality of truths (each limited to its own age) by asserting the absolute primacy of its own viewpoint at the cost of the very historical sense that gave rise to the truth in the first place. The challenge to remain *philosophically* grounded in the inexhaustibility of Being arises directly from threats posed by forms of thinking that submit reason to its instrumental use. If philosophy is to defend its validity, it must, in the words of Pareyson, take truth to be its origin rather than its object, and thereby recover its relevance in all realms of human activity: "saving [philosophy] from all of the attempts, today ever more widespread, to reduce it to thought that is merely pragmatic and historical, technical and instrumental, empirical and ideological" (4).

Enlightenment rationalism and Marxist historicism bear the brunt of Pareyson's critique, as these forms of thinking, in their own particular ways, submit thought to the service of politics and practical ends. A vindication of truth and philosophy liberates thinking from prescribed instrumental ends in favor of a more originary relation with Being that clarifies the philosopher's relation to and with politics. Pareyson asserted that the political relevance of the philosopher rests in simply *doing philosophy* without engaging in direct political action.[41] The philosopher battles ideologies, and thereby takes an explicit philosophical position. He or she is not afraid that action will destroy thought, but that action will forget Being and become its merely ontic shadow. All too often, however, one finds either the politician in the role of the philosopher's advisee, or the philosopher transformed into the tool of the politician. Both of these extremes presuppose as a point of departure the separation of thought and action, ultimately confusing truth with philosophy, or even worse, demanding from philosophy that which only truth can provide. Philosophy should not furnish reasons for political practice, but rather should relate to politics indirectly by exploring the "profound and originary solidarity of theory and praxis, which precedes the very distinction between thought and action, theoretical life and the practical life, cognitive world and active world" (154). The task of philosophy in the face of political and social pressures is therefore to explore and articulate the various ways that human activity remains continually open to revision and regeneration, to defend human activity against the reductive threats of dogmatism and relativism, and ultimately "to vindicate the revelatory and ontological character that every human activity, even practical action, has in itself" (160).

The other and perhaps even more widespread challenge to philosophy appears in its longstanding relation with "common sense." In the third section of *Truth and Interpretation*, Pareyson sought to identify the unique status of philosophy and argued that only through the interpretation of Being can philosophy also be "the philosophy of philosophy," namely, a critical endeavor that is committed to a position and yet remains open to dialogue. Although everything can be the subject of philosophy—art, science, religion, politics—philosophy is in no position to delegate expertise in any of them: Its unique role is precisely the protection of their autonomy and the maintenance of their mutual coexistence so that each

41. For more on Pareyson's thoughts regarding politics and their relation to his student Vattimo's political engagements, I refer the reader to my introduction in Gianni Vattimo, *A Farewell to Truth*, trans. William McCuaig (New York: Columbia University Press, 2011), vii–xxiv.

avoids its tendency to absolutization. Philosophy is in crisis today, Pareyson contended, not only because it has fallen from prominence and fails to limit the transgressions of the other disciplines, but even more importantly, because it has turned its critical function against itself: In the wake of the discovery of its own historical, personal, and linguistic conditionality, philosophy "has no other object than itself, nor any result other than its own destruction" (176). The answer to the crisis is once again a recovery of truth—not as the outcome of discourse, but properly as its origin and impulse in a manner similar to the way a seeming paradox opens up a moment of wonderment in the Socratic tradition of dialogue. The alternative, Pareyson warned, is philosophy construed as mere technics, as a method for thinking rather than as the richness of thought's ongoing discovery and development.

Perhaps the most pervasive and enticing threat to philosophy is nothing more than the allure of common sense that, fueled by a climate anti-intellectualism and free-market naturalism, has little patience for thinking that has been liberated from the tangible measures of practical action. The most salient feature of this phenomenon is the overvaluing of experience as an intrinsic measure. In an ironic turn, that which appears as the least abstract measure—the practical value of being immersed in experience—is taken blindly as an absolute value and as a result becomes the most abstract. In a manner more profound than Vattimo's critique of the *koiné* of hermeneutics,[42] Pareyson uncovered the ubiquity of common sense as the ultimate crisis of relativism turned absolute and declares the need for philosophy to recover and vindicate its own rigor. Philosophy does not take experience as the measure, but is rather the problematization and interpretation of experience and common sense. In this formulation, common sense is therefore a necessary but not sufficient condition for the revelation of truth. Its ontological value takes three forms: the inseparability of universality and historicity, the unity of the community with the individual person, and the originary identity of theory and praxis. Only

42. Gianni Vattimo, in *Beyond Interpretation* and elsewhere, argues that the prevalent feature of philosophy today is that interpretation has more or less become its common idiom at the cost of any rigorous definition of what hermeneutics actually is. For a more detailed account of Pareyson's understanding of "common sense" in relation to philosophy as interpretation, I refer the reader to my essay, "The Primacy of Interpretation in Luigi Pareyson's Hermeneutics of Common Sense," *Philosophy Today* 49 (Winter 2005): 333–341.

when philosophy interprets, rather than dismisses, the challenge of these incommensurable opposites will common sense be ushered in aid of philosophy's struggle to resolve its own crisis. In *Truth and Interpretation,* one rightly speaks of a vindication, rather than a foundation, for philosophical hermeneutics. As I suggested here, it is neither a political, and thus ultimately a pragmatic move that unashamedly prefers one vision of life over another. Nor is it, on the other hand, a traditionally philosophical move that seeks its *Grund* in some truth claim or compelling description of reality. If we follow Pareyson's lead, we not only recognize that all human activities can share in the revelation of Being, but that philosophy has the particular task of recovering ontological difference as a moral imperative for all human endeavors. Any vindication of philosophy and truth stands quite simply against those forms of thinking and acting that, in one manner or another, stifle philosophy's open and dialogical approach while simultaneously demeaning its ability to find relevance in the world today. Unlike forms of instrumental thinking that seek their justification in results that are hopelessly reduced to their historical conditions, the vindication of philosophy reflects a rigor peculiar to philosophy that seeks the legitimacy of its foundations and its own operations. Such an alternative is not, as some might suspect, an idealistic or utopian projection that ignores the harsher realities of modern life; nor is it a reduction of human choice to the cold standards of reason, namely, an instrumentalization of philosophy that would attempt to beat the various manifestations of religious fanaticism and post-industrial liberalism at their own game. It is, above all and appropriately for this work, a hermeneutic demand to be circumspect, to reflect, to listen, and to engage the voice of others in a way that is mindful of the risk and responsibility that attends any interpretation.

Truth and Interpretation

Preface

Gathered in this volume are some of my writings from the past six years. They were already conceived and thought out as chapters of a book, both in the unity of their argument and also in the continuity of their presentation. They all have a programmatic character, in the sense that they are at the same time a decisive stance within today's philosophical climate and also a work plan that in the upcoming years I would like to unfold and that I propose to others for their own elaboration. All of the lines of development are already present, however, even if they are sometimes expressed with deliberate brevity or other times merely suggested. Today, because of the elephantiasis of the mass media and the resulting cultural industry, one tends to write with an eye toward rapid and immediate consumption, intolerant of the delays required by re-reading and reflection. In contrast, the following pages are meant for a slow and meditative reading that is ready to develop and integrate the work's suggestive ideas; such reading therefore trusts in the collaboration of the reader. Many of these pages are the result of deep concentration, and are thus exposed to the risk expressed in the saying, *brevis esse laboro, obscurus fio* [In trying to be concise I become obscure].

These pages deal with topics that, if I am not mistaken, are extremely current and as timely as were the essays of *Esistenza e persona* [*Existence and Person*] twenty years ago, as the subsequent events demonstrated. They vindicate the necessity and autonomy of philosophy, today more than ever, in the face of the assault waged against it from all sides—from science, from religion, from politics. When they stray from their own fields, within which only philosophy can contain them, they lose their proper nature and degenerate into scientism, fideism, and panpoliticism, that is, precisely those things that represent the evils of our time: superstition, even when based on reason; fanaticism, both political and religious; and ideology, which turns thought into its instrument. From here emerge the various forms of relativism, skepticism, technicism, praxism, and nihilism that, under the guise of the most critical vigilance, are all outcomes of the decadence of philosophical thought. The defense of philosophy, this extreme but resolute vindication of its necessity, cannot be done without returning thought to its genuine principle—truth—and thereby saving it from all of the attempts, today ever more widespread, to reduce it to thought that is merely pragmatic and historical, technical and instrumental, empirical and ideological.

This book risks being unpopular because it speaks of truth at a time when one only speaks of action and reason—more precisely, of action without truth, namely praxism, and of reason without truth, namely technicism. And one knows that praxism and technicism are precisely the characteristic of the current world, so much so that today the suppression of the concept of truth has been brought about by philosophy itself, which has gone so far as to deny itself and theorize its own end. But the prejudice of historicism cannot go so far as to reserve the present for the denial of philosophy and the suppression of truth thereby confining truth and philosophy to the outdated remnants of the past, if for no other reason than the easily verifiable fact that the will to deny truth is just as old as the desire to affirm it.

Moreover, the vindication of truth is not by necessity a merely contemplative or theoretical attitude that would rightly be considered evasive and unilateral. The truth constitutive of thought is indispensable for both theory and praxis, above all when one knows how to grasp the profound and originary unity of these two terms. One should not forget that true thought, thought worthy of its name, is first of all thought of Being, and precisely by being such does thought derive its practical potentiality and its historical effectiveness [*efficacia*]. On the one hand, true thought is the originary unity of theory and praxis, prior to their division and thus prior to the opposition or reduction of one to the other; and on the other hand, true thought is authentic thought, concerned with what is its principle and origin, that is, its ontological rooting and its revelatory nature. For this very reason, such thought is able to direct and nourish experience, to master and transform the situation. In the end, truth cannot be understood as either objective or purely meta-historical. On the one side, truth is not the object but the origin of thought; it is not the result but the principle of reason; it is not the content but the source of contents. On the other side, truth appears only within a historical and personal interpretation that already formulates it in a determinate way, with which it coincides according to the situation, neither exhausted by nor reduced to it, inseparable from the pathway through which it is obtained, and thus from the historical form through which it appears in time.

In these terms, the concept of truth seems to me to be acceptable even to today's most careful and insightful critique, although it is still capable of restoring to thought that revelatory nature on which the survival of philosophy depends. Everything depends on the maintenance and the development of the concept of the ontological relation by which Heidegger has effectively revived and reinvigorated today's philosophy; nevertheless, one must avoid the blind alley in which he has trapped philosophy by proposing a solely negative ontology and by rejecting the totality of Western philosophy from Parmenides to Nietzsche. These two ideas end up jeopardizing the very existence of philosophy because in one sense, philosophical discourse disappears in silence, particular philosophical discourses become impossible, and most importantly, the possibility for an ethics is denied; and, in another sense, the rejection of all of Western thought becomes an invitation to total revolution rather than a solicitation to remember that at *each* point of the historical process there exists an alternative between positive and negative, and that the most important thing is freely to make the former prevail over the latter. By confusing inexhaustibility with ineffability and regeneration with revolution, Heidegger returns involuntarily to the indifference of historical forms and to the univocity of the temporal process affirmed by the very historicism that he had so victoriously defeated. This occurs because, by ignoring the personalistic aspect that is inseparable from a genuine ontology, he ultimately alters the relations between Being and time, between the atemporal and history.

The central point of my thinking is the originary solidarity of person and truth that comprises the genuine essence of the concept of "interpretation." I have now spent more than twenty years studying the concept of interpretation. To be exact, I began by reflecting on the problem of the unity of philosophy and the multiplicity of philosophies, and on the possibility of a dialogue among the diverse personal perspectives that may occur once we finally abandon the idea of objective truth. With respect to the concept of interpretation that resulted from that reflection, and that I deepened through its applications in other fields, above all in aesthetics, I emphasize the hermeneutic and thus ontological nuance of personalism that separates me from all forms of spiritualism, whether their origin is idealistic or intimistic. I have taken the fundamental idea for this book from such a concept of interpretation, that is, from the distinction between revelatory thought and expressive thought. This distinction invites us to restore thought to its originary truth-bearing function against the instrumentalization imposed on it by current technicism and ideologism. This theory of interpretation has had the good fortune of attracting the attention of foreign thinkers with whom I share the originary existentialistic inspiration and the constant meditation on Heidegger's thought. Furthermore, the distinction between revelatory thought and expressive thought has been welcomed by Italian scholars with whom I share a deep bond of affinity and whose consensus serves to validate my work.

I am aware that by defending philosophy and vindicating truth I have chosen the most difficult route. In a cultural climate like the present, it is far too easy to give up philosophy in favor of science or politics or religion, or to reduce philosophy to an empirical reflection on the so-called social sciences, such as sociology, psychology, and anthropology, or to sacrifice truth in favor of the multiple but indifferent variety of historical forms, or to deny truth in the dominant cult of action and efficiency. In philosophy, however, nothing is less true and nothing is more disgraceful than being simplistic; and often the deliberate search for what is difficult not only points to truth, but also ultimately guarantees it. When Plato exalts the beauty of the noble risk, he alludes to the fact that philosophy requires daring and courage. In more recent times, Schelling reminds us of a similar point: "*Wer wahrhaft philosophieren will, muss aller Hoffnung, alles Verlangens, aller Sehnsucht los sein; er muss nichts wollen, nichts wissen, sich ganz bloss und arm fühlen, alles dahingeben, um alles zu gewinnen*" ["The true philosopher must renounce every hope, every desire, every longing; he must neither want nor know anything; he must feel naked and poor, abandoning everything in order to gain everything"].

Notes

The writings collected in this book come from the following:

"Pensiero espressivo e pensiero rivelativo," opening address for a course in Theoretical Philosophy, delivered at the University of Turin on November 12, 1964, and published in *Giornale Critico della Filosofia Italiana*, 2 (1965).

"Valori permanenti e processo storico," opening address read in Campidoglio in Rome on October 3, 1968, as the inauguration for the *Convegno Internazionale sui valori permanenti nel divenire storico*, organized by the Academic Institute of Rome, and published with the title "Valori permanenti e storia" in the proceedings of the conference (Rome, 1969).

"Originarietà dell' interpretazione," enlarged edition of the essay with the same title published in *Hermeneutik und Dialektik* (Tübingen: Mohr, 1970).

"Filosofia e Ideologia," introductory lecture at the XXI Convegno del Centro di Studi Filosofici di Gallarate, read on September 5, 1966, and published in *Filosofia*, 2 (1967) and also in *Ideologia e Filosofia*, "Atti del XXI Convegno del Centro di Studi Filosofici di Gallarate" (Brescia: Morcelliana, 1967).

Appearing here with the title "Destino dell' ideologia" is the response and conclusion to the discussions of the conference cited above, published without a title in *Ideologia e Filosofia*, "Atti del XXI Convegno del Centro di Studi Filosofici di Gallarate" (Brescia: Morcelliana, 1967).

"Necessità della filosofia," a lecture held in February 1967 at the headquarters of the Italian Cultural Association with the title "Elogio della filosofia," and published in *Le conferenze dell' Associazione culturale italiana*, 19 (1967).

"Filosofia e senso comune," original edition of the academic speech delivered on November 6, 1967 for the beginning of the 1967–1968 academic year at the University of Turin, and published in *Annuario dell' Università degli Studi di Torino per l' anno accademico 1967–68: anno 564 della fondazione* (Torino, 1968).

The thinking advanced in this book was developed through continual contact and constant dialogue with the most prevalent theories of today and with those philosophies from the past that seem to retain a peculiar feature of timeliness. References are not always explicit, and often an entire debate is condensed into the space of a few lines. The informed and talented readers will notice them and make the necessary references on their own; in any case, I have furnished the notes with the elements needed to decipher some of the perhaps less-evident allusions and to reconstruct more specifically some of the cross-references. Beyond that, in the following notes I have limited myself to refer the exact citations to the places from which they were drawn and to present some useful comments for a better understanding of the text.

The first edition of my book *Esistenza e persona*, cited on page 3, came out in 1950: This year a reprinting of the third edition was released (Turin: Taylor, 1970). Allow me to point out some of the themes I discussed in the book, and that would become ever more central in the cultural and speculative debate of the subsequent years. Above all, there are the problems that emerged and became timely through the dissolution of Hegelianism: the multiplicity and historical conditionality of philosophies, the problem that follows for a concept of philosophical historiography, the dialogue among diverse perspectives on truth, the preoccupation with avoiding both fanaticism and skepticism, a pluralistic but not relativistic conception of truth; the possibility for a current "rediscovery" and a "recovery" (neither "renewal" nor "updating") of Christianity, the inevitably anti-Christian result of modern culture taken as the secularization of Christianity, the inseparability of Christianity from cultural contexts and the reaffirmation of its purely religious value but not, for that, as merely intimistic and "private," but Christianity as the inescapable alternative of every present conception that would be aware of the problems of today and atheism as the incontrovertible "internal" problem for every present profession of Christianity; the problems of a present-day personalism, as the convergence of concepts that seem opposed but are actually inseparable, such as those of individuality and community, the possibility of an interpersonal communication, the relation among person, society, and transcendence, and so on.

The following remarks concern the centrality of the concept of "interpretation," to which I allude on page 5. The type of attention that I devoted to existentialism in my early works already predisposed me to a theory of interpretation: On the one hand, my work on Heidegger had sent me back to reading Dilthey (which after that I never abandoned); and, on the other hand, in Jaspers I emphasized as particularly important and meaningful the theory of points of view, whether from the *Psychologie der Weltanschauungen* or from the antiperspectivist pluralism of *Logica filosofica*, as shown in my book *La filosofia dell' esistenza e Carlo Jaspers* (Naples: Loffredo, 1940), and in the essay "Ultimi sviluppi del pensiero di Jaspers," in *Rivista di filosofia*, 4 (1948), republished in the first edition of *Esistenza e persona*.

I sketched out the initial features of a theory of interpretation on the occasion of the problem of the unity of philosophy and the multiplicity of philosophies, as the basis for defining the nature of philosophical thought and proposing a new concept of philosophical historiography. Allow me to refer above all to "Il compito della filosofia oggi" in *Esistenza e persona*; *Fichte* (Turin: Editions of "Filosofia," 1950), XLV–LIII; "Unità della filosofia" in *Filosofia*, 1 (1952) ["The Unity of Philosophy" in *Cross Cur-*

rents IV, 1 (1953): 57–69]; *Prefazione e Conclusione* a G.W.F. Hegel, *Introduzione alla storia della filosofia* (Bari: Laterza, 1953). I offered further specifications when I extended—successfully, in my view—the concept of interpretation to the relation between the universal and the particular and to interpersonal relations, as occurred in general throughout *Esistenza e persona* and in the 1953 essay "La conoscenza degli altri," which was added to the book's second edition (1960).

But the decisive developments came to me from the field of aesthetics, where the concept of interpretation seemed to be particularly productive, and thereby contributed not only to the solution of problems relative to art, but also other problems such as the study of nature, historical knowledge, social life, and so on ("Filosofia della persona," 1958; added to the third edition of *Esistenza e persona*, 1966). Aesthetics, to which I devoted many years of study, revealed itself to me not as the proper sphere for the concept of interpretation, but rather as the greatest check of its originary and omnivalent nature: In fact, the issue is not that of extending a properly aesthetic concept to other fields but of drawing, from the particular clarity that the validity of the concept of interpretation achieves in the field of aesthetics, a confirmation of the validity that it possesses in all fields of human activity and in every human relation.

Here are the writings in which I deal specifically with the concept of interpretation in aesthetics: "Arte e conoscenza. Intuizione e interpretazione," in *Filosofia*, 2 (1950), and "Sui fondamenti dell' estetica," in *Atti del VII Convegno di Studi Filosofici di Gallarate 1951* (Padua: Liviana, 1952), both in *Teoria dell' arte: Saggi di estetica* (Milan: Marzorati, 1965); *Estetica: Teoria della formatività* (Turin: Edizioni di Filosofia, 1954; second edition: Bologna: Zanichelli, 1960), especially pages 35–37, 146–149, 151–238; "Il concetto di interpretazione nell' estetica crociana," in *Rivista di filosofia*, 3 (1953), also in *L' esperienza artistica: saggi di storia dell' estetica* (Milan: Marzorati, soon to be published); "L' interpretazione dell' opera d' arte," presented at III Congresso Internazionale di Estetica (Venezia, 1956), in *Rivista di Estetica*, 3 (1956), and "Interprétation et jugement," in *Revue philosophique*, 2 (1961), both in *Teoria dell' arte*, already cited; *I problemi dell' estetica*, written in 1958, published in 1961, and in its second edition Milan: Marzorati, 1966, 189–231; *Conversazioni di estetica* (Milan: Mursia, 1966), especially pages 33–39, 41–47, 55, 68–69, 71–78, 107–108, 112–113.

I hope that the explicit developments that I attempted to give to the concept of interpretation in this book will contribute to a better understanding of the theory of interpretation I outlined in my books on aesthetics; that is, that they invite and help the reader to consider it in its proper sense, as a *general* theory of interpretation, not *limited* to the field of aesthetics, as one can "read" it with a glance turned toward the whole of human activity and affirm its validity in all human situations and relations.

Among the foreign thinkers who have taken an interest in the theory of interpretation I have proposed, I recall with a particular spirit of kindredness Hans-Georg Gadamer, who wanted to cite it in his fundamental book *Truth and Method,* translated by Joel Weinsheimer and Donald G. Marshall (London: Continuum, 2004), 164. It is also cited in the essay *Hermeneutik*, in *Contemporary Philosophy*, edited by R. Klibansky (Florence: La Nuova Italia, 1969), 367.

The Italian scholars who have taken note of my distinction between expressive thought and revelatory thought are Augusto Del Noce, *Riforma cattolica e filosofia moderna: I. Cartesio* (Bologna: Il Mulino, 1965), 670–676 and Sergio Cotta, *La sfida tecnologica* (Bologna: Il Mulino, 1968), 105–106, 123 ff. The validity of the penetrating meditations that they drew from it is for me the most meaningful authentication of my proposal. In a certain way analogous to that distinction, I recall the problematic so fully developed by M.F. Sciacca in his book *Filosofia e antifilosofia* (Milan: Marzorati, 1968): Also by him I remember "Storicismo o storicità dei valori?," in *I valori permanenti nel divenire storico,* "Atti del convegno promosso dall' Istituto Accademico di Roma" (Rome, 1969).

Page 6: Plato's celebrated *kalos gar ho kindunos*, connected to the "noble risk" of philosophy, can be found, as noted, in *Phaedo* (114D). The passage from Schelling belongs to the *Erlanger Vorträge* (Schröter vol. 12), which seems to me to be among the best of his writings. In fact, these 1821 conferences kindled a genuine enthusiasm among its listeners, among whom was frequently the poet von Platen. An excellent effort was therefore made by Horst Fuhrmans, the most noted of Schelling's students, to publish a fascinating *Nachschrift* of this course in the winter semester of 1820–1821, entitled *Initia philosophiae universae* (Bonn: Bouvier, 1969). For a better understanding of the cited passage, it is worth recalling that just before it Schelling writes: "*Selbst Gott muss der lassen, der sich in den Anfangspunkt der wahrhaft freien Philosophie stellen will. Hier heisst es: Wer es erhalten will, der wird es verlieren, und wer es aufgibt, der wird es finden. Nur derjenige ist auf den Grund seiner selbst gekommen und hat die ganze Tiefe des Lebens erkannt, der einmal alles verlassen hatte, und selbst von allem verlassen war*" ["Whoever wants to place himself at the beginning point of a truly free philosophy must abandon even God. This means: whoever wants to acquire it, loses it, and whoever abandons it, finds it. Only this one has reached his own foundation and has known all of the profundity of life, has abandoned everything and has himself been abandoned by everything] (vol. 11; see *Initia philosophiae universae*, 18–19).

Introduction

Expressive Thought and Revelatory Thought

1. Historicistic Consideration and Speculative Discussion

One of the most common clichés in today's culture is the generically yet entirely historicist idea that every era has its philosophy and that the meaning of a philosophical thought resides in the adherence to its own time. This is no longer a case of classic historicism, which interprets history as a progressive manifestation of truth, which takes particular philosophies as steps leading toward absolute truth and then in the end confers a speculative significance to a specific philosophy's correspondence to its historical situation; rather, it is integral historicism through and through, one that withholds from philosophy the truth for which it longs by the very nature of its thinking and that assigns to [philosophy] no other value than that of being the expression of its own time.

This type of historicism, rather than draw its strength from a rigorous conceptual formulation, reflects the prevailing mentality today and a criterion more or less in tune with the current valuations of the majority of cultured individuals, that is, a real *idolum theatri*. I think that this historicism should neither be accepted nor repudiated totally; rather, one needs to find the limits within which it is right to apply it and beyond which it is necessary to repudiate it. To my mind, this distinction is inherent in the historical reality itself of philosophical thought. There are philosophies that, although they strive to attain a value of truth in their claims of a universal formulation, do nothing more than express their own time. Entertaining a speculative discussion with them is useless and inappropriate; instead, the only evaluation one can subject them to is whether their thought adheres to the historical situation. Here the critical function of the historicist method proves positive and useful: A profound need for sincerity allows us to see in their theoretical affirmations nothing more than a vain pretense, or an ignorant illusion, or an ambiguous masking. A living historical sense knows how to restore meaning to this form of thought, so radically emptied of its truth, by recognizing its capacity to express its own time. But there are also philosophies that, in the act of expressing their own time, are also and above all a revelation of truth: One cannot apply the historicist method, understood in that way, to these philosophies without completely misrepresenting their nature—a nature that requires, after an accurate historical positioning, a genuinely speculative discussion.

Historicistic consideration and speculative discussion should therefore not be taken as two different ways of doing the history of philosophical thought. These are not two exclusive methods that battle each other for the history of philosophy, but rather are two coexistent methods that share the task. *In actuality*, some philosophies are, in a manner of speaking, solely "expressive," and some philosophies are above all "revelatory." Only the former ones must be subjected to the historicization that is called for by the historicistic method, and all of their semblance or pretense of truth is not enough to make them worthy of philosophical discussion; only the latter ones rise to this level, meriting and at the same time provoking a speculative discussion. The "expressive" side, which is inevitably joined with their revelatory import, is not enough to legitimate a historicistic critique of them, intended to deprive them of truth and to measure them simply according to their correspondence to the historical situation.

Therefore, it is useful to examine thoroughly the difference between thought that is the mere product of history and thought that manifests truth, never forgetting that this distinction not only concerns philosophy, but also constitutes a dilemma that faces human beings in all of their activities. Human beings must choose to be history or to have history, must choose to be identified with their own situation or to make it a means for obtaining the origin, must choose to renounce truth or to give it an unrepeatable revelation. This choice depends—and I do not stop here to investigate the exceptional nature of this originary freedom where not only the being of human beings resides, but their very relation with Being—on the way in which one freely indicates one's own situation. One can indicate it as a solely historical position or as a primarily metaphysical one, as a simple boundary of existence or as an opening to Being, as an unavoidable and fatal limitation or as a pathway to truth. This choice offers the person the possibility to be reduced to a mere historical product or to become a living perspective on truth, and offers thought the possibility to be a simple expression of time or to be a personal revelation of truth.

2. Expression of Time and Revelation of Truth

Revelatory thought is always at one and the same time expressive, because truth offers itself only within each individual perspective: Truth is accessible only by means of an irreplaceable personal relation and can be formulated only through the personal pathway to it. Thought that starts from this originary solidarity of person and truth is at the same time ontological and personal, and therefore at the same time revelatory and expressive. Such thought expresses the person in the act of revealing truth and reveals truth to the degree that it expresses the person, without one of the two aspects prevailing over the other. We could superimpose ourselves on the truth, but then truth would be obscured rather than revealed, time would be transformed into an opaque and impenetrable screen, and we would become incomprehensible to ourselves. We could believe to discover truth by turning attention away from ourselves and from our own situation, but then truth would disappear because we have not employed the one organ we have for grasping it, namely, our very own person.

Far from being an obstacle to the knowledge of truth, one that might deform it by historicizing and multiplying it, the historical situation is truth's only vehicle, provided that one knows how to retrieve its originary ontological opening: Then the whole person, in its individuality, becomes the revelatory organ that, far from being superimposed on truth, grasps it within one's own perspective, and thus multiplies truth's formulation through the very act that allows it to be unique. In such a way, revelatory thought attests to its own fullness: Anchored to Being and rooted in truth, it derives its own contents and its own meaning directly from them, and the situation becomes the pathway to truth only insofar as it becomes the historical substance of the person.

Revelatory thought is such that in one sense *everyone* says *the same thing*, and yet in another sense *each individual* says *only one thing*: Everyone says the same thing, that is, truth, which can be in no other manner than as one and identical; and each individual says only one thing, that is, speaks the truth in one's own way, in the way that is one's *solum* [alone]. True thinkers are those who not only say the one truth, which in its infinity can very well unite all perspectives despite their diversity, but also strive their whole life to say and repeat that one thing that is their interpretation of truth, because that continual repetition is the sign that a thinker, far from being restricted to expressing the times, has achieved truth.

Truth is therefore one and atemporal within the multiple and historical formulations that are given of it. Such unicity however, which does not allow itself to be compromised by the multiplication of perspectives, is none other than an infinity that stimulates and feeds all such perspectives without letting itself be exhausted by any of the formulations and without privileging any one formulation. Thus, in revelatory thought, truth resides more as the source and the origin than as the object of discovery. As there is no revelation of truth that is not personal, likewise there is no truth that is not gathered as inexhaustible. Only as inexhaustible does truth entrust itself to the word that reveals it, granting it a profundity that can be neither explicated completely nor clarified fully.

3. Features of the Thought that Ignore the Bond between Person and Truth

The complete harmony that reigns over saying, revealing, and expressing therefore characterizes revelatory thought—saying is, at the same time and inseparably, to reveal and to express. That the word is revelatory is a sign of the fully speculative value of thought that does not forget Being; and that the word is expressive is a sign of the historical concreteness of thought that does not forget time. In revelatory thought, the word reveals truth in the act that expresses persons and their time, and vice versa. Not only is the expressive and historical aspect not damaging to the revelatory and theoretical aspect, but rather, it supports and nourishes it because the very situation is considered as a historical opening onto atemporal truth. In turn, the revelatory aspect cannot do without the expressive and historical aspect because there is no objective manifestation of truth; rather, one must grasp it always within a historical perspective, that is, within a personal interpretation.

When freedom ceases to support the originary bond between truth and person, however, everything changes. Truth disappears, leaving thought empty and unanchored, and the person also disappears, reduced to mere historical situation. The harmony among saying, revealing, and expressing breaks, and all relations become distorted and profoundly altered. Revelation and expression split definitively: Without truth, the revelatory aspect of the word is purely superficial and reduced to a rationality that is empty and devoid of content; and expression, no longer referred to the person in her revelatory opening, but to the situation in its mere temporality, becomes unwitting and abstruse. The nature of the word degenerates and falls apart: On the one side is a discourse whose empty rationality only serves a technical and instrumental utilization, and on the other side, masked behind explicit discourse, is its true meaning, that is, its being the expression of its time.

Following more closely this vicissitude through which historical thought replaces ontological thought, expressive discourse replaces speculative discourse, and the instrumental word replaces the revelatory word is helpful. Separated from truth, thought merely preserves the appearance of its revelatory character, that is, an empty rationality whose concepts must refer to the other aspect of thought for their proper meaning, specifically, to thought's expressive character. But the split between the revelation of truth and the expression of the person, by disturbing the intimate constitution of the word, produces a *disjunction* [*sfasamento*] *between explicit discourse and deep expression*—the word says one thing, but it means another. To find the true meaning of discourse one needs to consider not what thought says, but what thought betrays, that is, not the explicit conclusions of thought, its rational coherence, or the universality of its concepts, but the unconscious foundation that expresses itself there, that is, the situation, the historical moment, the time, the epoch.

This involves a second consequence: *the identification of thought with the situation*. Such thought is completely historicized because it merely expresses the historical situation and allows itself to be valued based on its adherence to the time in which it arises. What opens up are the way to culturalism, which encompasses all thought within a general history of culture that highlights the expressive aspect alone without any conception of its possible speculative value; the way to biographism, which reduces thought to an incommunicable expression of the situation in which everyone is inexorably immured as if in an inescapable prison; and the way to a more or less extreme historicism, which reduces all thought to a simple expression of the historical situation, denying it the possibility of escaping its own time.

In such a way we notice a third consequence: the interval that opens up between explicit discourse and deep expression is one of *masking*, that is, of that unconscious ingenuousness or bad faith by which thought makes a historical situation absolute, boasting the achievement of a speculative universality, but in the end only expressing the situation in its mere temporality. The conceptual discourse of historical thought, which always carries contents of truth—however degraded and emptied—within itself and which always presupposes a speculative intent—however frustrated or left unanswered—does nothing other than give an appearance of rationality and eternity to that which is actually pragmatic and temporal. Namely, it supports the conceptualization of historical conditions and the rationalization of practical attitudes.

As a result, historical thought displays its inevitable *pragmatic and instrumental outcome*. This is the fourth consequence we encounter, which appears clearly in the so-called demystifying philosophies, such as pan-political praxism that converts ideologies from mere expressions of the time into opportune instruments for action, or in the various forms of experimentalism that dissolve the function of thought into the elaboration of the most diverse rational techniques. These philosophies are the retrieval of rationalism after the demystification of solely expressive thought. If this thought, deprived of truth, wants to have a rational meaning that is not reduced to the masking of the historical situation, it cannot avoid becoming pragmatic and technical reason. The vicissitude of solely expressive and historical thought is thus over; the conscious refusal of truth necessarily culminates in the deliberate acceptance of the exclusively instrumental function of thought.

4. Cryptic Discourse and Semantic Discourse: Demystification and Interpretation

If we now examine more closely the characteristics of the two types of thought that I have briefly outlined (deliberately leaving aside science, which is a problem to itself)—on the one side, thought expert in truth, both ontological and personal, and thus inseparably revelatory and expressive; and on the other side, purely historical thought, where the absence of the revelatory nature ends up compromising even expression, reducing it to an indirect rationalization of the temporal situation with an unavoidable technical and instrumental vocation—the first thing we notice in them is a sort of interval between what is said and what is unsaid: in both, the word evokes something not explicit that contains the true meaning of discourse. In each, however, the significance and function of that which is not explicit is quite different.

First of all, in historical thought the word says one thing but means another; in revelatory thought, the word reveals much more than what it says. In the first case, the word expresses a conceptual construction, and its true meaning must be sought at the level of the unconscious and masked expression of the historical situation. The word neither reveals nor manifests nor illuminates, but covers, conceals, and hides: Its *legein* [saying] is a *kryptein* [hiding]. In the second case, the word is revealing and thus eloquent not only for what it says, but also for what it does not say. In fact, what it says is that very truth residing in it as inexhaustible and thus as unsaid much more than as said. As inexhaustible, truth resides in the word without being identified with it, but always holding itself in reserve, *kata parousian epistemes kreittona* [in a presence superior to knowledge]: It is a presence that does not identify itself with explication and thus opens the possibility of an ulterior and always new discourse. The presence of truth in the word has an originary nature. It is the source from which thought incessantly surges forth so that every new revelation, rather than move progressively closer to an impossible, total manifestation, is the promise for new revelations; and thus, its nature is more evocative than approximating. Here *legein* [saying] is *semainein* [meaning]: The word is meaningful because of its fertile pregnancy that reaches beyond the sphere of the explicit without diminishing it but radiating outward from it. When thought lacks truth, the explicit is so devoid of meaning that it must find its proper meaning in something else and thus refers to the expression hidden by discourse. In such a case, to understand means to unmask, that is, to replace the explicit with the implied. In revelatory thought, however, the explicit is so meaningful that one can clearly detect the presence of an inexhaustible source of meanings: Therefore, to understand means to interpret, that is, to examine deeply the explicit in order to grasp the infinity of the implicit that it both announces and contains.

Additionally, historical thought does not say what it does, and revelatory thought does not say everything. In the first case there is a real discrepancy between saying and doing due to ingenuousness or bad faith so that the rational assertion hides its true motivation: The explicit aspect, which feigns the revelation of truth, stands in open contrast to the implied reality, which is the situation expressed within it. Conversely, in the second case discourse carries its own meaning within itself as an incessant surging forth, so that what results is a continuous interval between what is said and what remains to be said. The terms *part* and *whole* are not the best suited to describe the revelation of truth: Revealing the truth means neither knowing it fully through the removal of a veil that impedes a complete view of it, nor seizing its simple parts in the desire for their progressive integration or the lament for their fatal inadequacy. Revelatory thought achieves its aim even if it never reaches a point where "everything is said" [*houto bathun logon echei*]. Its ideal is not the complete enunciation of a more or less corresponding reality, but the unceasing manifestation of an inexhaustible origin. Truth does not allow itself to be grasped but as inexhaustible, and this is precisely the only way to grasp it "whole." There is only ever revelation of the inexhaustible, and of the inexhaustible there can be nothing but a revelation, since the task is neither to grasp truth once and for all nor to lament the impossibility of giving it a definitive formulation; the task is rather to find an opening toward truth and draw from it a glimmer or a flash that, however faint or fleeting, is extremely diffusive, for the truth appearing there is inexhaustible.

Moreover, in historical thought the unsaid is outside of speech, whereas in revelatory thought the unsaid is present in the word itself. In historical thought, to understand means to cancel out the unsaid and to bring it to its full explication thus mending the discrepancy between saying and doing; conversely, in revelatory thought to understand means to realize that one does not possess truth lest it be in the form of something that still needs to be sought. If historical thought is a matter of canceling out the implied in the act of discovering it, of unmasking the divide between the said and the unsaid, of recovering the totality of discourse and its meaning—in a word, of performing a demystification so that the task is completed—conversely, the task of revelatory thought is infinite, because truth offers itself to the word precisely as something not completely explicable and makes discourse possible only to the extent that it resides there without ever being exhausted in it. Truth does not allow itself to be captured within a complete enunciation because it nourishes an unending revelation and puts forward, as an indication of its presence, the very interval between the explicit and the implicit. Thus, truth entrusts itself to the only one form of knowing capable of grasping and possessing an infinite, that is, to interpretation. Demystification retrieves the inferior irrationality of historical thought to the rationalistic cult of the explicit, whereas interpretation ensures the presence of truth in an unceasing process of revelation and in an infinity of penetrating perspectives. Demystification reestablishes a totality, whereas interpretation attests to the inexhaustible.

5. Unobjectifiability of Truth

At this point, one could be led to claim that, just as historical thought reveals its true meaning only when submitted to a process of demystification, so too revelatory thought appears in its true nature only when subjected to a demythification. In fact, revelatory thought seems to possess the traits of myth: Because truth offers itself only within a perspective and is grasped only as inexhaustible, the discourse that considers it has the double characteristic of always being multiple and never being fully explicit. It is always multiple, that is, personal and expressive; and is never fully explicit, that is, indirect and significative. Are not these, in fact, the traits of myth, in which the *vis veri* [the power of the truth] finds the most favorable environment for announcing itself in the expression of the person, and discourse speaks indirectly of its task by unveiling it in flashes rather than by exhausting it in an objective way?

Here a point of clarification is necessary so that the nebulosity of a poorly understood mysticism does not creep into philosophical discourse. Certainly, to affirm that truth offers itself only within each individual perspective without ever being identified with any one of them, and that truth can only be grasped as inexhaustible—it resides in the word not as a completely explicated presence, but as origin and source—means to affirm that truth is fundamentally unobjectifiable. On the one hand, in fact, if truth only gives itself within a personal perspective that already interprets and determines it, a comparison between truth in-itself and its formulation within an interpretation is impossible. For us, truth is inseparable from the personal interpretation we give of it, just as we ourselves are inseparable from the perspective in which we grasp it. We cannot depart from our point of view in order to grasp truth in a presumed independence that turns it into a criterion by which to measure our formulation of it from the outside. On the other hand, if truth is only grasped as inexhaustible, it is an origin and impulse more than it is an object and result; thought, rather than speak of truth as if it were a completed whole, must contain it, be moved by it, and nourish itself with it, discovering in it the impetus of its own course, the source of its own contents, and the measure of its own exercise. Truth resides in thought as a presence that is the more active and effective the less it is configurable and definable.

All of the aforementioned is not outside the limits of average experience, and the breadth of human activity presents numerous analogies for this. The impossibility of comparison characterizes interpretation in general. Take, for example, the performance of a work of art or the reconstruction of a historical event. The performance aims at rendering the artwork in the fullness of its sensible reality and the historical reconstruction aims at presenting the event as it actually was. They both do so to such an extent that these activities *are* themselves their object and not a copy of it. There is thus no possible comparison between the reality to be interpreted and the interpretation itself, because the work for the artist as well as the event for the historian do not offer themselves outside of the interpretations that artist and historian give of them. The full range of human experience is studded with these very active presences, even if they cannot be easily represented: Take for example the process of artistic production, where the work of art acts as forming before it ever exists as formed; or the reading of a book, where the understanding of the parts is made possible only through the idea of the whole, which, however, cannot be grasped even at the end of the reading, after traveling through all the parts, unless one has already divined it from the beginning; or the very frequent cases of a happy coincidence between anticipation and discovery, such as the solution of a problem, an unforeseen enlightenment, or love at first sight, which all flow from a state of fecundity, in which discovery is nothing other than the recognition of something that one already knew through a vague inkling, and does nothing more than satisfy and specify a waiting that already contained and laid claim to it.

The case of truth, however, is more radical than these already meaningful examples: Its unobjectifiability is originary and profound, and it manifests itself through an unyielding ulteriority. Truth hands itself over to the most diverse perspectives only in so far as it is identified with none of them, and makes discourse possible only in so far as it is not reduced to it. It is no wonder then that truth often has been entrusted to the impenetrability of silence and the mystery of nothing rather than to the *vis vocabuli* [power of the word]. One is thus led to say that truth hands itself over to the word only by escaping from it so as to take refuge in secrets, and that speech becomes eloquent only through this withdrawal; truly speaking is nothing but silence, the mute origin of every discourse. One also says that there is no revelation of truth without concealment, not only because truth only ever appears as something other than itself and what truth is in itself can only be hidden, but also because each one of its manifestations, inviting us to identify and confuse it with the revelatory word, is the very source of obfuscation and error. And some continue with the claim that thought can contain truth only by preserving it in its ineffability: Truth approaches us by exiting from mystery only in order to return and rest there, because its mode of being present is properly an absence, and its unobjectifiability is nothing other than the indication of its originary solidarity with nothing, and a persistent sign of mother night.

6. Not Mysticism of the Ineffable, but Ontology of the Inexhaustible

These terms of negative theology, no matter how suggestive and in their own way meaningful, are more suited to religious experience than to philosophical discourse, into which they cannot transfer without the risk for radical misunderstandings. First of all, the fact that truth is inseparable from individual interpretation, yet without ever identifying with it, authorizes neither the claim that truth never manifests itself as itself but only as other, nor the assertion that the word is the inadequate site of truth. On the one hand, if it is true that one cannot reveal truth but by interpreting and determining it, it is also true that this interpretation and formulation is precisely a *revelation* of truth, and therefore not something other than truth, but truth itself as personally possessed; and, it can appear in interpretation as a transformation or even a disguise not because it is *a* revelation, but because the interpretation is instead a possession of it, the more genuine the more personal and multiple it is. On the other hand, if it is true that the word can never be an exhaustive enunciation of truth, it is also true that the word is the site best suited for receiving and conserving it as inexhaustible because truth cannot escape the word and withdraw in secret; rather, truth grants itself to the word alone by stimulating it and granting it new revelations. Truth is not pure elusiveness, in respect to which our discourse would remain irreparably heterogeneous, and thus essentially indifferent and meaningful only to the extent that it could reduce itself to cipher, symbol, or allusion; rather, truth is an outward radiation of meanings that make themselves felt through a transvaluation of the word rather than a devaluation of it, conferring to it a new depth and breadth in which the explicit loses its own poverty, flees from the temptation to isolate itself in a presumptuous sufficiency, and declares the richness of the implicit that it carries within itself.

Furthermore, the philosophical exaltation of mystery, of silence, and of the cipher, risks being a simple overturning of the rationalistic cult of the explicit and preserving all of the nostalgia for it. If truth resides in the word without fully identifying with it, it is not because, frustrated by discourse, it loves to hide, but because no revelation worthy of the name exhausts it. *Unwissendes Wissen* [unknowing knowing], thought that aspires to know everything, inevitably leads to *Nichtwissen* [ignorance], whereas only *das sich selbst vernichtende Wissen* [the self-destroying knowing], a knowing that is aware of the inexhaustible, the *Überschwengliches* [inexhaustible] and that knows to renounce its own presumption, achieves a *vollendetes Wissen* [complete knowing]. That revelation implies an inseparability of disclosure and latency is undeniable, but the true foundation of that connection is inexhaustibility, which keeps disclosure, no longer nourished by the origin, from losing itself in an arrogant explication, and latency, by now already rescued from discourse, from being swallowed up in mystery. Inexhaustibility is that thanks to which, instead of presenting itself under the false appearance of concealment, absence, or obscurity, ulteriority shows its true origin, that is, its richness, fullness, and excess, through its inexhaustibility: not nothingness, but Being; not *steresis* [lack], but *hyperoche* [pre-eminence]; not *Abgrund* [abyss], but *Ungrund* [ungrounded ground]; not the *mustikos gnophos tes agnosias* [mystical darkness of the lack of knowledge], but the *anexichniaston ploutos* [unsearchable richness]: not the mysticism of the ineffable, but the ontology of the inexhaustible.

7. The Failure of Demythification: The Irrationalism of Reason Without Truth

Were some, not content with these clarifications, to insist that revelatory thought be demythified, they would find themselves faced with the irresolvable dilemma of choosing between a precarious rationalism and a questionable irrationalism. On the one hand, one might think it possible to replace myth with logos, never considering that this is the greatest of rationalistic prejudices because logos and myth have different functions. Logos cannot take the place of myth, nor can myth be considered an inferior form of logos. Myth that lets itself be destroyed by logos is not myth, but embryonic logos; and the logos that wants to destroy myth is not logos, but myth that lacks self-awareness. On the other hand, it would be absurd to derive from the so-called "mythic" aspect of revelatory thought the consequence, only seemingly more frank and critical, of a deliberate and programmatic mythology. That would entail shifting attention from truth to the means of accessing it, exchanging the goal for that which can only be its effect. The result would be that the word, no longer revelatory but now arbitrary and irrational, would be lost in the unforeseeable allusiveness of the symbol and the cipher.

In both cases, the originary connection of person and truth is broken, either because, due to a lack of confidence in thinking, one overemphasizes the personal aspect of it and closes it up in the incommunicability of an allegory or an experience, or because, due to the suspicion of reason, one aims at suppressing the inexhaustibility of thought by reducing it to perfect correspondence and complete explication. Either way, the outcome is essentially the same, that is, irrationalism, because what goes lost is the very thing that preserves thought from an irrational destination—namely, its ontological aspect, its rooting in truth.

What counts is truth, not reason. Reason without truth quickly leads to irrationalism because it is solely historical or technical thought in which even the more "theoretical" aspects, such as the purely cultural interest of the history of ideas or the strictly scientific rigor of methodological investigations, do not resist the radicalization that inevitably pushes them toward the irrationalistic outcomes of integral historicism or explicit praxism. The necessary demythologization of revelatory thought does not at all follow from the proper and necessary demystification of merely historical and expressive thought; in fact, from it one gains the awareness that if one does not want to reduce thought to a pure instrument of action or a mere temporal expression, one needs to preserve the indivisibly personal and ontological aspect of thought and welcome its originary rootedness in truth.

8. The Servitude of Technical Thought and the Freedom of Revelatory Thought

It will be said that the problematicity of human nature is lost because the reality of a secure and guaranteed possession of truth would eliminate the precariousness of the human situation and the tentative character of its investigation. The ontological nature of thought and the unobjectifiability of truth are, however, very far from offering such a peaceful and uncontested possession of truth because they instead solicit and appeal to freedom. They engage freedom in a vicissitude that, although it demands the courage of a personal formulation of truth, proves itself successful at its discovery only in so far as it does not ignore the risk for failure. Thus, human beings are confronted with their own responsibilities and must be ready to pay in person because theirs is not so much a discovery as it is a witnessing. In fact, risk, courage, responsibility—these are concepts that have meaning only in the presence of truth and that sharpen the problematicity of the human being by bringing such problematicity to the highest point of tension and thus rescuing it from the cold and impersonal process through which technical thought tests and corrects itself.

The protagonist in revelatory thought is certainly truth. Suprapersonal and atemporal, it towers over human beings and appeals to their approval, stimulates their quest, supports their efforts, and evaluates their results. Truth does all this within the very activity by which an individual seeks and formulates truth, so that truth addresses the freedom of the human beings and maintains them in their freedom. Not only does truth grant human beings the initiative, but in fact it claims and demands such an initiative. In the radical humanism of historical thought, instrumental discourse, and technical reason, it seems as if the protagonist were the human beings because it is a matter of a truly human thought that has relinquished absolute truth, that expresses historical situations, that acts on conditions of existence, and that elaborates rational methods. When deprived of truth, however, the constructions of reason overwhelm human beings and grow larger until they become their masters and exert on them an appalling and terrible power that reduces humans to the most monstrous slavery.

Certainly, the effectiveness of historical and pragmatic thought and of technical and instrumental thought is conspicuous and prominent because of its efficiency and success. This is not the standard, however, by which one should measure revelatory thought. An idea can be powerful even if it is not word of truth. Actually, only powerful ideas, that is, the products of historical and technical reason, can properly "have success." They have it, but only on the condition of exerting a power that enslaves humanity. Truth inspires human beings, whereas ideas master them. Truth lifts and exalts human beings beyond themselves, making even the humble capable of great things; ideas take possession of humans, subjugate them to the realization of their programs, and reduce them to mere tools, whether as cosmic-historical heroes or as faceless masses. No slavery compares with the slavery of human beings to their own ideas: One can think of the domination exercised by fashion, by commonplaces, by the cult of what is current, by the most diverse forms of conformity, and above all one can think of the violence of ideological battles, of political and religious fanaticism, and of so-called religious wars that should more aptly be termed wars of superstition, which is the purely human counterfeit of religion.

Human beings become slaves solely to themselves and their own ideas. Whereas obedience to reason lacking truth is the most intolerable of tyrannies, there is nothing servile about human beings' obedience to truth. In this case, obedience coincides with freedom because truth inspires rather than dominates, stimulates rather than imposes, supports rather than subjugates: It is a call that demands an answer and a witnessing, not an imposition that oppresses or constrains; it is an appeal that places human beings in front of their responsibilities and urges them freely to commit the self-assertive act that confirms their own being, recovers their origin, and indissolubly fastens the bond between person and truth: *he aletheia eleutherosei humas* [the truth will set you free].

Notes

Page 15: that in philosophy everyone says the same thing and that each individual says only one thing are theses that in a certain sense are found on the one hand in Heidegger and on the other hand in Bergson; but Heidegger affirms these theses on *solely* ontological grounds and Bergson on *non*-personalistic grounds. It is my intention to sustain them on the basis of an *ontological personalism*, where the two aspects, the first ontological and the other personalistic, are not only not to be disjoined, but also cannot be conceived other than as together.

Page 19: The indirect citations of Heraclitus and Plotinus are easily recognized. The terminology of "saying," "concealing," and "signifying" belongs to Heraclitus: The Oracle of Delphi, he says, *oute legei oute kruptei alla semainei:* "neither indicates clearly nor conceals, but gives a sign" (see fragment 93, Plutarch, *De Pythiae Oraculis* 404D from Heraclitus, *Fragments: A Text and Translation with Commentary*, by T.M. Robinson [Toronto: University of Toronto Press, 1987], 57). The concept of *kata parousian epistemes kreittona* [a presence transcending knowledge] is from Plotinus (VI ix 4): Cilento translates "by way of a presence worth much more than science."

Page 20: The Greek citation, *houto bathun logon echei*, is also from Heraclitus, and means "so deep a measure does it possess" (22 B 45 Diels/Robinson, 57).

Page 23: Regarding the beginning of the sixth section, one recalls the claim that "*vor solchen Mysterien zu warnen ist Pflicht*" [it is a duty to warn against these mysteries], a claim made by Schelling, that is, a thinker who also greatly indulged in the exaltation of obscurity and of not knowing (V 260), showing a caution equal to the resipiscence that causes Cusano to confess: "*putabam ego aliquando veritatem in obscuro melius reperiri* [I once thought it was better for truth to be found in the darkness]" *(De apice theoriae)*, and to defend the *vis vocabuli* [power of the term], however only in the *theologia sermocinalis* (*Idiota: De sapientia* II).

Pages 23–24: The German citations are from Schelling's *Munich Lectures on the History of Modern Philosophy*. They follow expressions connected to the whole history of negative theology (and also to Heidegger's negative ontology, already alluded to on page 22), and for which it is obviously useless to give precise references, as they are abundant in the history of thought. The "mystical darkness of unknowing," that is the *mustikos gnophos tes agnosias*, is from Pseudo-Dionysius (Migne, P.G. 1001 A), while the *anexichniaston ploutos*, the "unfathomable richness," the "*investigabiles divitiae*," are, as was noted, from Saint Paul (*Epistles*, III 8). One could continue by contrasting, for example, to the *huperphotos sighes gnophos*, to the "more than luminous obscurity of silence," of Pseudo-Dionysius (Migne, P.G. 997), the "infinite fullness" of Plato: *plethos apeiron* (*Parmenides* 144A).

Page 27: The Greek citation is the celebrated passage from Saint John the Evangelist: "The truth will set you free" (VIII 32).

Part I

Truth and History

1

Permanent Values and Historical Process

1. The Inadequacy of the Historicism and the Empiricism that Characterize Today's Culture

Widespread historicism and rampant empiricism, two of the most common characteristics of today's culture, acquire a particular relevance in light of the problem of the permanence of values in history.

Today's historicistic mindset does not take the form of a rigorous or precise theory, even though it derives from nineteenth- and twentieth-century historicism, whether in its idealistic, materialistic or culturalistic forms; rather, it gains its strength from being the more or less conscious criterion of current evaluations by the majority of cultured individuals, and compensates for its lack of philosophical rigor by being a truly integral form of historicism. This mindset carries the historicistic principle of *veritas filia temporis* [truth is the child of its time] to its most extreme consequences: that is, a historical form has no other value than its exact correspondence with the time in which it is born and of which it is simply a product; thus it possesses a momentary and ephemeral reality, and it is quickly confined to an irrevocable and definitive past.

This historicistic mindset often combines somewhat coherently with a form of practicism. When Nietzsche denounced the sterility of historicism, he correctly meant to show that it was impossible to confront the present with categories that belonged to the past: An understanding that justifies everything, and thus rejects judging and acting, might perhaps be able to penetrate the past, but on the present will only have a paralyzing effect. Nothing but a dangerous rift between thought and action could follow from it: On the one hand, action—which is in itself destined to the present—is released from thought, that is, it becomes pure praxis; on the other hand thought—once released from action—is kept in the past, in fact confined to it, and remains there, rendered sterile and infertile.

And so, the current way of doing politics is often nothing more than pure praxis, blind to every relation with theory that is not reduced to a complete instrumentalization of doctrines, and the current way of doing history is often inspired by an artificial neutrality that, rightly suspicious of rhetoric, nonetheless makes us incapable of evaluating the problems of the present. Another commonplace in today's culture is therefore explained, namely, the one according to which ideas are confined to the past while the present has room only for ideologies: Theory and speculative discussion would be things of the past, and the present day would only respect practical debates, whether political or religious. From this derives the increasingly frequent presence of philosophers as it were split in half—one half is culturalist, the other half is ideological—in whom the capacity for speculative philosophy and the understanding of the world live separately because the first, reduced to a neutral (albeit very critical) technique, serves only to deal with doctrines from the past, and the second constitutes nothing more than a practical choice, valid only in the present. Under the aegis of historicism, thought has divested itself of truth up to this extreme.

The other characteristic of today's culture, rampant empiricism, also can be understood easily, as it is nothing other than the logical result of the attempt by the so-called social sciences to replace philosophy. Today, to the degree to which it does not give way to action, thought tends to become empirical thought, which is precisely the kind of reflection that characterizes social sciences such as psychology, sociology, ethnology, cultural anthropology, linguistics, cultural history, and so on. These sciences have the greatest legitimacy when they remain within their proper limits, where they are truly irreplaceable, fulfilling an important function that is extremely useful for philosophy itself. The data that they collect, compare, and interpret reach such a high level of generalization as to demonstrate stable elements, recurrent features, permanent structures within the flux of human history, thus bringing about a valid contribution to the ever-growing knowledge about human beings. The investigation of human cultural forms as it is practiced in this field of studies certainly intensifies the experience that human beings have of themselves and the world. One might even say that philosophy could only benefit from the success of these sciences, and they are very useful to philosophy also in the sense that they increase the plurality of experiential fields on which philosophical thought must reflect, in contact with concrete questions and dealing with particular problems.

Some intellectuals today would, however, be pleased if the social sciences did not content themselves with this function and aimed to replace philosophy, going so far as to claim to be the only philosophy currently still possible. Truthfully, philosophy itself has allowed this to happen when it has accepted its role as a methodology for particular sciences. Taken in this way, philosophy becomes a rationality transparent to itself insofar as technically effective in individual fields of experience; that is, it becomes reason aware of itself but devoid of truth. In a word, it is *empty* thought, and as such, it is not only incapable of stopping the invasion of the social sciences, which are so rich with concrete contents, but is also ready to surrender its domain to them. At this point empirical thought—so useful when understood as the field on which to exercise a philosophical reflection committed to its own exquisitely speculative character—takes over philosophy entirely, purges it ever more of truth, and reduces it to the most resolute empiricism.

Now, if in today's culture there is some obstacle that keeps us from recognizing the presence of permanent values within the historical process, it is the historicist mindset and the triumphant empiricism. From a historicist point of view, the value of historical forms consists exclusively in their adherence to the time in which and from which they arise, that is, in their ability to express their own epoch. It is therefore a matter of a thoroughly transitory validity, rigorously limited to the narrow precincts and paltry duration of the historical situation. From an empiricist point of view, constant structures certainly exist in human history, verifiable beyond even the most subtle differences in situation, behavior, and civilization; but, these constants are nevertheless verifiable only in an empirical way and cannot be elevated above the level of a pure fact. In conclusion, in history there would exist on the one hand values that lack permanence, and on the other hand constant characteristics that do not suffice as values.

2. The Historicity of Values and Historical Durability

At this point it is necessary to submit the concept of permanent values in history to a rigorous philosophical critique, not only in order to protect it from ruin at the hands of historicism and empiricism, but also to correct and sharpen its meaning. Far too often we entertain, without critique, the rather naïve idea that history is the temporal realization of supra-temporal values, along with the simple distinction that follows from it between permanent insofar as supra-historical values and historical and thus temporal facts. If the problem is to distinguish in history what is truly permanent as a supra-historical value from what, as a historical fact, is solely temporal, one must recognize that in history everything is equally historical and temporal, including values, and that in the human world even permanence can mean nothing more than historical durability.

It is necessary to admit that in history all values are historical: They are born in time, surging forth from history, and live in time where they awaken new history. History is both that which flows into them and also that which moves from them; that is, it is both the substance of which they are formed and also the activity that they promote in their own footsteps because every value is simultaneously result and model, completion and beginning, and thus at the same time includes a past and opens up a future, concludes a process and begins new ones. The permanence of values consists precisely in their fully historical reality as for both origin and effectiveness; it consists in their capacity to endure in time after being born within time, and in their somewhat perpetual existence, whereby they condense the history that has nourished them into the stability of one historical form and also stimulate a new activity that is inspired by them and models itself after them. In a word, the permanence of values consists in a presence that is enduring in time because it generates history.

The dialectic of exemplarity and kindredness, which articulates the historical comportment of human beings, suffices to explain this sort of durability. On the one side, a human work that is not only new but truly original—where originality is the fortunate and indissoluble marriage of the universal and unquestionable feature of value with the singular and unrepeatable feature of success—becomes an exemplar and demands to be taken up and continued in a new activity; and on the other side, this exemplarity is effective only when it is welcomed within a historical environment spiritually akin to that from which the original value has emerged, so that only kindredness makes its original continuation possible.

On the one hand, it seems impossible to accept the still rather popular idea that the rhythm of human spirit consists in an alternation between innovative impulses and inactive pauses, as if the perpetuation of a successful result were tied to a passive habit. The exemplarity of value is not the immobile completeness of a perfection that could only allow its imitation; rather, it is the generative vigor of originality that not only demands but also even initiates an industrious and eager emulation. On the other hand, exemplarity bears fruit only when welcomed within an act of agreement and participation, the kind that only the communal feeling [*simpatia*] and awareness of belonging to a same spiritual community can inspire. Only at this point the new activity is in its turn original because, far from being subjected to the model, it instead seizes the opportunity to welcome and assimilate it so that the exemplarity of value, albeit an independent power, acts solely as internal stimulus and support for the activity that could discover and adopt it.

Thus, styles and customs establish themselves in all human activities as true lasting traces in the history of humanity, living incarnations of the very durability of values. But their duration is exactly historical: They last as long as the correspondence between exemplarity and kindredness ensures an equilibrium between conservation and innovation. When the kindredness weakens, this equilibrium breaks and the *synthesis* that inseparably united conservation and innovation gives way to the *dilemma* of repetition and revolt, and to the choice between conformity or rupture. Styles and customs, rigidified into manners and habits, degenerate toward death under the blows and refusals of a rebellious will.

3. Beyond Values and Beyond Durability: The Presence of Being

When speaking of permanent values in history, however, one does not mean the permanence mentioned above: In this case, one understands a presence far more originary and profound, of which historical durability can be in itself neither the effect nor the distinguishing mark.

It is a matter of a stimulating and regulating power internal to human industriousness [*operosità*]; it is so profound that it is inseparable from the acts that it produces and indistinguishable from the response that it receives, but it is also so peremptory that it is irreducible to human activity and present to it as its starting point and norm. In a word, it is presence without figure, yet powerful and unwavering—the presence of Being. Such a power need not appeal to external and preexistent values because it is inseparable from the activity that it stimulates and guides, nor does it need to be considered as its own value because it possesses and exercises a vigorous power in itself. We need not return to Heidegger's very severe yet persuasive critique of the concept of value in order to convince ourselves that ontology has no need for axiology, nor to understand that to conceive of Being as value does not exalt it, but degrades it.

Value is a quality of human works, and exemplarity is the power of historical values. To claim that Being should be endowed with exemplarity in order to have a stimulating power, and likewise that Being should be a value in order to possess normative vigor, amounts to attributing to Being qualities inferior to its nature and forgetting that the capacity for stimulation and regulation derives more from the *inexhaustibility* and *originarity* of *Being* than from the *exemplarity* and *originality* of *value*. Understanding Being as value turns everything upside down: Being is then subordinated to human needs and human beings are released from the service of Being; as a result, Being depreciates and falls into oblivion, whereas human beings are degraded and consigned to the negative because to believe that one has the power to exalt humanity while suppressing the ontological character of its activity actually means reducing the human to a position below itself. When humanity strives to make itself *super-human* [*superuomo*], its destiny is to become nothing but *sub-human* [*subuomo*].

It is also impossible to claim that historical durability is the sign or effect of Being's presence. First of all, it would be excessive optimism to believe that the durable is in itself positive. Frequently, truth is neither effective nor recognized in the human world, and evil is often more popular and successful than the good. Nor should one refrain from admitting that the negative can also be durable: In human history, the negative is certainly more persistent and tenacious than the positive. Indeed, in a certain sense, true persistence is precisely negativity because obstinacy and stubbornness are the orientations best suited to evil and error. Even if against our will, we must abandon the naïve trust that enduring things are always positive and that the good should be, in and of itself, enduring. This prejudice contradicts itself, as it is itself an effect of the persistence of the negative: *diabolicum est diabolum negare* [to deny the devil is a devil's activity].

Moreover, the presence of Being has so little to do with historical durability that one could just as easily attribute it to a simple instant. There is no reason why Being should reside in the enduring rather than in the momentary, and its presence neither extends the life of the enduring nor cuts short the momentary. It matters little whether Being appears in the rapidity of the instant or in the extension of time because it can make itself present in a single instant or remain absent from an entire epoch. Thus, the merely temporal distinction between the enduring and the ephemeral does not suffice to distinguish the ontological import of any temporal trait. It is true that time is the only venue for the appearance of Being, yet it is also true that the external traits of temporality are not transformed by the presence of Being. There is also no sign that could, from the outside, characterize the bearer of Being among the moments of time, as the temporal aspect of such a bearer is always the same. Similarly for Kierkegaard, the possession of the eternal does not change the everydayness of time, and the knight of faith has all the features of a tax collector or a grocer on vacation, of a shopkeeper who dedicates himself to his work with earthly perseverance and at night smokes his pipe content that the day is at its end. He possesses the infinite, but none of it leaks through to the outside, and no sign of the incommensurable betrays him, because he lives completely entrusted to the finite, as only the one who contains the eternal can do.

The problem is not to distinguish what in history would be permanent as a supra-historical value from what, as a historical fact, would be solely temporal. In history, *everything* is equally historical and temporal. The problem is rather to recognize the presence of Being in history, and thus to distinguish—in what is *entirely and equally* historical and expressive of its own time—between that which is *solely* historical and expressive and that which is *also* ontological and revelatory, between those things whose nature and value exhaust themselves in historicity, and those whose historicity is the opening and path to Being, and thus its site and apparition.

4. The Inexhaustibility of Being as Foundation of Its Presence and Ulteriority in Historical Forms

How is Being present in history? First and foremost we should exclude the metaphysical identification of the Absolute with the finite, which would impress on history a univocal and progressive direction and would recognize the manifestation of the Absolute in a series of historical moments. The problematicity of the relation between human beings and Being has nothing to do with an objective metaphysical glance that claims to see the Absolute unfold in the multiplicity of its manifestations. Although Being only ever appears in time, not all time is revelatory because Being abandons those who betray it, and thus whole epochs remain devoid of truth.

Nor is the presence of Being tied to the exercise of a pure formality, which according to a renewed transcendentalism would receive its content only from the circumstances, and would ensure the success of human activities on the ground of an intrinsic and autonomous criterion of reason and behavior. When removed from the vigor of their originary ontological rootedness, human thought and freedom sink to the neutrality of a purely instrumental reason or a mere technique for behavior.

Furthermore, Being is not present in history through its very own determinacy, in a form that is recognizable as unique and definitive, one that aids in the comparison of historical forms, thus rendering their appraisal swift, easy, and infallible. The presence of Being can be configured only historically, and Being has no other way to appear or place to reside but in historical forms. Being resides there in its *inexhaustibility*, that is, on the one hand with a *presence* that makes these forms its only way of appearing, and on the other hand with an *ulteriority* that allows none of them to contain it exclusively. Being resides there in such a way that it entrusts itself to the forms that reveal it, to the point of being inseparable from them; yet Being is never fully dissolved in a historical form, even though it gives itself over to it. This does not mean that when a historical form is revelatory one can separate, within it, a temporal and transient aspect from an atemporal and immutable substance, because everything in it is equally temporal and revelatory; nor does it mean that Being could distinguish itself from the historical form such that it could compare that form with another in order to judge them; rather, it means that Being resides in historical forms as an always ulterior presence, in all of the irrepressible force of its inexhaustibility.

There is no need to claim that this inexhaustibility of Being is, as one says today, a sort of meta-cultural permanence continually unformed and inaccessible so that it floats above all historical events, as if it feared contamination through contact with time and would retain its innovative and stimulatory power only if it were immune from every historical predicament. Aside from the fact that the meta-historicity of something appears less through its power to transcend its own historical forms and more from its power to be embodied in ever newer forms, it nevertheless remains the case that Being resists figuration to such a degree that it appears solely in historical determinations with which it truly coincides. Certainly, Being is present in such determinations in the only way that it can reside *wholly*, that is, in its inexhaustibility, which keeps it from dissolving into any one of these forms. This inexhaustibility does not tower over the historical forms, however; rather, it appears only *within* each one of them. And whereas Being only appears within a historical form, from which it is inseparable without being exhausted, it must also be said that this form is a *revelation* of Being, that is, neither its alteration nor disguise nor surrogate, but *Being itself as* historically determined.

5. Historical Forms as Interpretations of Being: The Elimination of Relativism

This presence of Being in history refers back to that concept of *interpretation* where the originary solidarity between human beings and truth is realized. Interpretation is also revelatory and historical at the same time, because on one hand truth is accessible only within each individual perspective, and on the other hand it is this same historical situation that is the pathway to truth. Truth cannot therefore be revealed unless one is already determining and formulating it, which only occurs personally and historically. The interpretation of truth is also the possession of an infinite: Truth offers itself only within the formulation that one gives of it and is inseparable from this formulation, such that it could not be presented with a determinacy and objectivity by which the formulation itself could be compared and judged from the outside; and that formulation, although unable to monopolize the inexhaustibility of truth that supports an infinity of other formulations, is *truth itself* in the form of a personal possession, and is nothing other than truth: not its image, nor its distortion, nor its replacement.

Interpretation is therefore born as revelatory and plural *at one and the same time*, and for this reason it escapes every accusation of relativism. Its plurality derives from the overabundant nature of the very truth that resides there, that is, it surges forth from the same source whence the manifestation of truth springs; and far from dispersing truth into a series of indifferent formulations, this plurality unveils truth in its inexhaustible richness. In its infinity, truth can offer itself to many diverse perspectives, and interpretation maintains its uniqueness in the very act that multiplies its formulations, in the same way that a work of art, far from dissolving in a plurality of arbitrary performances, remains the same work while entrusting itself to always newer interpretations that know how to grasp and render it, and while coinciding with them.

The final elimination of relativism becomes possible as soon as one grasps the *revelatory and at the same time plural* nature of interpretation, that is, when one understands fully that in interpretation the *revelatory* aspect is *inseparable* from the *historical* aspect. The interpretative relation between truth and its formulation is *at one and the same time* one of identity and ulteriority in perfect equilibrium. In one sense, truth coincides with its formulation so that it can be possessed in a revelatory way; yet this possession does not go so far as to authorize its exclusive and complete, let alone unique and final, presentation, for in such a case it would no longer be interpretation, but a surrogate for truth, that is, one of the many historical formulations that claim to be absolute and replace truth. In another sense, truth is always ulterior in respect to its formulation, but only so as to require a plurality of formulations. Truth does not convey a sense of its absolute ineffability, against which all formulations would remain fatally inadequate and irreparably insignificant, in a common and resigned equivalence and indifference, as relativism would have it, thereby cutting off any exit save an arbitrary and praxistic choice.

In the same way, a historical form—an epoch, civilization, or idea—can be an interpretation of Being, namely Being itself as historically determined, without implying an affirmation of relativism. Even the relation between Being and the historical form that reveals it is *interpretative*. That demonstrates, moreover, how the presence of Being in history is something much more radical and profound than any historical durability. Interpretation, in the very act that explains how a historical form is an epiphany of Being, grounds a reality that from the outside may even bear a resemblance to historical duration, but that possesses a nature much more substantial and originary—tradition.

6. The Originarity of Tradition

The possibility of tradition is tied *necessarily* to the interpretation of truth. In fact, interpretation gives a formulation of truth while possessing it as inexhaustible. That means that it contains *at one and the same time* a bottomless reserve of implicit possibilities and the indication of a specific manner of their realization. As possession of an inexhaustible, interpretation implies an immeasurable divide between explicit and implicit, said and unsaid, already thought and not yet thought. This divide grounds the difference between past, present, and future; but because it comes from that same inexhaustibility of the true that is originarily possessed by interpretation, it prevents the present from the possibility of finding the authentic meaning of the past unless [such a meaning] is referred back to the origin, and at the same time it offers [the present] the possibility of attaining the origin through its own reference to the past. Therefore, an interpretation necessarily grounds a tradition, because the unceasing deepening that it solicits ties the unraveling of present possibilities not only to the patrimony of possibilities already developed, but also to the very source of infinite possibilities. Thus a historical form is simultaneously a determinate interpretation of Being and a reserve of possibilities to be discovered and developed; and the stimulus to develop them, along with the way of discovering them, is suggested *at one and the same time* by the *past* and by *Being*: by the past, not as time gone by, but as historical reality referred back to its origin; and by Being, not in its alleged unrepresentability, but as that which is historically determined. A tradition gushes forth and flows precisely from that past recovered in its ontological rootedness and placed back within the temporal appearing of Being.

One can now see how far true tradition is from historical durability, even though it can assume its form and aspect. Consider, for example, loyalty to the past taken as heritage to be preserved, legacy to be worthy of, and wealth to be invested; or kindredness intended as a task, so that one knows how to project the past in its exemplarity and continue it in an original way; or the steady purpose of diligently cultivating the equilibrium between conservation and innovation: These are all noble and worthy things, but they have little to do with tradition, of which at best they can be the subjective form and exterior garment, destined to disappear in the void without tradition itself. Tradition is something far more profound because it does not limit itself to being the transmission of a historical result, but is fundamentally a listening to Being; that is, it is a dialogue with the past only insofar as it is an appeal to the origin. It traverses the centuries not because it is positioned in time, but because it is inserted at the heart of the temporal advent of Being.

Tradition has an essentially originary and ontological nature. It does not simply suggest loyalty to the past and transmission of a heritage; rather, it indicates the very conditions of such a loyalty and transmission, freeing them from a merely temporal dimension and returning them to their originarity. It shows that linking the present to a past and continuing a past in the present is truly possible and fertile only if the past is delivered from its mere temporality and recovered in a more originary manner, only if the past is considered to be a bearer of the implicit, and for that reason imbued with an ontological import, and only if the past is seen not as anterior to the present, but as close to Being. It shows that only the loyalty to Being can point out a possibility worthy of development in a historical form, and that a genuine invocation of the past means evoking the originary presence that it contains. The determining element in tradition is thus the call to the origin and the recovery of the ontological dimension of time, as it becomes manifest in the fact that the great traditions love to attribute a mythical character to their own beginnings and an esoteric character to their own means of transmission. The allegory in this is clear: On the one hand, one represents that which is originary and close to Being as primordial and distant in time, and on the other hand, one imagines as esoteric that which, due to its revelatory character, deserves a protection capable of preserving it from temporal dissipation.

7. Regeneration and Revolution

Tradition contains within itself the possibility of continual renewal due to its originarity, one that places it in direct contact with Being. True renewal of the past does not consist so much in a subjective act of originality inspired by kindredness in the person who welcomes and prolongs it, as it does in the fact that *by its very nature* tradition cannot hand something down if not through renewal of it, because tradition draws directly from the first spring of every authentic novelty that is the always fresh and inexhaustible source of Being, of that for which "every single day is as though it were the first." More than a renewal, this is the case of a true and proper *regeneration* that may even implicate or require profound transformations feared only by those who count on the durability of historical values and the constants in human behavior. The guardians of truth do not fear these transformations, for they know that they are due to a commitment to deepen the inexhaustibility of Being. At this level, the problem is no longer that of avoiding the loss of equilibrium between conservation and innovation but, much more radically, of choosing whether to remain faithful to Being or betray it because faithfulness is owed not to a historical and temporal form as such, but to the originary presence that is harbored there.

Tradition is the opposite of revolution not because it opposes revolution with conservation, but precisely because the originary and ontological regeneration that tradition demands differs completely from the regeneration advanced by revolution, regeneration that only has a temporal and secondary nature. First of all, revolution wants to start again from the *beginning*, whereas tradition is a continual recovery of the *origin*. The true object of a revolutionary stance is the *past* as such, whereas in tradition it is above all *Being*. Revolution longs for a new beginning *in time*, whereas tradition refers to the origin whence only a regeneration *of time* can come.

Furthermore, by virtue of the revelatory and plural nature of interpretation, tradition reaches the level where a formulation of truth and a historical formulation are affirmed over the recognition of other formulations and other forms through a free discussion with them. Conversely, grounding its own idea on the radical rejection of others, revolution removes such an idea from the pluralistic level of interpretation and turns it into a mere surrogate for truth, thus lowering itself to the level of temporality left to itself and immersed in the oblivion of Being.

Finally, revolution, in its most rigorous meaning today, is radical praxism that tries to institute the unity of theory and praxis *after* their separation, and that by proposing nothing more than their re-unification, remains still entangled within the lower register of division, unable to elevate itself to the ontological relation. Such a relation would be the *originary* unity of theory and praxis because it is indivisibly revelation of truth and decision for Being.

8. Being and Freedom

Certainly, by not appearing in a form that is its own, let alone unique and definitive, but always in the historical forms from which it is inseparable, Being opens the way to an apparent disorder wherein the lack of an extrinsic and objective criterion that could serve as an infallible point of reference seems to abandon everything to uncertainty and contestability, that is, exactly to what one wants to avoid when speaking of permanent values in history. This uncertainty and indeterminacy, however, are the exterior signs of an important and decisive fact: The interpretation of truth and the revelation of Being are entrusted to our freedom.

This does not mean that Being is abandoned to freedom, and thus that freedom is abandoned to itself: By its own exercise, freedom attests to the originary presence that solicits freedom in the very act in which such a presence entrusts itself to freedom, and that governs freedom in the very act in which such a presence accepts becoming the object of freedom's choice. The act through which freedom decides for or against Being is also the act by which it decides to either confirm itself or deny itself because it is a matter of confirming or rejecting the ontological relation that constitutes the very being of the human beings. Freedom is so tied to Being that freedom validates Being through its own decision for or against it, and it affirms it, albeit in the form of a betrayal, even when it rejects it thereby negating and destroying itself.

There is, therefore, something stable even if it does not establish itself as an absolute and permanent value or in a unique and definitive formulation—it is the stimulation and regulation, internal to human activity yet irreducible to it that is indebted to the presence of Being yet is set to work by human freedom. Such stimulation and regulation are attested in those rare and happy moments in human activities [*operare*] when entirely distinct attitudes like *audacity* and *humility* are joined *inseparably*, when the most silent and subdued listening to Being demands the courage to risk a personal formulation of truth.

Notes

Page 34: On the dialectic of exemplarity and kindredness, allow me to direct the reader to the treatment of that topic developed in Luigi Pareyson, *Estetica: teoria della formatività* (second edition, 115–150), and in the essay "Tradition and innovation" contained in Luigi Pareyson, *Conversazioni di estetica* (Milan: Mursia, 1966). Everything that I say there regarding aesthetics also applies to the whole of human activity. On the idea that forms give rise to styles, I refer the reader to the thought of Augusto Guzzo.

Page 35: Heidegger's critique of the concept of value can be found above all in Martin Heidegger, *An Introduction to Metaphysics*, translated by Ralph Manheim (New Haven: Yale University Press, 1959), 196–199; in "Letter on 'Humanism,'" translated by Frank Capuzzi in *Pathmarks*, ed. William McNeill (Cambridge: Cambridge University Press, 1999), 263–266; and in *Off the Beaten Track*, translated by Julian Young and Kenneth Haynes (Cambridge: Cambridge University Press, 2002), 168–173. Heidegger's critique is based on the principle that the attribution of value to Being supposes a subjectivistic conception that can have no coherent result other than the absolutization of the human point of view, and thus the most complete "forgetfulness of Being." On the one hand, the concept of value not only degrades entities once the concept is applied to them by not thinking Being in them, but it also forgets and suppresses Being itself because it does not let it open itself in its truth; instead, it reduces Being to a pure and simple fact, propped up vainly by an artificial and alternate event of attribution of value to Being and of Being to value. On the other hand, the ones who are degraded and changed in such a way are human beings themselves, who, neglecting Being, become the "killer[s] of God," able to utter "the biggest blasphemy possible against Being," and thus descend below themselves and are lost. Even Gabriel Marcel recalls the primacy of ontology: Axiology not rooted in ontology is false because it replaces authentic values, which are "mediators of transcendence," "incarnate essences," and "active evidences," with artificial values, which in their deceptive objectivity are nothing other than subjective projections: being, value, and freedom can only be saved together (Gabriel Marcel, "Apercus sur la liberté," in *La Nef*, 19 [1946], and "Ontologie et axiologie," in *Esistenzialismo cristiano* [Padua: Cedam, 1949]).

Page 36: The Latin expression that I used to clarify the concept of the "persistence of the negative," namely, *diabolicum est diabolum negare*, suggests from a different point of view and with a different emphasis the expression by Franz von Baader: "*Diabolum negare est Diabolo credere* [to deny the devil is to believe in the devil]" (in Franz von Bader, *Sämtliche Werke* IV 360).

Pages 36–37: Kierkegaard's beautiful pages on the everyday and earthly nature of the knight of faith are found in *Fear and Trembling*, translated by Howard and Edna Hong (Princeton, NJ: Princeton University Press, 1983), 47–50.

Page 42: The citation concerning the origin as that which "every single day is as though that day were its first" is from Martin Heidegger, *An Introduction to Metaphysics*, 97, when after having affirmed that "all thinkers in the history of philosophy have said fundamentally the same thing," he observes that what follows is not at all the necessity of "only one philosophy," as if "everything had already been said," because "*dieses 'dasselbe' hat allerdings den unausschöpfbaren Reichtum dessen zur inneren Warheit, was jeden Tag so ist, als sei es sein erster Tag*" [And yet this 'sameness' has an inner truth, namely the inexhaustible richness of what on every single day is as though that day were its first.]

2

The Originarity of Interpretation

1. Relation with Being and Interpretation of Truth: Ontology and Hermeneutics

Every human relation, whether it is knowing or acting, the understanding of art or interpersonal relations, historical knowledge or philosophical reflection, always has an interpretative character. This would not occur if interpretation were not in itself originary: It qualifies that relation with Being in which the very being of humanity resides; in it, the primigenial solidarity of human beings with the truth is realized. This originarity of interpretation not only explains the interpretative character of every human relation, but also the ontological character of every interpretation, no matter how determined and particular it might be: To interpret means to transcend, and one cannot speak authentically of entities without simultaneously referring to Being. In a word: The originary ontological relation is necessarily hermeneutic, and every interpretation necessarily has an ontological character.

This means that *of truth, there is only ever interpretation*, and that *there is no interpretation, lest it be of truth*. In interpretation, the *originality* that derives from the novelty of the person and time, and the *originarity* that derives from the primordial ontological relation, are indivisible and coessential. Interpretation is that form of knowledge that is *at one and the same time* and inseparably truth bearing and historical, ontological and personal, revelatory and expressive.

2. The Historical Aspect and the Revelatory Aspect of Interpretation are Co-Essential

It follows, first of all, that the only knowledge suitable for truth is interpretation, understood as a historical and personal form of knowledge in which the individual personality [*personalità*] and the historical situation, far from being an impediment or even a limit to knowledge, are its only possible condition and its only suitable organ. In a way, interpretation can be defined as that form of knowledge in which the "object" reveals itself to the degree that the "subject" expresses itself, and vice versa. Thus, the name "interpretation" does not apply when person and time, rather than becoming a medium and an opening towards truth, are the only true object of thought, which then becomes merely historical—whether it be ideological or technical—and destined to pass with time, as it is nothing but its image and product.

The proper character of interpretation is therefore to be *at the same time* revelatory and historical, and the nature of interpretation will not be fully comprehended if one does not understand completely the *coessentiality* of these two aspects—namely, how in interpretation the revelatory aspect is *inseparable* from the historical aspect.

Interpretation is that form of knowledge that is revelatory and ontological *insofar as* it is historical and personal. The personality and historicity of interpretation are not a superficial coloration, or a useless addition, or a careless accompaniment, or worse, an arbitrary superimposition, or a substantial limitation, or even an irreparable deformation, so that one could wish for their removal, plan their suppression, or belittle their fatal character. Regarding truth, person and situation are neither a lethal impediment nor a troublesome obstacle, but rather the sole pathway to it and the only means of knowledge; furthermore, they are an organ of penetration that, when used correctly, is capable and sensitive like no other, and completely suited to the purpose.

By virtue of interpretation, the anti-historicism that inevitably inheres within the investigation and discovery of truth does not and must not have an ascetic character, since the only way to approach the truth is not by exiting *from* history—an impossible task, as that would mean exiting from one's self and from one's own situation—but rather by making use *of* history, which is quite possible, even if it is uncomfortable, arduous, and is the origin of all the difficulties that challenge not only the knowledge of truth, but also every type of interpretation, no matter how particular and specific it might be.

Moreover, revelation of truth and expression of time are so inseparable in interpretation that they stand *in a direct rather than an inverse relation*, precisely because the historical aspect of interpretation, far from suppressing the revelatory aspect of it, is its only possible condition. One cannot say that interpretation would be less revelatory if it were more personal, because it is rather the more revelatory the more it is personal and historical. It is even impossible, in interpretation, to distinguish or claim to separate its temporal and transient aspect from an immutable and permanent nucleus because *everything* there is *equally* and *simultaneously* historical *and* revelatory, personal *and* ontological. If one grasps the truth, one does so not by exiting from history but rather by making use of history as an entrance and point of access, not by renouncing one's self but rather by becoming the very pathway and opening to truth.

In interpretation, revelation of truth and expression of time do not stand in a relation of contiguity or continuity or gradation, but of *synthesis*, in the sense that the one is the form of the other. It is true that the revelation of truth can only be personal and historical, and it is equally true that it, and only it, also contains the truth of time and of the person. Interpretation is *wholly* revelatory and *wholly* expressive, *all together* personal and ontological.

3. Interpretation Is Neither Subjectivistic nor Approximate

It is helpful to dwell for a moment on the fact that the historicity and personality of interpretation are quite far from granting it an arbitrary or approximate character, as though a subjectivism laden with relativistic or skeptical consequences followed from it.

If interpretation is always historical and personal, it is necessarily multiple. The plurality of interpretation, which is the first feature that stands out (*tot capita tot sententiae* [there are as many opinions as there are heads]; *my, your, his, her* interpretation), is often explained in manners that, seeming *prima facie* very natural and almost obvious to everyone, come to be universally accepted and repeated, engendering a series of dangerous ambiguities and inauspicious misunderstandings. For example, one might think that due to its plurality, interpretation dispels and disperses truth or remains irrevocably outside of it; on the one hand, one might say that if interpretations are always new and diverse, that is because they do not give us the truth but merely the image of it produced through our various personas and changeable reactions; and, on the other hand, one might say that if interpretation never appears as unique and definitive, it is because it does not penetrate the heart of truth, but only circles around it, letting its most intimate nature slip away. Considered in this way, interpretation would be limited to the realm of the arbitrary and approximate: the indifferent relativity of the realm of the debatable on the one side, and the shortcomings of a superficial and distorting knowledge on the other. It is quite true that interpretation might fall prey to the two extremes of relativism and skepticism when its own movement unfolds in the subjectivistic dissipation of arbitrary images or in the vain approximation of an object never reached; in such a case, however, interpretation is itself absent because personality, having become the object of expression more than the organ of penetration, superimposes itself on truth, helping to conceal and mask it rather than to capture and reveal it.

The fact is that the plurality of interpretation, far from being a defect or disadvantage, is the surest sign of the richness of human thought. Nothing is more absurd than to want to conceive of interpretation as one and definitive, as with those who would like to believe that knowledge is complete and full only if it is one and that the personal nature of knowledge is a disgraceful and fatal limitation. The error of these prejudices is to conceive of precision and evidence in such a pedestrian and banal way that they cannot then find any of them where the variety and novelty of human life thrives. The subjectivistic and approximate nature of knowledge is not remedied by the impossible option of the supposed unicity of interpretation; in fact, between these two extremes there is no dilemma but interpretation itself as the only genuine option. Interpretation is not less capable of grasping and revealing the truth because of its plurality, historicity and personality; nor does it give up its features of personality, historicity or plurality because of the fact that it reaches and possesses truth. The realm of the interpretable is based on the impossibility of an univocal and direct knowledge through which everyone would reach agreement without contention or dialogue; rather, such a realm presupposes that the only form of genuine knowledge is interpretation, which is in itself historical and personal and thus constitutively multiple and not definitive; and it implies that these traits of interpretation cannot be rejected, and that these features are to be considered not only essential and insuppressible, but also beneficial and favorable.

The fundamental principle of hermeneutics is precisely that interpretation is the only suitable knowledge of truth. This means that truth is accessible and attainable in many ways, and none of these ways, as long as it is worthy of the name "interpretation," is privileged in respect to the others so that it may claim to possess the truth in an exclusive, more complete or better manner. In order to reach its proper goal, interpretation need not be divested of its features of historicity and personality, something that it could not even do because such features cannot be eliminated. In it, the intervention of the person does not consist in self-suppression so that its place is relinquished in favor of an impersonal or depersonalized knowledge, and in order to "let truth be." Certainly, the task of the person in interpretation is precisely this, to "let truth be"; but that in no way means achieving an impersonal or depersonalized knowledge. That bit of "depersonalization," which seems to inhere necessarily in the "faithfulness" of an interpretation, is nothing more than a way to keep historicity and personality from gaining the upper hand, and thus becoming ends in themselves rather than pathways to truth, and concealing truth rather than opening access to it. In order to achieve this aim, however, the historical situation needs to be studied in greater depth and the substance of the person guided to the point of making it an apparatus of attunement and an organ for the penetration of truth. Truth is thus "left to be" inasmuch as it is "attuned to and captured," and it gives itself to interpretation to the degree that interpretation, through its openness and availability, has ensured acceptance of and consent to the truth.

4. The Impossibility of Distinguishing a Short-Lived Aspect and a Permanent Core in Interpretation

It is useful to insist also on another fact noted above, namely, that in interpretation it is impossible to distinguish or to claim to separate what would be its temporal and short-lived aspect from its immutable and permanent core.

Such a distinction would be possible only if in interpretation the historical aspect were separable from the revelatory aspect. Because interpretation is, however, such precisely because it approaches truth through the historicity of the situation and the personality of the thinker, the revelation of truth cannot occur independently from the expression of time, nor the latter without the former. For that reason, one cannot distinguish a "kernel" of interpretation that is atemporal and supra-historical, and thereby eternal and everlasting, nor a "shell" that is fleeting and ephemeral insofar as it is historical and temporal.

In human thought, *everything* is *equally* historical and temporal. If one wants to make a distinction, one could distinguish between the historicity that exhausts itself in the expression of time and the historicity that carries an ontological import, that is, between that which is *solely* historical and thus expressive of its own time without revealing truth, and that which is historical and *also* revelatory in the sense that the revelation of truth, according to the personality and historicity of interpretation, can only assume a historical form and have an expressive aspect. Such a distinction consists precisely in discerning between that which is interpretation and that which is not. The solely historical can do nothing more than express its own time; thus it is short-lived and fleeting, as it is gradually overwhelmed by time, of which it is nothing other than the mere product or image. In interpretation, however, the historical aspect and the revelatory aspect are so indissoluble—inseparably joined by the initiative of the person who makes itself and its own situation an organ of access to truth—that the historical element, indispensable for the manifestation and formulation of truth, is in a sense rescued from the flow of time. Truth is, without a doubt, supra-historical and atemporal, but its historicity and temporality assert themselves only within the historical and temporal formulation truth gradually assumes. Every formulation of truth is always historical and temporal, but its historicity and temporality, although not directly a manifestation or realization of truth, do not pass away with time because they are the opening and pathway to truth. Thus, they are marked by the originary and profound presence of Being.

Hermeneutics definitely excludes the idea that what is historical is thus ephemeral and short-lived, as well as the idea that the knowledge and formulation of truth are devoid of historical and temporal aspects. In interpretation, the historical element, although not ceasing to express time, is so little tied to its flow that it never loses its timeliness, inseparable as it is from the formulation of truth; in turn, the revelation of truth is so little abstracted from time that it rather moves from it and adopts it as an indispensable way and means for the achievement of its own purpose.

One should not cease to distinguish, in human thought, between the permanent and enduring elements and the fleeting and short-lived elements, nor should one stop considering as ephemeral those that are *solely* temporal and historical. One should keep in mind, however, that this close inspection, far from dividing a historical and transient "part" from an eternal and everlasting "part" in the interpretation of truth, does nothing but purify the undiluted and genuine interpretation of truth from the dross of merely historical and technical thought. The purification does not affect the necessity of grasping, in interpretation, the connection that inseparably joins the historical and temporal aspect with the ontological and revelatory aspect as both are essential to the very concept of interpretation.

5. The Unicity of Truth and the Multiplicity of Its Formulations Are Inseparable

The inseparability of the revelatory and historical aspects of interpretation explains how the *unicity of truth* and the *multiplicity of its formulations* can be united without contradiction, and even inseparably.

In fact, to say that interpretation is both and inseparably revelatory and historical is to say that truth is accessible solely within each individual perspective, which in its turn is that same situation as a pathway to truth. One cannot reveal truth without already formulating and determining it, which only happens historically and personally. Therefore truth, though one, never appears in its own determinacy, in a formulation that would be recognized as unique and definitive, but offers itself only within the formulation that it is given each time, and is inseparable from it, so that its only way of appearing is precisely the singularity of its personal and historical formulations.

Interpretation *arises* as both *revelatory* and *plural* precisely because it is simultaneously and inseparably ontological and personal. Its multiplicity, far from compromising the unicity of truth, secures and confirms it. Truth is one, but its formulation is always multiple. There is no contradiction between the unicity of truth and the multiplicity of its formulations because thanks to interpretation, which is always *at one and the same time* historical and revelatory, the unicity of truth asserts itself *only within* the historical and individual formulations that are given of it. It is precisely interpretation that maintains truth as one through the very act that endlessly multiplies its formulations. Interpretation is not, cannot, and must not be one. By definition, it is multiple. Its multiplicity is however the multiplicity of ever new and diverse formulations of truth, that is, the multiplicity that, far from compromising and dispelling the unicity of truth, maintains it and at the same time feeds off of it, protects it while at the same time drawing inspiration and suggestions from it. What is difficult yet necessary to understand is that due to interpretation, the unicity of truth and the multiplicity of its formulations are not only compatible, but indeed are coessential. The one finds its suitable form and its true meaning only in the other.

The formulations of truth are multiple, but their multiplicity does not compromise the unicity of truth. In fact, it supports it and lives from it. Analogously, the unicity of truth does not negate the multiplicity of its formulations, but lives in them and requires them. On the one hand, historical truths would not exist without the one truth of which *they are* interpretations: Without such truth, there would only be expressions of time, devoid of revelatory value, and, emptied of a hermeneutic function, devoid even of a speculative nature. They would be nothing other than merely historical thought, that is, thinking that is solely ideological, technical, and instrumental. On the other hand, that of which there is only one knowledge would not be truth: *The* one formulation of truth is the abolition of truth itself because it claims to confuse itself with truth while *being nothing other than* an interpretation *of it*, that is, *an* individual formulation, compossible with infinite others.

6. The Formulation of Truth Is Its Interpretation, Not Its Subrogation: Neither Its Monopoly nor Its Disguise

In order to have a precise understanding of this central tenet of hermeneutics, two fundamental circumstances must be kept in mind. First of all, truth and its formulation cannot do without each other; in fact, they are so tightly joined that they come to identify with each other. Precisely for that reason they cannot be confused, as would happen if the formulation, understood as something other than truth, were to claim to take truth's place or were to be its mere mask.

There is not one truth on the one side and its multiple formulations on the other, as two orders of things completely different from each other that just happen to meet and be joined at a given point in history. If this were so, there would be no true connection between truth and its formulation: Not only would truth be lost in its own separateness, which would fully justify the current and increasingly prevalent current tendency to deny the unicity of truth, and ultimately, to do away with it completely; but also the indissoluble bond that draws together and in fact identifies truth with its formulation would be dissolved because truth can only appear as formulated, and formulation of truth is only the one that is truth itself as interpreted. This is not to say that there is a unique truth with only one true formulation, and that this one would refract in multiple historical formulations that would more or less faithfully reflect it. The only way that the one truth appears and can appear is precisely in its multiple and historical formulations, which are not for that reason simple copies and tired reflections, but a real incarnation and concrete possession of truth.

By virtue of interpretation, truth and its formulation are constituted in such a way that between them *identity* is possible, and in fact, even necessary; their *confusion*, however, is impossible and, in fact, inadmissible. In their constitutive inseparability they are neither so "different" that they must not identify with each other, nor so "similar" that they can be confused. Indeed, as inseparable they are neither similar to nor different from each other, and precisely because they are identical they cannot be mixed up. It is not that truth only reveals itself *in something other* than itself or that it does not let itself be possessed except *as other* than itself; rather, truth entrusts itself to the historical forms capable of capturing it so such a degree that it gradually comes to identify with each one of them. Every formulation of truth that is worthy of such a name *is* truth itself as personally interpreted and possessed, so that the always new and diverse historical formulations of truth are at the same time the only way truth appears and exists, and our sole means of professing and possessing it.

A formulation of truth is what it is to the extent that it is an interpretation of truth. This means, on the one hand, that the formulation of truth is *nothing other than* interpretation, that is, *an* individual formulation of truth, historical and personal, that as such is compossible with an infinity of other formulations. Thus, it does not have the *right* to replace what properly belongs to truth, that is, its unicity and atemporality because truth can assert its own unicity and atemporality only within each of the individual formulations that it obtains and collects, or better, provokes and demands. On the other hand, this also means that the formulation of truth is, precisely, *interpretation*, that is, authentic and real *possession* that does not cease to be genuine and effective possession even if, as we will see, it presents itself as an unending and infinite task. Truth, already possessed in interpretation, has no *need* to present itself as different from itself and to confuse itself with its own formulations, concealing itself in them as if under a fickle and multicolored disguise that hides and deforms it rather than reveals and declares it.

Othering [*alterazione*] is the concept most detrimental to an exact understanding of hermeneutics, and thus the most misleading when one tries to define what a formulation of truth is. The relation between truth and its formulation is not one of alterity: as if truth could only reveal itself in something other, or present itself only as something other than itself; or as if the interpretation given of it were nothing but its copy or reflection, a picture or an image; or even as if it were to change its very nature—modifying, transforming, and deforming itself—due to the fact that it is formulated; or as if the fact that the various historical and personal formulations contain and possess it in their own specific way would destine it to an unceasing and chameleonesque disguise; or as if the richness of its revelations would turn into a phantasmagoric quick-change artistry. In fact, the two typically inadequate ways of thinking about interpretation and the formulation of truth—monopoly and disguise—can be traced back to this aberrant concept of othering. A formulation of the truth that claims to be the unique one, that is, that claims to monopolize truth in an exclusive possession, would thereby acknowledge its own being other than the truth, other to such a degree that it would want to replace truth. Conversely, to conceive of the various formulations of truth as its unceasing transformations or kaleidoscopic disguises still means to consider them as something other than truth, other to such an extent that they are simply its mere copy, indeed, its mask; or its image, indeed, its apparition; or its reflection, and even its deformation.

The interpretation of truth is one thing, but the subrogation of truth is quite another. As *interpretation*, the formulation of truth *is truth itself* and nothing other than truth. Certainly, it is truth as personally possessed and historically formulated, and not truth in its abstract and impossible separateness. Truth, however, does not alter and transform itself simply due to the fact that it is personally obtained and historically present because personal nature and historicity pertain to the pathway and the means of possession rather than to the source and content of the true. Insofar as it is capable of gathering it up to the point of fully *coinciding with it*, the formulation of truth is pure *revelation* and genuine *possession* of truth. As a *surrogate*, the formulation of truth is an othering of it, that is, nothing other than its copy, reflection, or image; hence the possibility of a *confusion* that mistakes them, that attributes to one of the many formulations the character of unicity that only belongs to truth, or that disperses truth into a multiplicity that properly belongs to its formulations. This leads, on the one hand, to the *substitution* of truth with one of its undeservedly *absolutized* formulations, and on the other hand, to the *dissimulation* of truth under the changing and protean variety of its formulations, enraptured by the maelstrom of an incessant and illusory metamorphosis.

What needs to be exposed is that both monopoly and disguise, far from being in any manner the revelation of truth, are its most radical and total falsification; rather than exhibit the hermeneutical connection that inseparably unites truth with its formulations, they oppose one to the other in a deceptive equivocation that will only degenerate into open duplicity. Here, in fact, a particular formulation claims to replace truth, that is, to possess it exclusively, and truth hides behind its formulations as if under the unstable mutability of a continual masking. These are two examples of how duplicity generates a deception because at this level monopoly and disguise are the most complete forgetfulness and the most resolute denial of truth. Monopoly is forgetfulness and denial due to its exclusionary character, which by absolutizing and eternalizing an individual formulation of truth removes all revelatory power from it and forces truth itself to disappear. Disguise is forgetfulness and denial due to its character—not so much mutable and multiform as much as inconstant and multiskinned—which renders the othering of allegories and symbols incapable of signifying the inexhaustible multiplicity of the revelatory perspectives of the true, incapable of representing a dialectic of hiding and manifestation such as the refined and subtle one found not only in Heidegger, but especially in Pascal, and capable, at best, of portraying chameleonesque behaviors and masking, slights of hand and fictions, that is, the vast realm of dissimulation where truth has no place, even if one were to think, absurdly, that the source of dissimulation were precisely truth itself.

7. The False Dilemma between the Unicity of Truth and the Multiplicity of Its Formulations

The fact that the formulations of truth in their historical multiplicity are an effective possession of the one and atemporal truth is surprising—and this is the second circumstance that should be kept in mind—only to an individual who is not aware of the interpretative nature of the relation between truth and its formulation. Due to an illusory desire for coherence, such an individual forgets that unicity belongs to truth and not to its formulations, and that multiplicity belongs to the formulations and not to truth. By confusing one with the other, this individual establishes a false dilemma between the two terms that is the source of perpetual equivocations regarding the nature of interpretation, particularly when truth is at stake.

Therefore, on the one side are those who, because of its unicity, not only consider truth to be atemporal but place it entirely outside of time; on the other side are those who consider truth to be multiple and changeable in itself, and even reduce it to a mere product of time because of the fact that truth only ever appears in its historical formulations. As a result, one is left with the imposed alternative of either the unwarranted and useless sacrifice of truth's multiple formulations in the name of the one truth or the sacrifice of atemporal truth in the name of its historical formulations. More precisely, the alternative is between those who, taking truth to be one and atemporal, claim that only one true philosophy, itself atemporal and one, exists, and those who, noting that philosophies are themselves multiple and historical, claim that truth itself can only be plural, and therefore that only historical truths exist. The result is that either one lifts an unduly absolutized historical philosophy to an atemporal empyrean, or one reduces history to a mere temporal succession that crushes its own products; either one deprives philosophy of its historical character, and thereby one deprives truth of its temporal appearance, or one eliminates the revelatory capacity from philosophy, thereby removing the ontological opening from history.

A dilemma ultimately arises between those who, in order to rescue the absolute nature of the one and atemporal truth, willingly risk falling into dogmatism, and those who, in order to preserve the historicity of these always new and diverse formulations, deliberately run the risk of relativism. This dilemma is pushed to the point where—and here we find the shortcoming of this way of reasoning—in the first case, dogmatism is preferred not to relativism, as would seem logical, but to *any* recognition of historicity and multiplicity, even in the formulation of truth, and in the second case, relativism is preferred not over dogmatism, as would seem natural, but over *any* recognition of unicity and atemporality, even in the truth as present and active in its historical forms.

These two positions are clearly opposed, and in fact do nothing but engage in continual polemic; in reality, however, they stand and fall together. They both ignore the possibility of other positions, forgetting that in order to preserve the historical multiplicity of truths it is not necessary to deny the unicity of truth, and in the same way, in order to protect the unicity of truth, it is not in any way necessary to disavow the multiplicity of historical truths. One need not risk relativism in order to avoid dogmatism, nor risk dogmatism in order to avoid relativism because since on the one hand, the one truth has no other means of presenting itself than within its individual formulations, and on the other hand, it is precisely the unicity of truth that preserves the historical truths in their individuality, creating communication and dialogue among them.

In fact, these two positions come together at a central point, that is, in the separation of truth from its formulation and the separation of the formulation from truth, and in the confusion of the one with the other, therefore ignoring the fact that they are unmistakable and incomparable precisely because they are inseparable, and that one cannot attribute to philosophy the unicity that only belongs to truth, and to truth a multiplicity that only belongs to philosophy. If unicity and atemporality, which are the essence of truth, are transferred to the formulation of truth, they become nothing more than an absurd presumption; and if multiplicity and historicity are transposed from the formulation of truth, to whose nature they belong, to truth itself, then truth itself is diminished. The false dilemma between the unicity of truth and the multiplicity of its formulations arises precisely through this undue confusion, as if, because truth is one, there should be only one legitimate formulation of it, and because the historical formulations of the truth are many, there also should be multiple truths. In other words, it is as if there were no other option than either fanaticism or relativism, as if every affirmation of truth should not take any form other than that of sectarianism, and as if tolerance should have no other foundation than skepticism.

8. The Hermeneutic Character of the Relation between Truth and Its Formulation

The most common experience should suffice to warn us about positions such as those mentioned above, which are unfortunately quite widespread, because it offers an obvious example of an interpretative relation, namely musical performance. In music too, interpretation is at once revelatory and plural. In music too, the work is accessible only within one of its performances. In music too, the multiplicity of the performances does not compromise the unicity of the work. In music too, the performance is neither a copy nor a reflection, but rather the life and the possession of the work. In music too, the performance is neither exclusive nor arbitrary.

This reference to aesthetics should not surprise us, since it is motivated by the fact that in artistic experience the structure of the concept of interpretation appears with striking clarity. The issue is not overextending or generalizing a concept born first and foremost in the realm of aesthetics, a concept that for that very reason is narrow and limited; rather, the issue is to take from the special clarity and particular effectiveness that it reveals in art the ground for verifying its deep originarity, an originarity that grants it a wide-ranging validity and fertile applicability in all fields.

The existence of the musical work consists in its living and sonorous performance, and not in the inert and mute pages of the score. The performance is always new and different, that is, multiple due to its necessarily personal and therefore interpretative character. But its multiplicity in no way prejudges the unicity of the musical work: In fact, the aim of the performance is to maintain the very individuality and unicity of the work without adding anything alien to it or dissolving it into ever different acts. The performance *renders* the work in the reality that truly belongs to it; the performance *is* the work itself, and neither just its representation or copy, nor just its simple approximation—this is its "revelatory" character. The performance succeeds precisely insofar as it engages in a performative act, an act geared to a realization, a taking possession that as unrepeatable and personal is aware of the possibility of other personal and novel performances—this is its "plural" character.

The work, far from dissolving into a multiplicity of arbitrary performances, remains identical to itself in the very act in which it offers itself to performances that know how to render it and bring it to life. These ever-new and diverse performances, far from being mere approximations or simple echoes of a unique performance claimed to be optimal or exemplary, are the very life of the work, that is the work as it speaks to everyone in the best manner that each can understand. Analogously truth, far from being dissolved in its own formulations, nourishes that very plurality while preserving itself as one and identical precisely as it is embodied in any one of them that knows how to grasp and reveal it. These historical and multiple formulations, far from rejecting the one and atemporal truth through the subtle and absurd nostalgia for an exclusive and perfect formulation, are rather the temporal arrival of truth, namely truth speaking to everyone, and yet to each one in its personal and inimitable language.

The relation between truth and its formulations is thus interpretative in the same way as the relation between the musical work and its performances is. This explains above all how truth, which only reveals itself in the act of granting itself to an individual perspective, is inseparable from its historical formulations. Moreover, truth does not have a unique and definitive formulation, which could only occur through an undue eternalization of that which is historical, or a monopolization of that which is communal. These features do not compromise truth, but rather support its unicity and atemporality. As a result, proclaiming the hermeneutic nature of the relation between truth and its formulation means that such a relation cannot be explained adequately with the current concepts of subject and object, form and content, virtuality and development, whole and parts.

9. Interpretation Is Not the Relation of Subject and Object

First of all, it is not a matter of a relation between subject and object, as appears yet again in the analogy with art. In the case of interpreters, whether actors or musicians, we neither expect that they be guided by the sole criterion of originality, as if a new performance were to be more interesting than the work itself, nor that they aim at impersonality, as if the performance were of no interest to us at all. We do not *demand* that they *ought* to deny themselves, nor do we *allow* that they *should want* to express themselves. We want *them* specifically to interpret *that* work, so that the performance is *both* the work *and* its interpretation. Moreover, for the interpreters, the work is not an object that stands before them in such a way that they could compare their performance and measure its value against it. For the interpreters, their performance *is* the work itself that through their faithful and penetrating effort is rendered in its full reality. This is so true that the work gives itself entirely to the performance capable of enlivening it with the life that is its own to the point of *coinciding* with it; yet, the work resides there, [i.e., in the performance,] with an *ulteriority* that prevents it from exhausting itself in the performance because the work, as regarding its own performances, allows *none* of them to monopolize it, nor does it dwell in *one* of them in a privileged or exclusive way—rather, the work provokes *all of them* and demands all of them.

It is clear that a relation of this kind cannot be described in terms of subject and object. The interpreters are not "subjects" who dissolve the work in their own act or who should depersonalize themselves in order to render the work faithfully as it is in itself, but are rather "persons" who know how to make use of their own historical substance and of their own irreplaceable activity and initiative in order to penetrate the work in its reality and enliven it with their own life. Nor is the work an "object" to which the interpreters should match their own representation from the outside, as the work is instead characterized by an "unobjectifiability" that it gains from its own being inseparable from the performance that brings it to life and at the same time from its being irreducible to any one of its own performances.

In the case of truth, the uselessness of the relation between subject and object is even more radical and profound. First of all, it is clear that a person's relation to truth is not the relation of subject to object, in which the subject can only attain the object by reducing it to its own activity, or in which the object can only be present to the subject when the subject divests itself of its own determinacy. The subject is enclosed either in its own particular actuality that reduces every object to subjective activity, or in an impersonal universality that alone would be the guarantor of a valid and communicable knowledge. Conversely, the person is open and always disclosed to the other, and in the very act of demanding that everything to which it relates must become interiorized, the person maintains everything in an irreducible independence, and to such an end the person uses its own inimitable and most singular historical substance. The relation of the person to truth is therefore a much more originary relation because the person is constituted as such by the very relation it has with Being, that is, by the person's rootedness in truth, and the person's destination is the very recognition of truth to the degree that this can be formulated only personally. And so the problem of truth is metaphysical before it is epistemological, and demands that one appeal to the ontological opening that belongs to the person rather than to the gnoseological closure one finds in the subject.

With that, the difficulties brought about by the closure of the subject within itself are completely overcome, namely, subjectivism with its arbitrariness, and impersonalism with its abstractedness. By granting personal activity a character that is more capturing than reductive, and by according personality itself a capacity more penetrating than deforming, the ontological opening of the person points out that the revelation [of truth] occurs neither through a narcissistic ideal of originality nor through an absurd duty of impersonality, as would be the case if one were to twist interpretation more toward self-expression and the study of the new than toward the encounter with truth, or if one were to expect discovery through a generic effort of depersonalization rather than through the intensification of one's own most personal gaze.

Far less can one consider truth to be an object, given that by its nature it is unobjectifiable, as between truth and the person no interval exists that allows the person to pull back until truth stands before the person in a complete and definitive figure, or to develop a formulation that explicates it completely and thus counts as definitive. First of all, truth does not exist in an objective form, with its own determinacy, which our formulations should approximate or on which they should be modeled. Every historical and personal formulation of truth is *at one and the same time* truth itself and the interpretation that is given of it, indivisibly. It is therefore impossible to distinguish truth from interpretation and interpretation from truth, and oppose one to the other, that is, truth as the objective standard for judging the validity of the formulation, and the formulation as the image and reproduction of an objective model. On the one hand, it is impossible to grasp truth in a presumed determinacy against which we would be able to measure our formulation of it from the outside; and on the other hand, truth only offers itself from within a personal perspective that already interprets and determines it. On one side, every historical formulation is a revelation of truth, that is, truth itself as personally possessed; and on the other side, as interpreted, truth can be distinguished from its formulation to such a small degree that it even identifies with its formulation. Thus, truth is unobjectifiable above all in the sense that it is *inseparable* from the interpretation that it is given and *incomparable* with its formulation.

Moreover, in each formulation truth dwells in a sort of irreducible transcendence, in the sense that truth entrusts itself to each formulation and even becomes the formulation without ever reducing itself to it or exhausting itself in it. In its formulations, truth dwells in its full inexhaustibility, that is, on the one hand, with a *presence* that turns the formulations into the only way for truth to appear and exist, and the only way for us to possess and announce truth, and on the other hand, with an *ulteriority* that permits none of the formulations to contain and possess the truth in an exclusive way, and that thus demands and provokes ever new and diverse formulations of itself. Truth is both present and ulterior, that is, at the same time formulated and unformulated, said and unsaid, existing *as* thought that is formulated and definite and residing *in* thought as it itself indefinite and unformulated. Truth is more present *in* thought as source and origin than present *to* thought as an object to be discovered. Thus, truth is unobjectifiable also due to its *inexhaustibility*, which denies its most revelatory formulations any privilege or monopoly and turns interpretation into the never-definitive possession of an infinite.

10. Interpretation Is Neither the Relation of Form and Content, nor the Relation of Virtuality and Development

Least apt to explain the hermeneutic character of the relation between truth and its formulation are the concepts of form and content or virtuality and development. These two pairs push the question back into the terms of subjectivism and objectivism, in the sense that subjectivistic would be a conception that considers truth to be a constant and common content to which every person confers its own form, and objectivistic would be the conception that sees an infinite virtuality of perspectives in truth, each one of which would develop one of the truth's powers.

The first conception is guilty of subjectivism when it admits of the person's intervention as a superimposition over a preexisting but unformed content rather than as an organ of penetration of a truth that reveals itself in the act of giving itself over to a perspective. This compromises the inseparability of the ontological and revelatory aspect from the expressive and historical aspect, which characterizes the interpretative formulation of truth and preserves it from every danger of subjectivism and arbitrariness.

The second conception is guilty of objectivism when it supposes a point of view from which it not only contemplates the infinity of the absolute unfolding in the multiplicity of its manifestations, but also recognizes a correspondence between the inexhaustible virtuality of truth and the plurality of its developments and perspectives. With this, the various perspectives, retracting the existential and personal link that ties them interpretatively to truth, and that burdens them with an infinite task of dialogue and exchange with other possible interpretations, would do nothing more than line up in the contiguousness and indifference of mere numerability, so as to put up a show on an idealistic and artificial stage.

Furthermore, both conceptions are guilty of an insufficient deepening, not only of the inexhaustibility of truth, but also of that indissoluble bond between inexhaustibility and human freedom, which is one of the fundamental cornerstones of a theory of interpretation. In the first conception, the person is considered in an isolated individualism where, in the best scenario, freedom is expressed in an affirmation of arbitrary subjectivism, whereas the inexhaustibility of truth would degrade to the level of the unformed and would have, at most, the appearance of chaotic confusion. In the second conception, the inexhaustibility of truth would lose its authentically originary and innovative character, lowered to a species of totality, however dynamic and preformed, more suited to simple expression than to genuine revelation. In fact, virtuality properly implies an element of totality and necessity, which presents the inexhaustible more as a reservoir or a deposit of possibility in waiting than as the source itself of novelty or the unceasing germination of ever new possibilities, and the person more as the lifeless tool of a necessary manifestation than as the free initiative of research and discovery. Both conceptions forget that inexhaustibility of truth and freedom of the person are inseparable because truth only offers itself and only functions within an individual formulation, which grants it a character both revelatory and diffusive, and the individual perspective finds the possibility of a continual renewal and the living realization of the inexhaustibility of truth only in the freedom of its own personal deepening and of an unceasing dialogue with other perspectives.

11. Interpretation Does Not Imply a Relation between Parts and Whole: The Insufficiency of Integration and Explication

One might think that between truth and its formulations there subsists a relation of totality, in the sense that the diverse formulations, unable to grasp truth entirely but only in one of its aspects, are by necessity partial and deficient, so that only through their reciprocal integration or their total completion can these formulations hope to attain a revelatory value. On the one hand, there would be the claim that the diverse formulations of truth, limiting themselves to grasp parts of truth bit by bit, are necessarily partial and fragmentary, to the point that their truth value would be compromised if it were not integrated into the totality of perspectives, the sole legitimate custodian of truth in its wholeness; on the other hand, one would affirm that in comparison to truth, every discourse falls short, implying a disjunction [*sfasamento*] and an interval between the said and unsaid, which necessarily results in its being deficient and incomplete, so that the only remedy would be a completion that would erase the interval between the tacit and the explicit because only in this way could one recover the totality of discourse and reestablish the wholeness of meaning.

This conception is still much more prevalent than one might believe, and it finds its way into apparently unobjectionable conceptions without raising suspicion; however, there is nothing more contrary to the interpretative nature of the knowledge of truth and the fundamental principles of a proper hermeneutics. First of all, that which is not fully present in each one of its aspects, no matter how minimal or small it is, is not truth; nor is that which requires the elimination of the unsaid in order to reveal itself, and furthermore, interpretation is neither that which fails to grasp the truth as a whole precisely from out of the lateral [*laterale*] perspective from which it begins, nor that which posits its own ideal in complete explication.

Above all, truth is such that a simple flash or a brief glimpse of it are not simply one "part" of it; in fact, the extreme diffusiveness and infinite possibility for deepening that these glimmers offer already confirm that in them the truth is possessed wholly. The only way to grasp the *whole* truth is to possess it *as* inexhaustible, in its surging and originary character, at the very source of continual renewal, not in one of its impossibly total pictures, but in a determinate perspective that is "lateral" without being "uni-lateral," and thus not in need of integration because it is already a totality in itself. The multiple and diverse formulations of truth have no need for a reciprocal integration that will add to or achieve their truth value because each one of them is already a totality, which as such does not attach itself to the others in an all-encompassing system, but engages in a dialogue with the others, recognizing them as totalities on their own terms.

Interpretation is neither a *part* of truth nor a *partial* truth, but is *the* truth itself as personally possessed. As such, interpretation not only has no need for integration, but also will not even tolerate it, and in fact, dismisses it, already having all that it can and must have. The very concept of interpretation rejects totality as *external* and as *one*: Either totality works within the individual human being, or it is individual and plural in itself. Truth is not *the* totality as the system of all its formulations: Each one of these formulations is *a* totality because it contains in itself *the* totality itself of the true, namely, each is *a whole* because it contains *the whole* truth, obviously in the sense of its inexhaustibility, as has already been stated. Truth neither divides nor shatters itself into a *multiplicity* of formulations, whose *totality* one should then recover as *external* to them; rather, truth resides *wholly* in each one of them. It is for this reason that truth can only offer itself in interpretation, which maintains the very wholeness of truth while it is realized as an individual interpretation, so that each formulation of truth is *a* totality precisely and solely because it possesses the *whole* truth.

Moreover, truth is neither a totality made in such a way that the thought that reveals it could consider itself diminished by not saying it *wholly*, nor is our formulation of truth such that we should consider it as inadequate and deficient if it does not achieve complete explication. Truth resides in its formulation not as the object of a completed statement, however ideal it may be, but as the stimulus for an unending revelation. It is true that there is no interpretation where the unsaid is missing; however, it is no less true that the unsaid of interpretation is not a residual implication that could be easily stated, but rather an implicit infinite that nourishes a continual and unending discourse. The ideal of the formulation of truth is neither a complete explication nor a definitive statement, but the unceasing manifestation of an inexhaustible origin. The absence of a perfect statement, which a formulation was never meant to furnish, is not one of its imperfections or deficiencies. Far from curing it of a deficiency or lack, the belief that one could carry truth to perfection through a complete and definitive exposition is nothing but an extraneous addition that, rather than completing it, destroys it. Lamenting or denigrating its presumed insufficiencies and shortcomings demonstrates that its nature is not understood, and that its perfection and essence have been mistaken for its defect and privation.

That which is not possessed as inexhaustible and that is explicated in a definitive enunciation is not truth; and that which, in order to possess truth, believes it must eliminate every unsaid, completing the discourse with a perfect and complete totality, is not interpretation. As a sign of its presence, truth points out precisely the unending and always ulterior nature of discourse; the enunciation of truth in a complete exposition would be the very sign of the inability to grasp it. Only as inexhaustible does truth offer itself to its formulation, namely, in such a way that it is impossible to attempt and absurd to realize a complete explication in it, whereas giving it an unending revelation is both more desirable and more feasible. This characteristic interminability of interpretation, far from being its defect or shortcoming, and far from attesting to its incompleteness or insufficiency, is rather its perfection and completion, and even its richness. The idea of achieving a totality by completing the deficiencies of the explicit with the complete explication of the unsaid is a fallacy and a vanity. Yet, it is just this idea that secretly hides itself in the theory of many relativists, both declared and unaware, who draw from the evidently indefinite and unending nature of the enunciation of truth not the confirmation of the indissoluble link between the inexhaustibility of truth and the freedom of the person, but the conclusion that the only existing truths are historical truths, considered in their relativistic and indifferent multiplicity. This demonstrates their imprisonment within a rationalistic myth of the definitive enunciation and the complete explication of truth, one that unknowingly preserves nostalgia for them.

The category of *totality* is therefore inadequate to explain the relation between truth and its formulations, either in the sense that the many and thus *partial* formulations find truth in their reciprocal *integration*, or in the sense that the individual formulation finds truth in a *completion* of the semantic *insufficiency* of the explicit by means of the exhaustive declaration of the implied, as if the ideal of the interpretation of truth were its *total system* or *complete explication*. Integration and completion are neither possible nor desirable when interpretation is properly understood. Interpretation is already, as explained, *total* and *complete* in itself, such that any integration would suddenly arrive from the outside and every completion would be an extraneous addition, and both would become not only superfluous and useless, but also indiscreet, tiresome, and ultimately prejudicial and lethal, so that the very character of the formulation of truth would be compromised.

It is not that interpretation, because it is total and complete, isolates itself from every *relation* with an other and rejects every *clarification* of the unsaid. Its nature excludes a relation only when it becomes a total integration, and a clarification only when it becomes a complete explication. But if the relation with others is one of dialogue, and if the clarification of itself is a development of the implicit, no such danger exists. In the forthcoming sections, I return to the idea of truth as a demand for dialogue, and to the deepening of the implicit as distinct from the implied; for the time being, however, I highlight the following.

First of all, the personal and interpretative nature of the knowledge of truth indissolubly joins *each* individual perspective with the necessity for recognizing infinite *other* possible formulations and the demand for a continual conversation with them. The confirmation of this multiplicity of perspectives can and must be made only within each individual perspective as the real experience of dialogue and the concrete exercise of alterity: Only in this way can *all* of the perspectives really be formulations of truth, thereby preserving their interpretative and thus revelatory character. The recognition of other perspectives must occur on the basis of the affirmation of one's own, otherwise the very nature of the perspective as such—as the personal possession of truth—will be lost, both regarding other perspectives and regarding one's own, which would then devolve into a simple and hypothetical point of view from which one could contemplate the others. Alterity would disappear along with one's selfhood [*proprietà*], namely, personality itself as the existential root and interpretative link that characterizes and qualifies every formulation of truth. Only an externally viewed multiplicity would remain, namely, a sheer number of substitutable possibilities, able to be borrowed and exchanged, and thereby indifferent and equally valid, all placed on the same level, and the object of an impersonal, objective, and ultimately falsifying consideration.

There exists, however, a reciprocal relation between the diverse formulations of truth, one that has nothing to do with their total integration, which is certainly unbecoming of the dignity of interpretation. This relation is dialogue, understood in the sense already clarified—the performance of a communication that holds together all perspectives so that each one is present to each of the others, without summarizing them from the outside or integrating them into a total system, as is the case with interlocutors and collaborators in a shared project. Each perspective is thus respected in its inimitable totality as the very personal possession of truth. Only such a *free opening of dialogue* constitutes a relation adequate to the order and nature of interpretation.

Moreover, interpretation is an unending process that requires a continual and unceasing investigation. This is so precisely because it is the possession of truth: as inexhaustible, truth offers itself solely to a possession constituted in such a way that it does not cease to be possession simply because it presents itself as an infinite task. In fact, such a possession is an infinite task exactly because it is not a simple approximation or image of truth, but its real and effective possession. Certainly, this feature of interpretation can seem contradictory and paradoxical: It is at the same time effective possession and unending process, and thus at the same point it unites stability and mobility, steadfastness and continuation, achievement and pursuit. Here the analogy with art is again helpful, in which reading is undoubtedly a true possession of the work, yet the meaning of reading consists in its being an invitation to read it again; the awareness of having penetrated the work is accompanied by the awareness of having to proceed onward to yet another deepening, and every revelation is a reward and a success only as stimulus and promise for new revelations. The very inexhaustibility of the work of art is what allows it to unite possession and pursuit without contradiction; the case is so much more so with respect to the interpretation of truth, given the even more intense, profound, and originary character of its inexhaustibility. The compatibility of possession and process, of conquest and pursuit, of mastery and investigation—in fact, their coessentiality—now clearly emerges as one of the fundamental cornerstones of hermeneutics.

12. The Constitution of Interpretation

At this point it is helpful to gather together the results of our investigation so far in order to delineate the fundamental principles of hermeneutics and clarify the structure of interpretation.

The relation between truth and its formulation is therefore interpretative: The formulation of the true is in one respect the *personal* possession of *the* truth, and in another respect the *possession* of an *infinite*. On the one hand, that which is possessed is *the truth*, and it is possessed in the only way that one could possess it, that is, *personally*, to the point that the formulation that is given of it *is* truth itself, that is, truth *as* personally possessed and formulated; on the other hand, the formulation of truth is truly a *possession* and not a simple approximation, yet truth resides in such formulation in the only way it can reside, that is, *as* inexhaustible, to the point that an *infinite* is what is possessed there. Interpretation is in fact the only form of knowledge that is in one way capable of giving a personal and thus *plural* formulation of something that is *one* and indivisible without compromising or losing its unity, and in another way capable of grasping and revealing an *infinite* by truly possessing it rather than merely alluding to it or circling around it. That of which only one adequate knowledge is possible, or which *eludes* all possible knowledge, is not truth. Interpretation occurs only when truth actually *coincides* with its formulation without *being confused* with it, so that it maintains its *plurality*, and only when truth is always irreducibly *ulterior* in relation to its formulation albeit without *going outside of it*, so that its *presence* is safeguarded.

Truth offers itself only within one of its formulations—*with* which it *coincides* each time and *in* which it always resides as *inexhaustible*. But if the *identification* between truth and its formulation gives way to *confusion*, or the relation of *ulteriority* becomes one of *exteriority*, the interpretative relation disappears because in such cases the inseparability of truth and its formulation is destroyed: Either one replaces the other by pretending to *substitute it*, or both separate, remaining without relation due to the *inaccessibility* of one of them.

In the first case, there is no longer the *coincidence* between truth and its formulation that, by pointing out that very truth as personally possessed and historically formulated in every formulation, guarantees *at one and the same time* the *unicity* of truth and the *plurality* of its formulations. A formulation presents itself as unique and exclusive while supplanting all of the others, that is, it absolutizes itself by assuming that unicity that only belongs to truth; there follows a *confusion* between the two terms, in the sense that a formulation, rather than interpret and reveal the truth, attempts to replace it and usurp its position, and thus they both, namely, the betrayed truth and its formulation, disappear. The formulation, which is a *subrogation* of truth rather than its interpretation, loses every revelatory characteristic and expresses nothing other than itself, and therefore not only the plurality of formulations but even truth in its unicity vanishes. In the second case, the *ulteriority* of truth regarding its formulations is accentuated in such a way that it results in the lack of all *presence* of the true in the interpretation given of it. The two terms are separated from each other and rigidified in a reciprocal *exteriority* that distances them from each other and deprives them of any relation. Truth is pushed into a meta-historical *inaccessibility* where it remains ineffable and unrepresentable. The diverse formulations of truth remain irreparably inadequate and equally insufficient in the face of this *ineffability*, to the point that erroneous, weak, and unfaithful formulations can no longer be singled out, thereby removing every distinction between true and false. Deprived of its revelatory character, interpretation disappears along with the very *ulteriority* of truth, which is lost in the fog of the ineffable.

As we have seen, in interpretation the relation between truth and its formulation is one of identity and ulteriority *at one and the same time*, in perfect balance. On the one hand, truth coincides with its formulation, thereby allowing it to possess it in a revelatory way, but never to the point of authorizing it to present itself as complete and exclusive, or even unique and definitive, for that would not be interpretation but *subrogation* of truth, namely, one of the many historical formulations that pretends to absolutize itself and usurp the position of truth. On the other hand, truth is always ulterior to its formulation, but only so that it requires and permits a plurality of formulations, and never in the sense of an absolute *ineffability* that would render all formulations fatally inadequate and irreparably insignificant in a shared and resigned equivalence and indifference.

It would still be useful to investigate fully the personality of interpretation and the ulteriority of the true, for they present us with a rich problem. In the following section, however, a very brief outline of this issue will suffice.

13. Consequences of the Personality of Interpretation

To say that every perspective is always a *personal* possession of truth, that is, *the* truth as personally formulated, means that the person engages in interpretation primarily as a pathway and organ of knowledge, as an instrument of organization and a probing antenna, as a revelatory beacon and means of penetration. Interpretation adds *nothing extraneous* to truth, nor anything that does not belong there because its very task is to reveal it, to possess it, or even *to be it*. That means that interpretation is an extremely *active* and performative process, both because in interpretation the person is no less an initiative than an organ—the person is free to turn his or her own historical individuality either into a prison and obstacle to the knowledge of truth, or into an extremely valid instrument for indicating and revealing truth—and because the formulation of truth demands a lively and intense exercise of *productivity*, intended to invent and formulate schema, to verify their adequacy, and give them coherence and structure until the personal possession of truth coalesces in an organic and living form, capable of its own reactions, endowed with an autonomous life, and rich with further proliferations. The meaning of all of this free and voluntary activity consists in a constant *listening* because truth is something that human beings neither invent nor produce, nor something that could be invented or produced in general. One needs to *let truth be* and not claim to invent it. The reason why the person becomes the *organ of truth's revelation* is above all so as to be able to be the *site of its coming*.

Certainly, personality can be an obstacle to the penetration of truth, as far as it closes itself in mere temporality or is concerned more with expressing itself than with grasping the truth; in that case truth flees, neglected and obscured, along with the person who is reduced to a product of time and rendered incomprehensible to him or herself. Interpretation is therefore a type of knowledge intimately constituted by the constant risk for failure, where the revelation is obtained only as a victory over the ever-present menace of concealment. This precariousness of interpretation is not due to its personality and plurality, which is a form of richness rather than an imperfection, but to the alternatives presented by the very freedom of the person, who can become his or her own narrow prison, blind to the coming of truth, or instead an airy opening, attuned to truth's revelation. When the person in fact chooses to become the intermediary of truth, there is no other organ of knowledge that can be so sharp, penetrating, and certain. This originary and profound opening-out inheres in the nature of interpretation, so that its condition can also serve as its limit; and the more its outcome is favorable and the truth offers itself to it, the more it faces the possibility of falsification and the risk for error, to the point that the danger of error is never so menacing as when one is in the closest proximity to truth; the possibility of the most abyssal and extreme error is inexorably tied to the most successful conquest of truth. In this the validity of Heidegger's saying is apparent: "*Wer gross denkt, muss gross irren*" [the one who thinks greatly must err greatly].

In this sense, the concept of interpretation is the only one able to unite truth and history without reducing one to the other or sacrificing one for the other, which would mean to lose both. This happens when, due to excessive care for the unicity of truth, one does not pay attention to the changeability and variety of historical situations, or when due to the concern for understanding the various historical formulations, one denies the existence of error, thereby dispersing truth within history. In particular, the concept of interpretation, affirming at once and inseparably the surging and originary unicity of truth and the essential and constitutive plurality of its formulations, is able to escape the indifferentism of historicism because it maintains the distinction between true and false in the very act by which it grants history its rights by accepting it as a pathway to truth. The indifference of historicism arises with the expression *veritas filias temporis* [truth is the daughter of its time], which by eliminating error—because in history everything is equally expressive of time—also abolishes truth. At a close analysis, however, one cannot say that time generates truth; rather, time favors, promotes, and facilitates truth's historical occurrence because, as Milton says, time is "the midwife rather than the mother of Truth." That is exactly the content of the concept of interpretation, which presents itself as the only way to reconcile the plurality of historical truths with the distinction between true and false.

The ideal of interpretation therefore cannot be depersonalization, which would deprive interpretation of its organ. In order to grasp the truth, interpretation has no other recourse than to the development of the person in its historical substance: the understanding of time and the possession of the true, the awareness of the situation and the penetration of truth, the consciousness of the self and the revelation of Being proceed together and condition each other. When one deals with truth, the supposed "objectivity" of science and the proclaimed "neutrality" of knowledge no longer make any sense. As interpretation, the knowledge of truth is always compromising, in that it requires a personal choice and a commitment. This is the most evident and trembling consequence of the fact that truth is accessible only within an individual formulation and that it can be possessed only as personally interpreted. Knowing and possessing the truth are impossible without commitment, without taking a side, without personal exposure. This occurs not only in philosophy understood as the formulation of truth, but also in every single interpretation worthy of the name, no matter how marginal and insignificant it might be because truth is engaged in every hermeneutic process, and even the most meager interpretation carries an ontological import.

It is true that, because it offers itself only within an individual perspective, truth can be grasped only within a personal and concrete viewpoint; it is also true, however, that only from a personal and concrete point of view can one consider a perspective to be a personal possession of truth, and thus understand anyone's point of view. Thus, not only is a personal formulation of truth compromising, but so is the communication between various and diverse formulations, because only if truth is possessed in one of its formulations can one understand that truth is present also in a different formulation. One needs to take or have taken a position in order to understand another position, and any interpretation can be understood solely from another interpretation. Thus, only those who have their own philosophy can have access to the philosophy of another, and in general, the philosopher is the only one who can understand philosophies—indeed, only philosophy understands philosophy. Similarly, only the person who has a religion can understand another religion, and only the religious person can understand a religious experience, and so on. On every count, this notion of interpretation flies in the face of one of the most tenacious and obstinate idioms in today's culture, one that has not only reduced all knowledge to history, but has also idealized the historian as the model of the intellectual, who with "historical objectivity" should comprehend without judging, understand without discussing, conclude without taking sides, or in other words, become ultimately disinterested in the truth.

By virtue of its interpretative character, a formulation of truth can be communicated solely through empathy, kindredness, and elective affinity. It cannot rely on a presupposed universality, such as a previous impersonal reason or a given historical community; rather, it relies on the unifying and diffusive force of truth, namely on that unicity and universality of the true as it holds true within every single formulation as the appeal to freedom rather than the constriction to evidence, as the demand for communion and dialogue rather than as a respect for habitual conventions. It is thus not the case of a preexisting universality but of a universality to be established. This can be accomplished only by instituting a community of kindred persons, brought together by a similar interpretation of truth, and precisely for that reason able to understand and communicate reciprocally.

What follows from this is the founding and innovative character of interpretation, which could never modify a situation, or even less initiate an epoch, were it to limit itself to expressing its time and being historical consciousness. Interpretation succeeds only because it is a perspective on Being and a revelation of truth, thus offering to today's world, impregnated with activism and praxism, the example of a knowledge that as such is initiating and transforming. Interpretation can be such initiation and transformation to the extent to which it preserves itself as theory and avoids becoming mere praxis. Interpretation is in fact contemplative not in the lifeless sense of the simple consciousness of the past or of the mere expression of the present, but in the effective sense of the revelation of truth, which is the very source of renewal and the principle for every valid transformation beyond every sterile and secondary opposition between praxism and theoreticism and beyond every artificial and derivative resolution of theory into praxis—a beginning, rather than an end to history, a master rather than a disciple of time, a provoker rather than a depiction of situations.

14. Consequences of the Ulteriority of Truth

Regarding the ulteriority of truth present in every single formulation, it must be noted that there would be no interpretation if truth were either completely hidden or completely evident, because both total concealing and complete explication would suppress the truth either by imprisoning it in a definition more fitted to its corruption than to its declaration, or by dissolving it in an ineffability as misleading as any exclusive definition. Revelation supposes an inseparability of disclosure and latency, because the process of illumination could not start from an obscurity so dense that it would not even contain a hint of a glimmer, and conversely truth's inexhaustible origin would be lost were evidence so obvious that it would lack even the most minute secret. Total secrecy, in which silence alone would be the speaker and the truth would only be assigned the feature of ineffability, would collapse into the most obscure mystery and open the way to the most reckless arbitrariness of symbols. A complete manifestation, which were to culminate in the "everything said" and wish upon truth a definitive clarity, would renounce the implicit as the source of the new and would wind up relying on the objective univocity of the utterance. On the one hand, we would have a cult of mystery that leads finally to *Schwärmerei*, namely, deliberately resigning to an imaginary mythology, since abysmal silence and bottomless night are a false richness, which far from Augustine's *canorum et facundum silentium veritatis* [canorous and eloquent silence of truth] only yields to the obscurity of arbitrary and fleeting allusions. On the other hand, there would be a cult of the obvious that even reaches superstition, namely, valuing the explicit for its own sake; this is clearly idolatry because the completely exhausted word, lacking depth and being unaware of the implicit, is extremely poor, and to value it as revelatory, that is, as the locus of truth, would amount to overestimating it. *Depth without clarity* versus *clarity without depth*: Both are degenerations because they are ignorant of the nature of interpretation and are confident either in the irrationalism of absolute ineffability and the arbitrary allusiveness of ciphers, or in the rationalism of complete enunciations and objective communicability of the explicit.

The inseparability of disclosure and latency regains all of its hermeneutic significance only if it supposes as its own foundation the inexhaustibility of Being and if it involves a radical distinction between the implicit and the implied. In one respect, the obscurity from which the process of illumination begins is not the absence of light, but its abundance: It is the abundance of light itself, which as the source of vision eludes sight, and indeed the more it escapes sight, and even blinds it, the more intensely it illuminates. In another respect, the evidence that completes illumination is not the suppression of the implicit, but its locus and indeed its care, not as a simple implied that one could easily denounce and declare, but as the unsaid in which the very meaning of the said resides.

Truth escapes, yet it does this only so as to offer itself. More than escape, it ultimately holds itself in reserve. Far from concealing itself in order to disappear, it rather gathers itself in order to better reveal itself. It is not a greedy jealousy of its own secrecy, but the generosity of a promise and an appeal. That is the sign of fullness rather than absence. The ground of the ulteriority of truth is inexhaustibility and not ineffability, richness rather than poverty. That which is originary is positivity, and every negativity is treachery, degradation, forgetting. To say that truth resides as origin in its own formulation means that truth urges by escaping and escapes by urging. Its ulteriority is not so much the ironic and negative possibility of slowly undoing its own formulations, abandoning them and surpassing them all in order to take refuge in a remote and nocturnal informulation; rather, it is the extremely free and productive possibility of embodying itself in always newer forms, with an inexhaustible abundance, so that it never ceases to coincide with each one of them over time, even though it provokes and transcends them all. That is the opposite of the ineffability of negative ontology, which carries within itself, as its logical consequence, the praise of silence, the glorification of the night, the exaltation of nothingness, that is, more concretely, historical indifference, the primacy of praxis, the practice of negation. In the end, it carries within itself skeptical relativism, revolutionary praxism, and radical nihilism, which are closely bound to one another through their common origin in the ineffable.

What constitutes interpretation is then the difference between the implicit and the implied. The implied is a margin that is temporarily missing from the perfection of knowledge, and that requires its own suppression, being in itself destined to disappear in complete explication and total evidence. Conversely, there exists neither any explicitness nor any evidence that could exhaust the implicit, which resides in such explicitness and evidence precisely in order to renew their meanings again and again, since it supposes that interpretation is destined to contain truth as inexhaustible, and not to exhaust it in an objective statement. Both "demystification" and "interpretation" consist in making the "unsaid" speak. But whereas demystification makes it speak by suppressing the implied in total evidence, interpretation makes it speak insofar as it develops the implicit while sustaining its inexhaustibility. A philosophy of interpretation can be nothing other than a philosophy of the implicit, aware that one cannot *possess* truth except in the form of having *yet to search* for it, since interpretation is not the complete enunciation of the implied, but the unending revelation of the implicit, where everyone sees the poverty, weakness, and limitation of the former in relation to the richness, abundance, and infinity of the latter.

Notes

Pages 59–60: I theorized musical interpretation in *Estetica: teoria della formatività*, 189–214, 226–233 and in *I problemi dell'estetica*, 195–223); see also "Il concetto di interpretazione nell'estetica crociana," in *Rivista di filosofia* 3 (1953).

Page 62: An example of that dialectic of interiority and independence to which I allude and that should eliminate every intimist and subjectivistic conception of personalism, can be seen both in the critique I made of the aesthetics of Stefanini on this point (see *Conversazioni di estetica*, 92–102), and also in the theory that I proposed of the dialogue of the artists with their material (*Teoria dell'arte*, 151–158), a theory that can be easily "transposed" from the field of aesthetics to every other field of human activity.

Page 72: The saying, "*Wer gross denkt, muss gross irren*," which could perhaps be translated, "Great thoughts are matched by great mistakes" [this would be the literal translation of Pareyson's own translation], can be found in Martin Heidegger, *Aus der Erfahrung des Denkens* (Pfullingen: Neske, 1954), 17. As Schelling recalls, only the one who takes a risk in the adventure of thinking can make an error, such that it is an honor to consider someone capable of error: "*Wer irren will, der muss wenigstens auf dem Wege sein; wer aber gar nicht einmal sich auf den Weg macht, sondern völlig zu Hause sitzen bleibt, kann nicht irren:*" [Only the one already on his way can make an error; the one who has not even set out on his way, and who sits comfortable at home, cannot make an error] (V 5). That is perhaps even clearer in the rendering published by H. Fuhrmans: "*Auch Irren ist ehrenvoll. Wer irren, vom Weg abirren kann, der kann doch gehen. Wer hinter dem Ofen sitzen bleibt, ist nicht fähig zu irren:*" [To err is also something honorable. The one who can err, wandering off course, can also move forward. The one who sits comfortable by the stove is not capable of error] (*Initia philosophiae universae*, cit. 11). On the extreme proximity of truth and error, one should always keep in mind Pascal's profound observations: "Truth, we know, is so delicate that, if we make the slightest deviation from it, we fall into error; but this alleged error is so extremely finespun that, if we diverge from it in the slightest degree, we fall back upon the truth"; see Blaise Pascal, *The Provincial Letters*, translated by Thomas M'Crie (Kessinger Publishing, 2004), 24.

Page 73: The citation from Milton is taken from the first "Treatise of the doctrine and discipline of divorce" (*Complete Works*, Yale University Press, 1959, vol. II, 225).

Page 75: The expression from St. Augustine is situated in the following context: "*Mentibus nostris sine ullo strepitu, ut ita dicam, canorum et facundum quoddam silentium veritatis illabitur*" (*De libero arbitrio*, II, 13, 35): [So when the silent eloquence of truth flows over us without the clamor of voices . . .] *On the free Choice of the Will*, translated by Thomas Williams (Indianapolis, IN: Hackett Publishing Company, 1993), 56.

Part II

Truth and Ideology

3

Philosophy and Ideology

1. Expressive Thought and Revelatory Thought

The term *ideology* has been around for more than a century and a half, during which time it has slowly assumed the most diverse and often conflicting meanings, up to the semantic chaos into which it has fallen today, due not to the natural wear and tear on the concept, but rather to the impudence and imprecision of those who use it. Through this changing variety, however, one can say that from the first ideologues to the most recent sociologists, two conceptions remain relatively constant in the term's long history: first, an as-it-were "material" origin of ideas and second, the political purpose of ideology. Over time, these two concepts, without losing their determinacy, grew into the more general concepts of the historicity and the pragmaticity of thought, thereby confronting philosophy with the two problems of the relation between thought and situation and the relation between theory and praxis. Under these conditions it is clear that the theme in question has an unavoidably political bent; but, it cannot have an adequate treatment if not handled philosophically. Such a treatment is precisely what I propose to give.

The two characteristics I outlined above belong to the realm of what I have already referred to as expressive thought. There are "philosophies" that do nothing more than express their epoch, serving simultaneously as its conceptualization and guide, its product and awareness, its image and its instrument. They are products of human reason, on the one hand inseparably connected to the historical situation from which they are born and in which they live, and on the other hand hungry for power, that is, effectiveness in the historical world. These allegedly historical and pragmatic philosophies are countered by authentically philosophical thought, which due to its speculative nature takes on the task of revealing truth. I believe that the difference between ideology and philosophy can be explained fully if one retraces it to the difference that I am proposing between expressive thought and revelatory thought. With this purpose in mind, I intend to examine the two fundamental aspects of ideological thought in order to connect them to the two essential properties of expressive thought.

2. The Historicization of Thought in Ideology

Let us first deal with historicity. In purely expressive discourse, historicity exhausts the very essence of thought. From an ideological point of view, such is the function of ideas, which do nothing other than express the historical situation, translating it into conceptual terms, and accepting to be themselves evaluated solely in terms of their adherence to the time from which they emerge. That is historically verified by the development of the concept of ideology: from Destutt de Tracy, who concentrated his attention not so much on the value and content of ideas as on their origin and sensible origin, to Marx, who instituted an organic and dialectic connection between the material foundation and the ideal superstructure that is its product, all the way to Mannheim, with his concept of a *Seinsverbundenheit* not only of ideas and beliefs, but also of principles, categories, and judgments.

The first task faced by expressive thought is therefore its "historicization": singling out its "meaning" in its being a representation of its time, its "value" in its ability to conceptualize the conditions of existence, its "truth" in its correspondence or adherence or conformity to the historical situation. It is well suited to this treatment because it is already radically and exclusively historical, that is, stripped of every concern for reaching truth and vested merely with the ability to express the situation. And this is precisely the treatment to which these ideologies subject themselves: One tries to present precisely their fundamental "historicity," which resides not so much in the simple historical conditionality of thought, but rather in its complete identification with the situation.

In order to avoid, on this point, an equally vain and superficial rebuttal of Marxism, let it be noted that the historicization of which we are speaking has nothing to do with a reductive explanation, for which reconnecting the spiritual productions to their material basis would amount to dissolving them in a merely accidental and superfluous appearance instead of seeing them in their historical essentiality and undeniable reality. The identification of expressive thought with the historical situation does not nullify it, but rather considers it, in its "expressivity," as the very situation insofar as conceptualized, and, in its "specificity," as an integral part of the situation that, without it, would not be what it is. This means reconstituting a structural unity and an organic totality that, although guaranteeing the inseparability of consciousness from reality, preserves spiritual productions in their irreducibility and irreplaceability, to the point that one could say that there is nothing in the superstructure that was not already in the base, except the superstructure itself.

It is true that, when so understood, historicization loses every reductive trait. It is no less true, however, that it confirms precisely the fact that expressive thought, for the very reason that it is connected by organic and necessary links with the other aspects of the situation, lives in such situation only in so far as it cannot take leave from it, and it is inseparable from it because it is a prisoner there; expressive thought is all the more valid the more empty it is in itself, and, albeit full of the historical reality of which it is the reflection and awareness, it is nevertheless empty of truth.

3. The Technicization of Reason in Ideology

Let us now deal with pragmaticity. Expressive thought necessarily has a pragmatic character because its fundamental historicity, logically carrying with itself a devaluation of the theoretical aspect of thought, consequently provokes the exaggeration of its practical aspect, amplifying it to the point of an extreme pragmaticity that expresses itself in the most pronounced instrumentalism or in the most radical praxism. This is proven by the very history of the concept of ideology, in which the practical and political aspects become ever more prominent, up to the extreme outcomes that can be found in the merely technical conception of thought and in panpoliticism. Destutt de Tracy had already realized the importance of his inquiry in terms of the consequences that, in his view, it would inevitably provoke in the pedagogical, social, and political fields; and the well-known contempt Napoleon had for ideologues, treated as mere theoreticians and sterile dogmatic scholars, was an implicit recognition of the political purpose of their thought, and for that reason he opposed them.

For Marx, the very relation between ideology and philosophy bears practical and political efficacy. From this follow the by now classic conceptions regarding the instrumental feature that all ideologies have always had in the course of history in order to justify the preservation or the overthrow of an order, and regarding the interaction between the superstructure and the base, according to which the idea produced by reality reacts against it until it finally guides it. From here also follows a form of Marxism that, by emphasizing the moment of struggle and considering the proletariat as a class, presents itself as ideology, namely, as a committed and militant conception, and enslaves philosophy to political power, thus professing an explicit instrumentalism. There is also a form of Marxism that, emphasizing the final moment and recognizing the complete human being in the proletariat, presents itself as the realization of philosophy and identifies philosophy and politics, culminating in an integral praxis. That is to say, there is a Marxism that, by reducing philosophy to ideology without any remainder, and by conceiving of ideology solely as of a means for political action, denies philosophy without realizing it, in the sense that it turns it into a mere instrument for political power. And there is a Marxism that, by differentiating between philosophy and ideology, proclaims the end of ideologies because it has reached the final unity of theory and praxis; by having abolished philosophy precisely through the complete realization of it, it makes philosophy identify itself completely with politics, in the sense that philosophy is the revolution itself. Finally, there is a "metaphysical" Marxism that, in order to avoid a realization of philosophy that either realizes it without overcoming it through its suppression, or that overcomes it by suppressing it without its realization, is concerned with realizing it as "technical thought." And there is a "prophetic" Marxism, for which ideological knowledge in its culmination contains not only the reflection of historical reality, but also an "educated hope," a not yet clear knowledge that critically anticipates what has not yet become.

Finally, in Mannheim these diverse ideologies, always growing to the point of encompassing those vital or organic or systematic complexes of ideas that travel under the name of *Weltanschauungen*, perspectives, or philosophies, are considered in their practical efficacy and in their political importance, allowing them to become valid instruments of an action that may be preserving and justifying as well as revolutionary and appealing, in order to restrain or to guide the movement of history.

There is a necessary connection between the expressivity and historicity of thought and its pragmatic purpose. The very concept of expression has in itself such an instrumental nature that, as pantheism shows, its employment even in metaphysics is unable to avoid engendering equivocations. A metaphysics that wishes to use the concept of expression instead of revelation finds itself inevitably forced to culminate in a sort of pantheism where individual entities are nothing more than instruments of the absolute. Expression is so instrumental in itself that it cannot be applied to the relation between the finite and the infinite without turning the finite into an instrument of the infinite. Replacing the concept of revelation with that of expression, pantheism suppresses the transcendence of the absolute precisely because it conceives of finite entities as expressions, and thus as instruments, of the infinite.

Moreover, by emptying thought of the very thing that makes it thought, namely its relation to truth, historicity prepares and provokes its complete pragmaticization. Even if the connection between thought and situation is conceived as organic, there is no doubt that historicity demeans the theoretical aspect of thought, depriving it of its true speculative value and placing it in a condition to search for compensation in its pragmatic efficacy, namely, in its capacity to act on the situation itself—the instrument of action as the mirror of the situation. The privation of truth and the pragmaticization of thought are tightly and undeniably connected, moving forward in direct proportion: A thought emptied of truth cannot find a "truth" other than that of its own subordination to action, and inversely, thought reaches its complete technicization only to the degree that it gradually loosens its relation with truth. Thought deprived of truth, if it wants to have a rational meaning that is not reduced to mere historical expressivity or to an empty and superficial rationality, can do nothing other than become pragmatic and technical reason, not only in the sense of being capable of projecting and verifying an action to the degree that it can control and correct itself, but above all in the sense that it enslaves itself to action in the very act of promoting and guiding it, or even in the sense that it dissolves into action and is identified with it.

At this point we are no longer dealing with pragmatism, where truth still survives, either in the sense that truth is the criterion of efficiency or in the sense that efficiency is the mark of truth. Here there is no truth other than efficiency, whether instrumental or praxistic. That is, there is no truth because praxis completely exhausts either the scope or the very essence of theory. Asking whether ideologies are true or false, or saying that they are neither true nor false makes sense only insofar as all of them are considered false, namely, corrupted by the fundamental error of having renounced truth, and thus of having accepted being exhaustively qualified through historicity and pragmaticity—they are products of history and instruments of action. The technicization of reason corresponds to the historicization of thought. Action without truth, which is technics, corresponds to thought without truth, which is ultimately ideology. And so, it is solely on the basis of the elimination of truth that one arrives at the technicization of reason, either in an instrumental sense as enslavement of the idea to action, of ideology to politics, of philosophy to political power, or in a praxistic sense as the identification of thought and action, theory and praxis, philosophy and politics.

4. The Inseparability of the Historical and the Revelatory Aspects in Ontological Thought: Truth and Interpretation

The historicization of thought and the technicization of reason are therefore the two traits of expressive and ideological thought, in which the absence of truth ensured that the problems of the relation between thought and situation and of the relation between theory and praxis were to have no other solution than the amplification of one of the two terms to the detriment of the other, in the sense that the situation has prevailed over thought, and praxis over theory. Revelatory thought, to which alone philosophical thought can be traced back, opposes them with two completely different traits and relations.

The first difference concerns the diverse function of historicity in the two forms of discourse. In an ideological discourse, which is *merely* expressive, historicity exhausts the very essence of thought. Conversely, in a philosophical discourse, the historical situation participates only in so far as the person freely puts it forward as a pathway to truth, so that it is *at one and the same time* revelatory and expressive because it reveals truth in the very act of expressing the person. This thought begins from an originary solidarity of person and truth, and thus is at the same time ontological and personal. Such originary complicity explains, within this thought, the inseparability of the expressive and the revelatory aspects, and qualifies them in their reciprocal relation. The historical aspect of philosophical thought is inseparable from the revelatory aspect because what it expresses is the very person who views her own situation as a historical opening to atemporal truth. The revelatory aspect of philosophical thought is inseparable from the expressive aspect because there is no objective manifestation of truth as a complete and evident whole, as truth can be accessed only through an irreplaceable personal relation and can be formulated only through the personal way of approaching it. From this, two consequences follow.

The first consequence is that the expressivity of thought no longer consists in the simple capacity to express its own time, and its historicity no longer consists in its complete identification with the historical situation, because what is expressed here is the person, who on the one hand interprets his or her own time, and on the other hand makes him or herself the unique revelatory organ of truth. First of all, time is not expressed directly, but only through the free mediation of the person, who does not suffer from the problems of the time as if time were imposing them on him or her as already configured, but lets him or herself be faced with their proposal, and it is the very person who gives them life and configures them, so that there is a leap from the situation to the question even before there is ever a leap from the question to the answer. Furthermore, the means of viewing the situation depends on the person, who turns it into either a fatal and obscuring limitation of truth or a luminous opening onto truth, either isolating it in a presumed self-sufficiency that would reduce thought to a mere reflection or awareness of time, or recovering the originary ontological opening that restores the revelatory function to thought. And it remains in the person's power to turn his or her own individuality into a pathway to the truth, multiplying its formulations even while letting it be one in its inconfigurable yet soliciting presence.

The second consequence is that truth is unobjectifiable, that is, it only offers itself within a personal perspective that already interprets and determines it. That means, above all, that one cannot grasp and reveal truth unless one is *already* formulating it, and thus it is inseparable from the personal interpretation that we give of it. It is also impossible to grasp truth in an imaginary independence and determinacy that would allow us to measure, against it and *from the outside*, our own formulation of the truth in order to judge its value; thus the truth is incomparable with the enunciation that is given of it. And still, the interpretations of truth, as always personal, are multiple and thus truth's unicity, atemporality, and universality are such *only within* the multiple, historical, and worthy philosophies that formulate it. To conclude, truth's existence *as* thought that is formulated and definite presupposes that truth cannot reside *in* thought except as indefinite and unformulated.

Clearly this all implies the end of ontic and objective metaphysics and its replacement with an ontological and indirect metaphysics, which is the only way today to preserve the universal and speculative nature of philosophy, and thus ensure the survival of metaphysics. The fact that ideological thought is merely expressive and historical, and that the historicization of thought implies the technicization of reason, indicates in the ideology that claims to replace philosophy the final and coherent result of historicism, namely, the end of metaphysics *tout court*. If today the end of metaphysics is tied to the replacement of philosophy with ideology, and to the necessity of the connection between merely expressive and historical thought and its pragmatic and instrumental purpose, then the survival of metaphysics is tied to the recovery of the speculative nature of philosophy, which can be sustained only through the abandonment of ontic and objective metaphysics, through the affirmation of the unobjectifiability of truth, and through the recognition of the indivisibility of revelation and expression.

The declared unobjectifiability of truth in no way endangers its transcendence because personalism, far from being a subjectivism or an intimism with more or less idealistic or spiritualistic origins and an inevitably narcissistic bent, completely reveals its nature only when taken as "ontological personalism," according to which the person is constituted by the relation with Being. Such a relation is essentially the, albeit active and revelatory, listening to truth. The destination [*destino*] of the person is the recognition of truth to the degree that this can be formulated solely personally. By contrast, subjectivism and intimism are the exact opposite of ontological personalism, which, more than concern itself with every affirmation's unavoidably subjective nature or with truth's intimacy with the human mind, wishes to confer a character of personality not so much to truth, which in itself is beyond the personal, but to the always individual interpretation that is given of it, which truth itself provokes and solicits and from which it is always inseparable. Ontological personalism is concerned, if anything, with the multiplicity of pathways to truth, among which dialogue is guaranteed due to the uniting force of truth itself, which institutes a commonality as far from subjectivism as it is from impersonalism. Truth in fact offers itself to everyone, addressing each one in one's own manner, which is the most difficult concept of sociality and of community to realize, but also the truest and most authentic. More than anything, ontological personalism dwells on the fact that truth, although irreducible to each interpretation, can nevertheless offer itself only within the personal formulation of it that is given. All of this attests to the fact that truth is originary and as such, unobjectifiable, more present *in* thought as source and origin than present *to* thought as the object of discovery. Truth is so ulterior that it does not identify itself with any one of the perspectives that reveal and formulate it, and in fact escapes any consideration that claims to speak of it as of a complete and obvious object and to possess it in a unique and exclusive way. Truth is so inexhaustible that it solicits the most diverse revelations and entrusts itself to an infinite variety of formulations, without ever running the risk that it might lose its unicity.

Therefore, *interpretation* is the first trait of revelatory thought, in which the relation between thought and situation confers a place to the historical element without any undue amplification of it. Interpretation is always characterized by the inseparability of expression and revelation, that is, on the one side, by the personality of its subject who expresses him or herself in the act of becoming the organ of revelation, and on the other side, by the inexhaustibility of its object, which reveals itself in the very act of affirming its own unobjectifiability, as inseparable from the interpretation that is given of it and yet always ulterior to the interpretations that it engenders.

5. The Originary Unity of Theory and Praxis in Ontological Thought: Being and Testimony

The second difference that separates revelatory and philosophical thought from expressive and ideological thought rests in a different way of viewing the relations between theory and praxis. Just as the historicity of ideological thought cannot be opposed through its symmetrical error, namely, the elimination of any historical element from philosophical thought, so too can pragmaticity not be refuted through the revaluation of pure theory, ignorant of all practical elements. Here too the matter is not simply that of the relation between theory and praxis; rather, it is the very question of truth, truth that is so originary that it places itself beyond the distinction between theory and praxis, indicating the primordial unity of the two terms that alone is capable of explaining and directing their derived distinction and their genuine reciprocal relation at every level.

Faced with the technicization of reason, which appears especially in the extreme conceptions of the pragmaticization of thought—whether in the instrumentalist sense of furnishing ideas that serve political action or above all in the praxistic sense of identifying philosophy with politics itself—it is not a matter of reclaiming the purely speculative or contemplative character of philosophy, as if one were required to do so *in mere antithesis* to an undue accentuation or to a more or less radical exaggeration of its possible practical aspects. At the base of these conceptions, in fact, there is not a privileging of the practical dimension in antithesis to a privileging of the cognitive attitude, as one might think from so-called "vulgar Marxism"; rather, at the base is the need to grasp and realize the unity of theory and praxis, so as to solve the problem of the relation between philosophy and historical reality. Not that today one should not accentuate, in the face of rampant activism and praxism, the need, in fact the necessity, for theory and contemplation: Indeed, the irreducibility of contemplation to practice, and thus even of practice to contemplation, needs to be defended because at a certain level of specification the mixture of the two is hybrid and ambiguous. Still, one must not forget that in the true human being theory and praxis are indivisible at every level because every thought ultimately has practical consequences and every action presupposes thought, to the point that both theoreticism and activism stand out only if understood in a reactive sense. Above all, one needs to recognize that there is a just demand for postulating the unity of theory and praxis. In order to satisfy it truly, one needs to descend to a more profound and originary level: that is, one needs to reach the ontological relation that, precisely in the act in which it offers truth both to theory and to praxis, completely overcomes the distinction between them, being instead its root and originary norm.

Praxism, however, never reaches such an originary depth, although it has the merit of demanding the unity of theory and praxis. When such a unity is conceived of as futural in respect to the present duality, that is, as a (basically seeming) remedy to a (basically persistent) degradation, one remains in the ontic sphere, which far from ascending to the origin substitutes the originary with the chiliastic and precisely for that reason ends up reducing the realization of philosophy, which should overcome it as mere theory, to its true suppression. At the ontic level, one should clearly distinguish theory and praxis, and if anything one should emphasize their indivisibility in that distinction. Yet the genuine sense of such a distinction—and the necessity of holding them carefully distinct without confusing them or contaminating one with the other, while at the same time putting forward their indivisibility as the profound sense of that same distinction—is nevertheless only attained at the originary level because such a level is anterior to the distinction between theory and praxis, and the unity, in order to be such, must be grasped before the duality. When one arrives at the level of the ontological relation, the very problem of the relation between theory and praxis is brought back to the deeper question of the originary bond between person and truth. And here the problem splits into two questions, which are better addressed separately.

In the first place, what is at stake in praxism is neither theory nor truth. What is of concern in it is not only the reduction of theory to praxis, but above all the suppression of truth *also* in praxis. What is called into question is not just the realization of philosophy or the relation between philosophy and historical reality, but rather the ontological import of all human activity, both theoretical and practical, in the sense that we find ourselves facing an alternative for which either everything, even philosophy, is reduced to technics or everything, even practical action, has an ontological import. One can reach truth directly within any of the specific human activities, whether philosophy, morality, or art. Each has its own originary truth because each is equally qualified to being revelatory. The essential point is that in all of these activities there should reside and operate true thought, which is the ontological relation, the primary link between person and truth, the revelation of truth in an originary way, preceding the distinction between the various activities. What matters is to point out the ontological import and the revelatory character of any human activity. This can only be done if one reclaims, in each one of them, the presence of that originary thought that is the revelation of truth.

The issue is then that of finding the truth of thought as well as of action, of guaranteeing the genuine ontological dimension both of theory and of praxis, without which both are reduced to technics, and both become identical with the universal technicization of reason. This is what panpolitical praxism would like. In this sense, reclaiming the speculative nature of philosophy does not mean relinquishing praxis to irrationality, but rather restoring an ontological dimension to praxis. The alternative is not between speculation so rarefied that it results in scientific indifference and a practicity so opaque that it falls into irrationality, as would seem to be the concern of sociological historicism; rather, the alternative is between truth and technics, between the revelation of truth and the technicization of reason, between the revelatory and ontological character and the instrumental or praxisitc character of thought engrained in every human activity.

In the second place, rescuing the unity of theory and praxis from an ontic ordering of the future and restoring its originary ontological dimension means to push ourselves toward a still deeper level, in the very heart of the ontological relation, which is theory and praxis together in the sense that—if one could say this with respect to a level prior to the distinction—theoretically, the ontological relation is revelation of truth and practically, it is decision for Being. Nor is it one without the other, because the revelation of truth, as personal interpretation of it, is the originary act of freedom, and there is no act of freedom more originary than the very decision for Being. First of all, as it is only accessible through a personal pathway truth demands a choice and an option, so that one must choose: whether one identifies oneself with one's own situation and reduces oneself to a mere historical product, or whether one grants such a situation a revelatory power and elevates oneself to being a living perspective on truth; whether one grants an instrumental and praxistic character to the thought engrained in every human activity, thereby confining it to mere technics, or whether one assigns to it an ontological import and a revelatory capacity, opening it up to truth. As unobjectifiable, truth demands freedom and decision because it is not a matter of re-cognizing a definite object, but of determining a presence without figure, which confronts us with the responsibility of personally formulating truth. Furthermore, the revelation of truth, by implying the courage to give truth one's own formulation, and thus assuming the character more of a testimony than of a discovery, coincides with the decision for Being, that is, it coincides with the exercise of that radical and deep freedom through which one turns Being into the goal of an approval or a refusal.

This is clearly the most primal freedom within which the gift of Being always is, just as truth is always within the interpretation that is given of it, in the sense that just as there is no interpretation if not of truth, so there is no freedom without the gift of Being. Because of this freedom, the human being is initiated initiative, given to oneself as always self-giving [*dato a se stesso come dantesi*], at once self-relation and relation to the other, coincidence of reception and exercise of freedom, synthesis of receptivity and activity, a response to a call, obedience that creates. Because of this freedom, one is reduplicated in one's being, in the sense that one both is and consents to being, at the same time is and welcomes Being, simultaneously is in a relation with Being and is the relation itself. But we are also dealing with that freedom, no less originary, by which the human being, in respect to Being, chooses between approval and refusal, with a fundamental and profound choice that enables all conscious and determinate choices, so that the approval, which consists in consciously confirming one's own being, is the revelatory opening to truth and faithfulness to Being, whereas the refusal, often isolating itself in unconsciousness, is the conscious and deliberate or unconscious and obscure path of the forgetting of Being and of the betrayal of truth.

Here we find the second trait of revelatory thought, in which the relation between theory and praxis welcomes the practical element without undue exaggerations: It is *testimony*. By resolving the alternative between truth and technics through the choice of truth, and by delivering the freedom necessarily implied in the revelation of truth back to the decision for Being, testimony is certainly the unity of theory and praxis, yet it is an originary unity anterior to any distinction and thus protected from the danger of being limited to opposing or reducing one term to the other.

6. False Consciousness and Mystification in Ideological Thought

Opposed to the constitutive historicity and pragmaticity of ideological and expressive thought are the concepts of interpretation and testimony that characterize revelatory and philosophical thought. I will now develop some points that, while identifying the difference between ideology and philosophy with new evidence, aim at showing the attitude of revelatory thought toward the multiplicity of ideologies.

First of all is the problem of "mystification." The historicity of expressive thought is necessarily tied to the feature of mystification, which the nineteenth-century history of the concept of ideology has slowly refined until it has become its typical and essential feature. In the very concept of expressive thought there inheres a distinction between conscious, explicit thought and deep, hidden reality, and thus an interval between the expressed claim and the secret motivation, so that in a given situation, the expressive import of the discourse can be understood only according to the discovery of these implied and masked conditions. As is well known, this is not the simplistic denunciation of imposture that belongs to the Enlightenment, with its trademark and notorious rhetorical bag of lights that uncover the "lies of priests" ("*notre crédulité fait toute leur science*" [our credulity constitutes their science]). Here the "lie" is deeper, removed from deliberate calculation and reaching the level of the unconscious, not limited to individual conceptions and motivations but extended to the very derivation of thought from its historical conditions. The explanation given of the unconscious must also explain the simultaneity of expression and masking that distinguishes ideology from the situation.

The "psychology of interests" does not suffice here. In the very field of psychology, psychoanalysis has gone deeper, has identified the indirect ways such as slips, failed acts, and dreams through which instinctual needs tend to carve a path into consciousness, and has inventoried the unconscious mechanisms of the I's self-defense such as remorse, denial, projection, and rationalization—all mechanisms that due to their unconsciousness confer the form of masking to expression and point to a value of expression in masking. The very inseparability of expression and masking due to a necessary unconsciousness is theorized by Nietzsche, according to whom the concealing function is essential to reason, which as an instrument of the will to power, through a spontaneous and unconscious fable-producing activity, produces fictions that by falsifying and distorting reality manifest instincts in the very act of covering them up. This is accomplished by virtue of a substitution of true motives with acceptable motives, so that every spiritual form has two meanings, one immediate, evident, and well known, the other secret, hidden, and intimate. It is on the ground of this divide that some psychologists have been able to propose a schizophrenic interpretation of ideological discourse.

The very same sociological historicism indicates *Seinsverbundenheit* as the key for explaining the process of ideological deformation, in the sense that "the conceiving and thinking subject is prevented from becoming aware of the incongruence of his ideas with reality by the whole body of axioms involved in his historically and socially determined thought." From here arises the apparent paradox of an anachronistic thought that expresses its own time, which obviously can occur only in the form of a masking, because as anachronistic it masks and deforms it, and as adopted for unconscious historical determination, it expresses and represents it. A typology of the various forms of masking, through which human beings hide their instincts in the act of justifying their satisfaction with apparent rationality, is contained in Vilfredo Pareto's noted theory of residues and derivations. Conversely Kelsen, by judging ideologies to be contradictory because they mask reality in the very act of partially reflecting it, still recognizes the inseparability of expression and dissimulation, due to a necessary unconscious, as an essential trait of ideology.

For Marx, who is the most profound theorizer and the most lucid expositor of this problematic, "falsehood" is still more deeply embedded in the unconscious, and lurks in the very principle of ideological thought, because it is due to that fundamental alienation that is the cause of the very necessity of the unconscious. Due to its alienation, thought, even if it never ceases to be a product of historical reality and thus to express and represent it, falsifies and deforms such a reality because it is a "false consciousness" of it. Thought unaware of its own material origin is also unaware of its own nature: It then believes and pretends to be founded on itself, and presents its own product as reality, that is, it transforms things into ideas and then it considers them as things—it hypostasizes its merely ideal products, and with them covers and dissembles reality through a process of scotomization that is as intense as the process of hypostatization has been profound. Unaware of the reality that it reflects, it expresses it in an unfaithful and inadequate, or even an illusory and deforming way, and is thus constitutively mystifying. False consciousness is therefore a sort of profound bad faith, by which the very concealing, covering, and hiding obtain an expressive function and by which the transformation is presented only as deformation, and representation assumes the look of a disguise, so the historical can pass as eternal, the particular and partial as universal and total, and the material as rational. From here comes the fundamental trait of ideological mystification: the existence of an interval between the explicit and the hidden, the outright and the implied, and the superficial and the profound is presented as a discrepancy between the apparent and the real, between the false and the true—whence the necessity of demystification. Unawareness of its own historical origin, incapacity to call itself for what it is, illusion and pretense of unconditionality, hypostatization of its own products and denial of reality, eternalizing, universalizing, and rationalizing mystification, interval between the explicit meaning and a hidden one—this is the complex mechanism of ideological mystification theorized by Marx.

That mystification is a necessary consequence of the historicity of expressive thought seems clear from the fact that the loss of its originary connection with truth inevitably condemns thought to a sort of degradation. Historicity, depriving thought of truth, which is its natural element, proceeds toward the emptying out of reason, abandoning it to its mere discursivity and stripping it of its ontological import, that is, reducing it to the empty form of discourse and taking away from it the source of its contents. Separated from truth, thought retains only the semblance of its revelatory nature, that is, an empty rationality whose concepts must refer to the other face of thought, namely its expressive side, for their own meaning. That means that discourse becomes adept at expressing things different than what it says, in the sense that expression, hidden by the explicit face of discourse, becomes unaware and concealed, whereas the rational apparatus does nothing more than conceptualize the historical conditions that gave rise to it. Therefore reason, left without truth, far from clarifying the historical situation, simply obfuscates and masks it, and, in the very act of depending on it completely and deriving all of its substance from it, can only express it in the form of masking and mystification. In conclusion, diverting thought away from truth and reducing it to empty rationality is an invitation to search for its meaning in something different than its explicit discourse, and to destine its conceptual universality, reduced to mere appearance, to rationalizing a secret history by expressing and hiding it at the same time. Speaking of historicity in a radical and intensive sense therefore necessarily entails speaking of mystification and false consciousness.

7. The Falsification of Time in Ideological Thought

If things are so, one could nevertheless think that ideological thought, as expressive and historical, contains the genuine truth of its time, and that an appropriate treatment of demystification that sheds light on the true meaning implied in explicit discourse is all one needs to find such a truth. Yet, despite every appearance to the contrary, merely expressive and historical thought does not say the truth about its time because it lacks an interpretative character, and interpretation occurs only within ontological thought, in the originary bond between person and truth. Genuine historical rootedness and authentic ontological relation are indivisible in the originary nexus of person and truth: Thus the idea emptied of truth, namely the one marked by the forgetting of Being, also loses its true contact with history, becoming not only the principle of the masking of reality, but also the reason behind the falsification of time. There can be neither true contact with history without contact with truth, nor interpretation of time without revelatory thought. When ontological rootedness is missing, historical rootedness is also altered, and the expression of time assumes a falsifying character. Thought devoid of truth does not speak the truth, not even about time. And saying that, no matter how devoid of truth, such a thought is nevertheless full of time is to no avail; it is surely full of time, but time that has been falsified.

Ideological thought, in so far as it elaborates and exercises a conceptual apparatus founded upon an empty rationality and a purely formal discourse, is the counterfeiting of truth, and precisely as the counterfeiting of truth it is also the falsification of time. Even if it coincides with the historical situation, it does not contain the truth about time because in it the explicit discourse masks and thus falsifies what is expressed there, and that happens *precisely because* it *is nothing other than* the expression of time. Nor should one think that searching for the true meaning of the explicit in the implied amounts to finding the truth: Ideology is so radically deceptive that its demystification is a denunciation rather than a rendering it true [*inveramento*]. In no way can the distinction between apparent and real, explicit and implied, declared and secret, evident and hidden be traced back to the distinction between true and false. Certainly, there is no other understanding of ideology than demystification, as it reduces it to time, of which it is simultaneously product, expression, and masking. What is thus discovered is not truth, but weak and tired surrogates for truth: that is, the "truth" of mere historicity as the correspondence between an idea and a situation; the "truth" of false consciousness as the masking that denounces deep motivation; the pragmatic and technical "truth" as efficiency of action and experimental performativity. Ideology cannot, therefore, reach an authentic knowledge or furnish a genuine understanding of time because there can be no interpretation of time if not within the limits of the interpretation of truth, that is, in thought that, by being ontological and revelatory, is properly philosophical.

Only through the distinction between expressive thought and revelatory thought can one therefore understand the origin of mystification, what the so-called demystifying conceptions have not ultimately succeeded to explain. That the unconscious is not enough to explain the simultaneity of expression and masking because it requires in its turn an ulterior foundation, is accurately demonstrated by Marx, who pointed out such a foundation in alienation. Marx did well to denounce ideological mystification, to bring it back to alienation, and to conceive of alienation as the separation of thought from reality. Real alienation, however, is the forgetting of Being and the loss of truth, that is, precisely that which distinguishes expressive or ideological thought from revelatory or philosophical thought. The true "alienation" is the individual's separation from Being and the splitting of the originary nexus of person and truth, the ontological closure and the relinquishment of interpretation: In their freedom, human beings reject Being and renounce truth. In such a way, on the one hand, they identify themselves with their own situation and are reduced to merely historical products, and thus they replace their own freedom with their own "reification"; on the other hand, individuals make themselves incapable of turning their own situation into an opening to Being and a pathway to truth, and replace interpretation, which is the profound essence of thought, with abstraction, namely, the "exteriorization" of their own thought.

Only the opposition of revelatory thought to expressive thought can explain ideological mystification, and only revelatory thought also speaks the truth about time, as is seen in Vico. Today his thought could invite us to replace mystification with myth, to replace the masking of historical reality by thought with the presence of the *vis veri* [power of truth] in fables, to replace the momentary and fleeting historicity of ideology with the constancy of common sense and tradition, and to replace the disguising and dissembling of our interests with their transfiguration and sublimation. How far philosophy, as ontological thought and revelation of truth, is from ideology as expressive thought and from the mystification of reality can be seen through the distance that separates Vico and Marx, since for Vico, in historical reality the idea is not product but stimulus, not reflection but model, not masking but elevation. Between Marx and Vico the terms are even reversed, because whereas Marx sets out to find the "irrational" *under* the (apparent) rationality, Vico wants to point out reason *in* the "irrational," the true as being operative even in the most basic manifestations of human activity. Whereas the former remains thus tied to that philosophy of the implied that ultimately remains without development, the latter opens the way to that philosophy of the implicit that is very rich in possibilities, explanations, and insights for the human life. The presence of the *vis veri* in myth, in common sense, and in tradition is the extreme opposite of mystification, because here a conceptual apparatus does not mask historical reality and its material conditions; rather, truth, in an inchoate yet no less effective way, is already operative in the most basic human activities: Poetry is the first working manifestation of the *vis veri*; the "vulgar traditions" contain "public grounds of truth," and common sense offers a "criterion of truth" for which "vulgar wisdom has no more certain rule than civil prudence"; the obfuscation of the truth is given not through thought, but through ignorance, which makes us "attain the truth covered in falsity"; and this is not masking, but the sublimation of interest, because the idea acts not so as to cover interests, but so as to turn a vice into a virtue.

8. The Complete Explication of the Implied and the Infinite Interpretation of the Implicit

One could think moreover that the difference between ideology and philosophy is not so great given that in both expressive and revelatory thought there is a disjunction between the said and the unsaid; in both, the word refers to something not explicit that contains the real meaning of the discourse. But the difference could not be greater, because the interval between the said and the unsaid is presented in the first instance as the divergence between the explicit and the implied, and in the second instance as the discrepancy between the explicit and the implicit. In expressive thought, the word does not say everything because it masks the temporal basis that it secretly expresses; in revelatory thought, the word does not say everything because the truth that resides there is inexhaustible, and it gives itself over only in the form of having to be sought out further.

In the first case, because of the difference between saying and expressing, the word does not reveal, but hides, in the sense that it says one thing but means another. What is meaningful is not the explicit but the implied, which has nothing to do with the first, to the point that understanding means on the one hand completely getting rid of the explicit, and on the other hand negating the implied as such and achieving its complete explication. In the second case, because there is a coincidence among saying, expressing, and revealing, the word reveals truth as inexhaustible, and thus it is eloquent not only as for that which it says, but also for that which it does not say. The explicit is so meaningful that it appears as an unceasing radiating outward of meanings, continually nourished by the infinite richness of the implicit, so that understanding means deepening the explicit in order to harvest the inexhaustible fecundity of the implicit without ever reaching complete explication, due to truth's overabundance. The lack of complete explication is not due to the inadequacy of the word, but to its very capacity to possess an infinite, a pregnancy of revelations that, despite their growth in numbers, never move closer to a total manifestation, which is in itself impossible.

It follows that mystification, precisely because it covers the implied over with the explicit and conceives of the unsaid as a simple, hidden implied, not only is not opposed to complete explication, but even requires and forces it. Conversely revelation, precisely because it renders the explicit more meaningful than its very explicitness requires and conceives of the unsaid as the finite richness of the implicit, eludes every attempt at total explication. In the first case, the relation between the explicit and the implied consists in the fact that the latter must progressively and definitively take the place of the former. In the second case, the relation between the explicit and the implicit consists in the fact that the importance of the former is constituted by the inexhaustibility of the latter. The understanding of an ideology is nothing other than demystification, that is, it consists merely in the unmasking of the expression hidden by discourse and in the definitive replacement of the explicit with the implicit. Conversely, the understanding of a philosophy is a genuine interpretation, because it consists in the unending deepening of a discourse rendered inexhaustible by an infinite presence.

This distinction should eliminate or at least to circumscribe what has become one of the cravings of philosophical historiography today, almost entirely based on the "art of mistrust" and on the "school of suspicion," namely, on Nietzsche's *Kunst des Misstrauens* and *Schule des Verdachtes*, which prevent interpreters from considering explicit discourse and lead them to submit philosophical theories to a sort of psychoanalytic treatment—no theory is considered for what it says but rather for that which one presumes it unconsciously and secretly expresses. This treatment, highly fit for ideological thought and expressive thought in general, does not apply at all to genuine philosophical thought, in which the presence of the unsaid, far from authorizing that explication of the implied that is ultimately the demonstration of the falsity of expressive thought, instead demands that interpretation of the implicit, which is the sure sign of the profound nature of revelatory thought. With an adequate philological and historical preparation, but without historicist complexes or sociological preoccupations or culturalist prejudices, one should begin reading the philosophers as one reads the Bible; that is, one should read them for what they say explicitly and declaredly while one is careful to live up to the infinite depth of their speech. That is, one should pay heed *at one and the same time* to the letter and the spirit, to the explicitness and the profundity of the word, to that which it says explicitly and to the infinite message that it contains and announces; one should not disassociate one from the other, relativizing the word to its time and giving it no other meaning than such a relativization.

At this point a clarification is in order, one that is important for those who, aware of Heidegger's work, want to push it beyond the *impasse* of negative ontology into which he has unfortunately and hopelessly forced it. The fact that truth eludes complete explication should not force one to consider it as ineffable, as if its natural site were silence, as if its only mode of conferring itself to the word were that of eluding it, and as if it could never reveal itself without hiding itself because it would have no other means of being present than through absence, and also because every one of its appearances would ultimately be a betrayal of it. The word is the inadequate site of truth only if one understands it rationalistically as total explication; but, if one takes stock of its infinite capacity, it appears rather as the most appropriate site for welcoming truth and preserving it as inexhaustible.

I am well aware of the importance that the concept of the ineffability of truth has had in the history of philosophy, but I think that its aim was not so much the exaltation of silence as the only manifestation adequate to Being, as much as the sense of the inexhaustibility of truth. And in fact, if I have emphasized the ulteriority of Being and the unobjectifiability of truth, I have done it not so as to assert its ineffability, but so as to affirm its inexhaustibility, that is, its ability to reside in the word without identifying itself with it but always holding itself in reserve, to confer itself to every formulation without ever being exhausted in it, and to enter into discourse only to radiate outward ever new meanings of it. I am also well aware that the ineffability of truth would be nothing other than the pure and simple reversal of its complete explication, and thus would not avoid the problems associated with it. One needs to take note that the only way to possess and preserve truth is precisely that of welcoming it as infinite: That which is not gathered as inexhaustible cannot be truth. The revelation of truth resists both the rationalistic ideal of total explication, because then we would no longer have truth, which is inexhaustible, and also the irrationalistic demand for ineffability, because then we would no longer have revelation, that is, a possession. Revelatory thought supposes not the mysticism of the ineffable, but the ontology of the inexhaustible.

9. The Problem of the End of Ideological Struggles Is Resolved Neither by Sociological Historicism nor by Historical Materialism

A second and final problem that has yet to be faced is that of the end of ideological struggles that, in the view of many, should constitute a positive fact of daily life. In today's world, this concept seems essentially and principally to take two forms: that of sociological historicism and that of historical materialism. The first proposes, on the basis of an ultimately relativistic perspectivism, a demystification and particularization of ideologies that would make their integration and synthesis possible. The second, on the basis of an identification of philosophy with politics, would confine the multiplicity of ideologies to an alienated past. In both cases, the multiplicity of historical ideologies would be replaced by the totality of their anticipated integration or by the unity of philosophy finally realized.

The connection between particularization and integration is not understood well by sociological historicism. The particularization of ideologies, namely, the becoming aware of the historicity not only of other ideologies, but also of one's own, requires the taking on of a point of view that, by eliminating ideologies as such, is logically superior to those of the ideologies themselves. But one might ask, what meaning could the integration of ideologies still have from this superior point of view, which sociological historicism is concerned neither with clarifying further nor with making it be critically self-aware? First of all, becoming aware of the historicity of one's own ideology can be practically useful, as it places desires and unconscious beliefs under the control of consciousness. But far from validating the ideology, such becoming aware destroys that very thing, to which lack of awareness or false consciousness is essential. Ideology must be taken as true, lest it become a toy for scholars or a contrivance of cynics. As soon as it is unmasked, far from remaining in one of its supposedly new truths or genuine forms, ideology dissolves and no longer carries out its function, which is to be the instrument of action as the unconscious expression of historical conditions. This in fact means that the becoming aware of the historicity of ideologies can only be carried out from a point of view that is outside of and superior to that of ideologies. But sociological historicism does not nor can say what this point of view might be, because without any critical justification of its own point of view, it merely ends up with demystification: On the one hand, the historical conditions in their sheer practicity, and on the other hand, the conceptual apparatus in its empty rationality. And then, what should be integrated: bare interests, openly in conflict and susceptible only to be directed by a *Realpolitik* or empty ideas, rendered useless and superfluous? The very possibility of integration, of synthesis, of dialogue exists nowhere because there are no integratable, open, or communicating elements.

Marxism, through the realization of philosophy, denies that perspectives aware of their own historicity may still have enough positive value to make their integration desirable. Moreover, it offers a critical point of view that explains, in one breath, the historical multiplicity of ideologies, the need to demystify them, and the inevitability of their end—a point of view that is the end of alienation, namely the unity of theory and praxis, the unity of consciousness and reality, the realization-suppression of philosophy through its identification with politics. However, it also falls prey to the problem of affirming the unicity and conclusiveness of a specific philosophy, even if this philosophy is praxistically realized and definitively becomes "world," and coincides with the process of history and political action. With that, the possibility of dialogue is suppressed together with the elimination of the plurality of perspectives.

Sociological historicism and historical materialism are still tied, therefore, to archaic philosophical solutions, because the former does not justify the point of view from which it embraces the multiplicity of perspectives, whereas the latter does not abandon the concept of the unicity and conclusiveness of philosophy. The first identifies both ideologies and philosophies with the concept of perspective; in so doing, it ends up lacking a critical point of view on the multiplicity of perspectives, a point of view that could only come from philosophical thought accurately distinct from ideological thought. The second makes the distinction between philosophy and ideology, and thus critically reaches the point of view from which to observe the multiplicity of ideologies; but it can only do this by identifying philosophy with praxis, that is, by dissolving philosophy into praxis and considering praxis itself *as* philosophy. That still means, even if involuntarily, to conceive of philosophy as one and definitive and thus to betray, in the name of praxistic thinking, the nature of philosophical thought, which as such requires the plurality of philosophies. Due either to the a-critical confusion of ideology and philosophy, or to the extreme pragmaticization of philosophy, both have, in the end, reduced revelatory and ontological thought to historical and technical thought, thus compromising the hope that the end of ideologies would bring about a dialogue capable of resolving conflicts and struggles.

10. The End of Ideological Struggles Increases the Technicization of Thought

As a matter of fact, ideologies persist and continue to struggle vigorously against one another. The very idea of an integration of perspectives becomes an ideology, at least in the sense that it uses its own program in order to criticize other ideologies that do not adopt it. Marxism itself ends up presenting itself as ideology, indeed it splits into a multiplicity of ideologies that even turn against one another. This is the function and destiny of ideologies, however. They are closed and exclusive systems, and thus essentially in conflict with one another. They cannot bear a speculative critique, recognize only the errors of others, and ignore any refutation that is not in the form of a struggle. They present their own principle as unquestionable, and will not admit of other principles, whose very existence amounts not to an invitation to discover compatibility, but to a reason for negative critique. The multiplicity of ideologies does not teach dialogue, communication, and collaboration; rather, when it does not advise compromises, deals, and complicity, it admits only of struggles, oppositions, and conflicts.

This happens because ideologies are by their nature totalizing, that is, they claim to be a complete and total vision of the world. This fact is a necessary facet of their mode of conceiving and enacting thought, in the sense that they all abide by an ideal of complete explication, and thus believe that truth can be fully explicated; that is, that truth is the possible object of an exclusive possession. Thus arises the spectacle in the ideological camp, that any one of them is the sole possessor of truth and thus accuses all others of ideology. This is clearly a counterfeiting and a parody of the interpretation of truth, which, albeit one in its inexhaustibility, can hold together all perspectives, however diverse they may be, and can institute a multiplicity of them that, equally distant from simple compromise and a declaration of war, is shared possibility, dialogue, and communication.

One might think that in order to achieve a healthy collaboration, it would be enough to deprive ideology of that totalizing nature that makes it an imposter and at the same time the surrogate of philosophy or religion. This is surely the intention of contemporary sociological attitudes, when on the one hand, based on a conception of science as neutral thinking, they hope that political programs will conform to a political theory or a sociology of a scientific nature, and on the other hand, discerning in the ever-more technological nature of today's society a cooling off of ideological struggles, they foretell also a technicization of political life. In this way, they believe to be installing, under the form of science, a sort of vague liberalism that ensures the supremacy of intellectuals and, under the auspices of technics, a political life void of myths and ideas but well versed in self-control and tests.

Now, it is rather clear that in a society inspired by scientific neutrality and the technicization of politics, ideologies would eventually weaken and disappear as totalizing and surrogating conceptions, and thus the ideological struggle would fade and eventually die out. But one must take note of the fact that every theorization is motivated by a speculative intention, even if in an inchoate form and with the opposite result; thus, it is always susceptible to a speculative redemption even if it is faked, and that even ideological and historical thought after all employs philosophical assertions, albeit degraded, emptied, and instrumentalized. In light of this consideration, one can see that the sociological program that is inspired by the "neutrality" of science and of technics simply brings to completion the technicization of reason that, together with the historicization of thought, is the extreme result of the forgetting of Being and the obscuring of truth. From this, it is clear that the point in need of striking is deeper; if ideology's seductive force is increased and even instituted by its totalizing tendencies, one must above all avoid the birth of equivocations regarding the ontological nature of truth and the confusion over revelatory thought and expressive thought.

11. Only Philosophy as the Guardian of Truth Makes Dialogue Possible

We can therefore let ideologies bury ideologies, and turn rather to the safekeeping of truth. In order to do that, we need to make sure that the name "ideology" is in no way used to qualify revelatory thought, and above all that no ideological function is ever attributed to revelatory thought.

In the first place, if ideology is a simple surrogate for philosophy, there is no need for ideology where there is philosophy. The guardians of truth have no need for ideology, and must not even use its name in order to denounce the difference that separates them from the followers of some ideology, as when they carelessly speak of "ideological differences" that would separate them from the others. We are not dealing with "ideological differences," but with a radically different way of understanding thought, which is expressive for those followers and revelatory for the guardians of truth. Accepting the name "ideology" as a common platform for discussion is like forfeiting the game, because it means giving up *a priori* the defense of the fundamental point of divergence.

In the second place, the guardians of truth must in no way let philosophy become ideology. In order to combat ideologies, it is not enough to turn non-ideological positions, such as philosophy or religion, into ideologies, as if in this way they would become more effective in the struggle. In general, one does not fight one ideology by embracing another. Not only is philosophy not an ideology, but in fact becoming one would bring to an end what philosophy is. Historicists and sociologists already reduce all thought to expressive and ideological thinking, whether they do it for scientific and historiographic reasons, as with the various historians of ideas and culture, or whether they do it for purely political reasons, as with theorists and practitioners of politics. In order to fight ideologies, should we therefore add to this distortion of philosophical thought a programmatic ideologization of philosophy? Even if expressive thought happens to take the place of revelatory thought, and ideologies happen to become the surrogates for philosophy, these are not good reasons why philosophy should degrade itself by itself to the range of ideology, or why one should wish to ideologize revelatory thought. The organism regains its health only if political ideology resists overtaking philosophy, and only if philosophy resists intervening *directly* in politics, that is, only if each is restored in its own function without reciprocal invasions and confusions of realms.

There are no good ideologies that can be used to combat the bad ones. All ideologies are bad, and all of them are false because they have betrayed the essence of thought. The struggle against ideologies is not fought on an ideological level, but on the level of philosophy which, in order to win, has no need to ideologize itself because doing so would guarantee its defeat. What needs to be fought is not a single ideology, but that which stands at the base of the concept of ideology, namely, the substitution of revelatory and ontological thought with historical and pragmatic, expressive and mystifying, instrumental and technical thought.

Philosophy has no need for ideology because it is radically incompatible with ideologies. In this sense, there is no passage between ideology and philosophy. Just as ideology cannot and fails to transform itself into philosophy even if it attempts to replace it, so too philosophy cannot and must not transform itself into ideology, even if it commits itself to the struggle against it.

Philosophy, however, even when it escapes the attempt at its own ideologization, does not thereby reject worldly action. Philosophers as such are not theorists of disengagement, as those who accuse them of escapism would claim. Choosing the truth requires much more courage than choosing success. Revelatory thought demands an originary commitment, through which one complies with Being rather than rejects it, and one agrees to bear witness to it rather than to sacrifice it to history. Revelatory thought demands the clear awareness that it is up to time to make itself worthy of listening to the eternal, instead of it being up to the eternal to make itself heard by time. It demands a radical decision, by which one turns one's own person into the very organ of affirmation of truth in a way proper to one's own time rather than into the manager of the idea force that guides the time of which one is a product. One becomes the herald of a renewal that is, above all, personal, rather than the prophet of a merely terrestrial regeneration. Certainly, if in order to combat ideology one needs to ideologize philosophy, that is, renounce philosophers as such, and consider them as real philosophers only to the extent that they become political militants, then the battle is lost because one has compromised the truth, running the risk of preferring, over and against the truth, thought that is convenient at the moment and action that is geared toward success. One can win the battle only on the philosophical level; in fact, the best allies of panpolitical praxism are the so-called theorists of the "engagement" who, by accusing the defenders of the revelatory and ontological function of thought of escapism, end up bringing about the technicization of reason, which is the very aim of praxists.

Furthermore, it is precisely philosophy, as revelatory and ontological thought, that makes dialogue possible, unlike the mystifying and instrumental thought of ideologies that does not allow and even excludes dialogue. This discloses the exclusive and polemic power of historical and technical reason, and the uniting and cooperative power of ontological and revelatory thought. Truth as inexhaustible offers itself to infinite interpretations, soliciting all of them personally and opening all of them to dialogue. The particular, albeit aware of its own historicity and partiality, will never offer itself to the compatibility of an agreement or to the opening of a communication. There is here an apparent paradox: *It seems* that philosophies should be exclusive and at odds with one another because they are complete, and instead they are compossible for the very reason that they draw from truth that, as infinite, places all interpretations in dialogue; and, *it seems* that ideologies may be compossible because partial and therefore integratable, but instead their very partiality, masking totality, is the cause of the continual struggle among them.

The action that philosophy can perform in the world is precisely the realization of the dialogue that is not possible on the level of ideology, where on the one hand the recognition of the multiplicity of perspectives makes it impossible to adopt one, and on the other hand the adoption of a point of view excludes the recognition of those of others. To critique the "totalizing" tendencies of philosophy and oppose them with an "opening" is to remain tied to an ideal of ontic metaphysics and of rationalistic explication, even if one denies it. The concept of revelatory thought as personal interpretation of the inexhaustible truth corrects an extrinsic concept of multiplicity with a more profound concept of singularity, in which totality and plurality find themselves reconciled. Thus, on the level of philosophy it is possible to do philosophy of philosophy, whereas on the ideological level doing an *Ideologienlehre* [a doctrine of ideology] is impossible. In fact, philosophy is born as the awareness of the ontological relation, in which the connection with truth is *total* and the formulation that is given of it is *personal*. Ontological thought is the only one that allows philosophical thought to be both *philosophy of philosophy*, that is, a point of view on the multiplicity of philosophies that is critical, aware, and justified and thus is recognition of the personality, alterity, and intersubjectivity of perspectives, and also *philosophy*, that is, the taking of a position, the rejection of any pseudoscientific neutrality, and the personal and responsible formulation of truth. And so, only in philosophy is it possible to acknowledge other philosophies while adopting one of them, and thus truly open up those perspectives to dialogue.

Notes

In this chapter, all of the most important theories on the concept of ideology are taken into consideration and often discussed explicitly: The by now classic texts of the ideologues, of Marx and Engels, of Max Scheler, and of the sociologists of knowledge, of Karl Manheim, of Vilfredo Pareto. With respect to Marxism, I recall with particular emphasis the developments of Karl Korsch and Ernst Bloch and the interpretation of Kostas Axelos. Among the sociologists, I remember especially R.K. Merton, *Social Theory and Social Structure* (1957) and W. Stark, *The Sociology of Knowledge* (1958), and naturally the Frankfurt School, with the works by Max Horkheimer and Theodor Wiesengrund Adorno in the *Frankfurter Beiträge zur Soziologie*. On the problem of ideology in general, I limit myself to the following citations: Hans Barth, *Warheit und Ideologie* (Erlenbach-Zürich: Rentsch, 1945, 1961); Leo Kofler, *Marxismus und Sprache* (Cologne: 1952); Hans Joachim Lieber, *Wissen und Gesellschaft* (Tübingen: 1952); Theodor Geiger, *Ideologie und Warheit* (Stuttgart: 1953); Helmut Plessner, *Zwischen Philosophie und Gesellschaft* (Bern: Francke, 1953); Werner Knuth, *Ideen, Ideale, Ideologien* (Hamburg: Holsten, 1955); Jeanne Hersch, *Die Ideologien und die Wirklichkeit* (Munich: Piper, 1957); Ernst Topisch, *Vom Ursprung und Ende der Metaphysik* (Vienna: Springer, 1958); Leszek Kolakowski, *Der Mensch ohne Alternative* (Munich: Piper, 1960); Carl August Emge, *Das Wesen der Ideologie* (Wiesbaden: Steiner, 1961); Kurt Lenk, *Ideologie* (Neuwied: Luchterland, 1961, 1964); Daniel Bell, *The End of Ideology* (New York: Free Press, 1961, 1965); Ernst Topisch, *Sozialphilosophie zwischen Ideologie und Wissenschaft* (Neuwied: Luchterland, 1961); Robert E. Lane, *Political Ideology* (New York: Free Press, 1962, 1967); Joseph Gabel, *La fausse conscience* (Paris: Editions de Minuit, 1962); Jürgen Habermas, *Theorie und Praxis* (Neuwied: Luchterland, 1963); Jakob Barion, *Was ist Ideologie?* (Bonn: Bouvier, 1964); Reinhard Lauth, *Zur Idee der Transzendentalphilosophie* (Munich-Salzburg: Pustet, 1965); Hans Joachim Lieber, *Philosophie Soziologie Gesellschaft* (Berlin: De Gruyter, 1965).

Page 82: It would be useless to list the notable texts by Marx. As for Mannheim, see *Ideology and Utopia: An Introduction to the Sociology of Knowledge*, translated by Louis Wirth and Edward Shils (New York: Harcourt, Brace and World, 1968).

Page 83: A clear example of this skillful interpretation of Marxism, intended to shed light on the organic character of every historic moment, and *thus* the specific character of spiritual productions, is the Marxism of Karl Korsch. In the attempt to avoid the so-called denigrated "vulgar Marxism," precisely in the act of affirming the organic relation that in the totality of the situation inextricably ties its various aspects together, and thus also the ideal apparatus, he insists on the impossibility of considering the ideal products as chimerical, in the sense that their specificity is required by the historical situation as the integrating part of this and as the differentiated element of its complexity, to the point that one can speak of a "spiritual-intellectual structure." In such a way, although it is held that the dialectical treatment of ideology consists in the organic insertion of it in the total picture of the situation, it is also claimed that action is conducted not only at the level of economic structures, but also at the level of philosophical critique. See especially Karl Korsch, *Marxismus und Philosophie* (Leipzig, 1923). The assertion that "in the superstructure there is nothing that was not already in the base with the exception of the superstructure itself" (*"nichts sei im Ueberbau, was nicht auch in der Basis angelegt ist, mit Ausnahme des Ueberbaus selber"*) was said by Habermas regarding Ernst Bloch (Habermas, *Theorie und Praxis*, 338).

Page 84: By "metaphysical Marxism" I understand a conception like that of Kostas Axelos, *Marx penseur de la technique* (Paris: Editions de Minuit, 1961); *Vers la pensée planétaire*, (Paris: Editions de Minuit, 1964). For "prophetic" Marxism I obviously mean the thought of Ernst Bloch (in general the *Gesamtausgabe* in 15 volumes, and in particular *Das Prinzip Hoffnung* [Berlin: Aufbau Verlag, 1954–1959, 2nd edition Frankfurt: Suhrkamp, 1959]).

Page 88: The emphasis on "commonality" [comunanza] can also be found in St. Augustine, who is the great theorist of interiority: *"Verita tua nec mea est nec illius aut illius, sed omnium nostrum, quos ad eius communionem publice vocas, terribiliter admonens nos, ut eam nolimus habere privatam, ne privemur ea. Nam quisquis id, quod tu omnibus as fruendum proponis, sibi proprie vindicat et suum vult esse quod omnium est, a communi propellitur ad sua, hoc est a veritate ad mendacium"* ["Your truth belongs neither to me nor to this one or that one, but to all of us, as you call all of us publicly to share in it, warning us terribly not to take it as our private possession, lest we be deprived of it. Whomever takes for himself that which is there for the enjoyment of everyone, and claims as his that which belongs to everyone, is driven from what is held in common to what is his own, namely, from truth to a lie"] (Augustine, *Confessions*, XII, 25, 34); *"Communis est omnibus veritas. Non est nec mea, nec tua, non est illius, aut illius: omnibus communis est"* ["Truth is common to us all. It belongs neither to me, nor you, nor this one or that one: to all it is common"] (*Enarrationes in Psalmos*, 75, 17). These citations confirm the clearly anti-subjectivistic character of personalism, and the possibility of interpreting the same Augustinian doctrine of the interiority of truth to the mind in the ontological sense, rather than an intimistic one; nevertheless, this is challenged by the fact that in St. Augustine there is no hermeneutic concept of truth, namely the idea that truth only offers itself within the personal and historical formulation that is given of it. See also page 199.

Page 92: For the concepts of "gift" and "testimony" tied to the concept of freedóm, I refer the reader to the third edition of my book *Esistenza e persona*, 176–182.

Page 93: The French quotation is a verse from Voltaire (*Oedipe*, act IV, sc.1).

Page 94: The schizophrenic interpretation of ideology is found in J. Gabel, *La fausse conscience*, cit., 68–96. The citation regarding sociological historicism is taken from the already cited book by Mannheim, *Ideology and Utopia*, cit. 175. Pareto's theory of residues and derivations is found, as I noted, in the great *Trattato di sociologia generale* of 1916 (3rd edition: Milano: Edizioni di Comunità, 1964). Regarding Kelsen's theory of ideology see *Reine Rechtslehre* and *General Theory of Law and State* from 1945. See also *Aufsätze zur Ideologiekritik*, ed. Ernst Topisch (Neuwied: Luchterhand, 1962). Regarding Marx, it would be superfluous to list his many well-known texts.

Page 99: The expression "art of mistrust" is contained in one of the posthumous fragments of Nietzsche from 1885 to 1888: "Hier kommt eine Philosophie—eine von meinen Philosophien—zu worte, welche durchaus nict 'Liebe zur Weisheit' genannt sein will, sondern sich, aus Stolz vielleicht, einen bescheideneren Namen ausbittet . . . Diese Philosophie nämlich heisst sich selber: die Kunst des Misstrauens und schreibt über Haustür: memnes hapistein." ["Here a philosophy comes into language—one of my philosophies—which has no desire to be called 'the love of wisdom,' but perhaps from pride begs for a more modest name. . . . These philosophies, as you know, call themselves the art of mistrust and write over their front door: memnes hapistein"] (the Greek citation is from Epicurus, 250 K). The expression "school of suspicion" is contained in the preface of the first volume of *Human, All Too Human*: "Man hat meine Schriften eine Schule des Verdachtes genannt, noch mehr der Verachtung, glücklicherweise auch des Mutes, ja der Verwegenheit" ["My writings have been called a schooling in suspicion, even more in contempt, but fortunately also in courage, indeed in audacity"], *Human, All Too Human*, translated by R. J. Hollingdale (Cambridge: Cambridge University Press, 1996), 5. Certainly, the Nietzschean "mistrust" is something other than the claimed "unmasking" to which certain critics of today would like to submit even great speculation, also because Nietzsche's need of "truth" or of "veracity" is much more radical and generous, and above all absolutely lacking of every projective and autobiographical character. The same cannot be said instead of many of today's self-styled "demystifications." Remember that Nietzsche recommends to the higher man, in *Thus Spoke Zarathustra*, precisely that mistrust: "Habt heute ein gutes Misstrauen, ihr höheren Menschen!" ["Have a good mistrust today, you higher men!"] *Thus Spoke Zarathustra*, translated by Adrian Del Caro (Cambridge: Cambridge University Press, 2006), 235. In fact, "mistrust" is "the only way to truth" ("der einzige Weg zur Warheit"), it is the "source of veracity" ("Misstrauen als Quelle der Wahrhaftigkeit"), to the point that one can affirm that "As there is mistrust, so there is philosophy" ("So viel Misstrauen, so viel Philosophie") (Ed. Colli-Montinari, IV, III, 283; VII, III, 383; V, II, 262).

Page 100: On the reading of the Bible as an infinite message, see Gianni Vattimo, *Art's Claim to Truth*, translated by Luca D'Isanto (New York: Columbia University Press, 2007), 118–122.

4

The Destiny of Ideology

1. The Ambiguity of the Neutral or Positive Meaning of Ideology

In all debates about ideology, the greatest disagreement exists over the very meaning of the term. Surely there is a primary and constant meaning, in use for more than a century, which one could call derogatory, for it is particularly suited to a form of weakened and inferior thought. This is indeed ideology when it is understood as conceptual abstraction, destined to cover up and at the same time express determinate aims, or when it is considered as theory that is completely subservient to politics or completely dissolved in it. Alongside this disparaging meaning, however, there emerges one that supports a neutral or possibly positive meaning, which not only does not deem dangerous the weakening of the theoretical aspect of thought that arises in ideology, but in fact encourages and even praises the practical and political aims that inhere essentially within ideological thought.

In order to validate their claim, supporters of these new meanings must maintain that ideology is the demonstration of the practical fecundity of thought and of the power of ideas in the human world, as opposed to the sterility of thought that is abstract and detached from reality, and opposed to the uselessness of a form of philosophy that is academic and forgetful of life. As far as I am concerned, I remain faithful to the first meaning, and I think that ideology is nothing more than an instance of a more general and unfortunately ever more diffuse phenomenon—the historicization and technicization of thought. The result of this trend is the obfuscation of truth and the abandonment of speculative thought in favor of purely technical and instrumental reason, or a hybrid mix and confusion of theory and praxis.

Whatever the case may be, it is clear that only misunderstanding and confusion can result from the multiplication of diverse and equivocal meanings for the same term. For example, the conceptual apparatus of "ideologies" is considered as a system of "ideas," and their practical purpose is taken as a realization of "ideals": ideologies would essentially be *Weltanschauungen* that translate into practical schemes or programs of political action; there is no one who could not see how perfunctory and confused this hasty assimilation of heterogenous terms such as "ideas," "ideals," *Weltanschauungen*, practical schemes, programs for action, and so forth is. In such a situation, philosophy is called upon to define and clarify the terms of the question, and philosophers would not live up to their precise duty if, rather than bring about precision and clarification, they were to increase the confusion by indulging in the abuse of words, maybe with the specious pretense that the meaning of a term follows from the use one makes of it, and that one cannot challenge the use, but can only accept and approve of it.

As I see it, the clarification that in this situation philosophy must make is precisely that of differentiating between speculative thought and technical thought. The former is far from being abstract, detached from life, "academic," or "professorial," because such thought is revelatory and ontological, rooted in Being and in truth. Whereas its speculative character is derived from its being truth-bearing, it is no less certain that, just as it is truth-bearing, it also is and succeeds in being the guide for action. Conversely, technical thought only appears to be thought because it does nothing other than express its time and submit itself to action or become dissolved in it; that is, its conceptual apparatus has no other value than as instrumental and expressive, historical and technical, and thus in one respect it neither knows nor reveals anything, but only expresses temporal situations, and in another respect, it is not the guide for action, but only its technical and operative instrument.

The first type of thought is philosophical thought, whereas the second is ideological thought. Ideology is not a valid alternative to philosophy, even when one wants to reprimand philosophy for a presumed abstractness and a claimed detachment from life. It is clear that a philosophy that is truly abstract and out of touch is not worthy of the name "philosophy," nor could one say that it truly has a speculative character. In fact, philosophy attains concreteness and adherence to life through truth, and philosophy worthy of the name is always historical and personal revelation of truth. Philosophy, which by virtue of truth deserves to be a guide for action, is much more concrete and fertile for human beings than ideology, which betrays truth and amounts to nothing more than an instrument of action. Furthermore, so-called professorial and academic thought cannot avoid being part of ideological thought, because in its abstract and empty conceptuality, deprived of content, it is sustained simply by the historical situation, which it unknowingly expresses in its own way; nor does it have any function other than the rationalization of interests that remain hidden and unconscious, but nonetheless present and influential. The most striking feature of "academic" thought is its very emptiness and abstractness, and the most obvious way to fill this void and this abstraction is by considering its conceptual apparatus as the masking of a so-called "secret life."

In light of this fundamental distinction between speculative and technical thought, it seems clear that ideas and ideals, *Weltanschauungen* and projects for action, cannot be easily assimilated to ideology. Only through a previous degradation can ideas and *Weltanschauungen* become ideological, and only through a tendentious exaltation can one think that ideologies may be elevated to the richness of an ideal and the pregnancy of a practical plan. What characterizes ideology as such is its radically historicistic and potentially praxistic character; the same can be said univocally neither of ideas and *Weltanschauungen* nor of ideals and programs of action. Softening my proposed distinction by introducing a neutral or even a positive sense alongside a negative meaning of ideology and by assimilating to ideology realities rather far from it as those I mentioned, means mitigating the urgency of the problem posed by the reality of ideologies and letting go of the concern for a truly philosophical and moreover very concrete problem emerging from our time's turbulent reality. In the end, it means replacing concepts that are loaded with a genuinely speculative problematic with concepts that are too dull and neutral to be of interest to philosophy.

2. The Problem of the Concrete Distinction between Ideology and Philosophy

If someone asks me, as often occurs, how one might determine whether a particular thought is philosophical or ideological, that is, revelatory and ontological rather than expressive and technical, I respond by saying that this very question is not philosophical. First of all, one cannot expect that from a definition—let's say a definition of art—there automatically follows a division between beautiful and ugly works, or successful and unsuccessful ones. This distinction, possible only on a case by case basis, is a single act of judgment, whose responsibility is not attributable to a definition assumed as a criterion, but to the person who makes the judgment; for this very reason, the judgment is the object of continual revisions and discussions and of frequent disagreements and denials. In this sense, it is absurd to presume that from the *philosophical* distinction between philosophy and ideology one can derive an infallible criterion in order to distinguish concretely the one from the other in determinate cases, and to make the *historical* assignment of this or that particular thought to philosophy or ideology refer to such a criterion.

Furthermore, historical reality is always very complex, such that within it the distinction is not always operable in clear and precise terms. Both speculative and pragmatic aims find themselves mixed and confused within it, and they are indeed so intimately enmeshed that it is difficult to separate them out because every theorization, even if oriented toward openly or seemingly practical ends, is motivated by a speculative intention. Ideological thought also consists of conceptual elements, however degraded or instrumentalized they may be. The concepts and distinctions elaborated by philosophy have precisely the task of clarifying and illuminating historical reality to the degree that it is possible within the chaotic and confused state in which historical reality finds itself due to its extreme complexity.

Moreover, it is not the definition that must serve as criterion, but truth itself, which entrusts itself to revelatory thought and eludes merely expressive thought. In this sense, it is *index sui* [the mark of itself]. We are not dealing, however, with an *external* criterion that could somehow from the outside measure and commensurate diverse theories with precision, incontestably assigning some of them to the realm of philosophical and ontological thought and some others to the realm of ideological and pragmatic thought because truth always and only presents itself within an interpretation, and only there can it be *index sui*. Truth appears only to those who know how to see it, and seeing it means already to give an interpretation of it. Truth can only operate as an *internal* criterion, and we can even call it doubly internal, that is, embedded, in the end, in the very thing that one judges, and present only in the interpretation of the very person who must judge. Briefly, the criterion is, in the end, inseparable from both the "object" and the "subject" of judgment. Evidently, such a position is not only the most difficult for reaching and ensuring the incontrovertibility of a judgment, which rather requires a clear distinction and separation between the object judged, the judging subject, and the criterion of judgment; but it is also an occasion for, and even an invitation to and a request for the most open debate and the most avowed contention.

We are thus rather far from the availability of a criterion that is rigorous because it is rigid, or infallible because it is external. Nor do we have that "Lesbic rule" mentioned often by Vico, namely, a ductile and flexible criterion that achieves precision through its malleability and rejection of rigidity. Here, we find ourselves at a much more profound level where truth itself encounters human freedom, both sustaining and offering itself to it, and where human freedom appears possible only as the site of truth—we are at the very root of interpretation, which is to say, at the root of "revelation" and "contention" *at one and the same time.* Certainly, human beings have the great benefit of always being in some way *within* truth, tied to it by an originary bond that always concretizes itself historically, either through the situation, provided it is ontologically oriented, or through a tradition, provided it is continually renewed and refreshed. But the possibility of their failing this relation through the very freedom that confirms them in it, exposes human beings to a problematicity that has nothing to do with doubt, and to an uncertainty that has little to do with ambiguity; rather, the two derive from the bond that, as we saw, indissolubly joins revelation and contention together in interpretation.

Those who ask, however, how one determines concretely whether a particular thought is philosophical or ideological are perhaps driven to such a question by a subtler and more precise reason. It might be that in the definitions and distinctions elaborated by philosophy, one searches not only for a truth content, but rather for functionality [*operatività*], and thus one is ready to accept the distinction proposed above between revelatory thought and expressive thought only to the degree that it is functional, that is, conducive to the formulation of suitable historical judgments. It is clear, however, that this reservation is already a blatant and flagrant violation of the proposed distinction, because it accepts the traits of functionality and pragmaticity as the only ones essential to thought. Submitting the distinction between philosophy and ideology to the criterion of functionality signifies that one has already annulled and rejected it, because it means denying philosophy a revelatory and truth-bearing character and ascribing to it a merely technical and pragmatic character. The distinction between philosophy and ideology is possible only from the point of view of philosophy, not from the point of view of ideology. Thus, the revelatory character of thought appears only to the one who knows how to distinguish it from its expressive character. This means that at the level of ideology and of the technicisitc conception of thought, the question of the functionality of that distinction cannot even arise, and that the one who raises it once the distinction has been advanced, does so only in order to give or receive a negative answer.

3. The Deliberate Confusion of Philosophy and Ideology

Rather than resorting to philosophy in order to attain some needed clarifications when confronted with the multiplicity of meanings for the term *ideology*, one could say that it is nothing more than a question of words. To use the same word for different, if not even opposed meanings is never advisable, however, because it engenders a useless and shameful confusion; furthermore, it solves nothing, given that the task of definition not only remains, but is left ever more urgent and pressing. In this case, one cannot say that it is a mere question of terminology. At stake here is the very way in which philosophy is understood: whether philosophy should be conceived as one and definitive, or whether it should be reduced to pure methodology or to a simple technics, or whether it could be rather conceived as plural and truth-bearing *at one and the same time.*

For this very reason, one cannot ignore the possibility that there may be good reasons why the same word might be used for two things that at the very beginning seem equal but are instead different *toto coelo* [under all aspects], indeed diametrically opposed. In such a case, the many meanings of the term *ideology* would have a more profound aim and decidedly philosophical meaning, because the matter would then be that of finding out which problem hides behind the possibility or the intention of using the same word to designate opposing things, one of them clearly negative and the other, at least potentially, positive. The use of the term *idea* in Dostoevsky provides a vivid example of how one and the same word can serve to indicate both a negative and positive reality. In fact, for Dostoevsky, ideas can be either divine or demoniacal, that is, either they can be those "seeds of other worlds" that "God has sown on this earth while tending his garden," as the elder Zosima says in *The Brothers Karamazov*, or they can be ideas that take possession of human beings, similar to demons who when exiting from the possessed enter into pigs such that the whole herd throws itself into the lake and drowns there, as one reads in the passage from the Gospel that serves as the motto for *Demons* and on which Stepan Trofimovic remarks before dying. For

Dostoevsky, divine ideas are originary and profound truths, suited to be a constant inspiration for a human being and constitute the task of that individual's whole life, able to provoke a devotion to which a person dedicates oneself constructively affirming oneself in one's own coherence and vigor. Conversely, demoniacal ideas are illusions of an errant and decayed human being, artificial constructions that would more aptly be called "ideologies" than "ideas," scattered and scattering opinions in which the personality of the human being dissolves and is annihilated or solidifies into a stubborn and arrogant individuality. The fact that Dostoevsky designates with a single word two very different realities of the spiritual and historic life is not due to carelessness or absent-mindedness; rather, it is in order to demonstrate the very ambiguous and contradictory nature of all human things, in which opposing realities are often hidden under one appearance, and anything can assume the aspect of its opposite. This is an expression of Dostoevsky's most profound conceptions regarding the dialectical nature of reality, the antinomic nature of human beings, and the human exercise of freedom.

Now, the co-presence of opposed meanings in the same and identical term *ideology*, although not hiding a problem as profound as the one perceived by Dostoevsky, could nevertheless be the sign of a deliberate will to equivocation that manifests a prevalent tendency in today's world: that is, the will to exalt ideology to the level of philosophy and lower philosophy to the level of ideology; the will to sacrifice the revelatory nature of thought to its merely historical and expressive nature, that is, to sacrifice its connection with truth to its collocation in time; the will to mix thought and action so that one cannot be discerned from the other, placing thought in the service of action or even dissolving the former into the latter; and finally, the will to politicize thought, not only in the sense of turning it into a form of panpolitical praxism, but also in the sense of valuing it solely to the extent that it sets itself up—or pretends to set itself up—as the norm and guide for political action.

Unfortunately, one needs to recognize that this will to equivocation works its way into everything, even where one would least expect to find any concession to these forms of historicism, sociologism, and praxism, that is, in the supporters of the revelatory and speculative nature of philosophical thought. And it even succeeds in imposing itself, albeit inadvertently, on those who never should accept it, such as the Christians who, were they truly faithful to their principles, should never speak of "ideological differences" that would separate them from the disciples of some ideology, as for example from communists or followers of the

Enlightenment, and should rather speak, if ever, of "doctrinal differences," because religion is neither an ideology, nor does it have a need to ideologize itself in order to make its battle against ideologies more effective; indeed, it is radically incompatible with any ideology, that is, with any form of thought that has rejected all truth in order to embrace its historical, technical, and pragmatic nature. Christianity is called to take action in the world, where it must animate a philosophy, a morality, or an art; not for this reason, however, does it ideologize itself because it becomes active only by instilling itself in consciences, where it does not fail to undertake a total renewal, which in all movements of intense religious experience is called "rebirth." Such a personal rebirth, far from reducing philosophy, art, or morality to mere technics or purely expressive thought, rather lifts them up and reinvigorates them in their nature.

In the end, it may even happen that one also condemns what constituted Croce's greatest source of pride during his long presence in Italian philosophy, namely, the double but ultimately unique and indivisible battle that he courageously and tirelessly waged on the one side against abstract and empty philosophy, and on the other side against empirical and pragmatic philosophy: With praiseworthy and clear resolve he said, on the one side, that "the scholar of philosophy, in order to be truly such, must not be a pure philosopher, but develop some skill, and first of all the skill of being a human being," and, on the other side, that he himself "felt disgust, and sometimes hatred, for those philosophies that immediately give birth to actions and programs of practical action from their corrupt womb."

4. The Nonphilosophical Character of Ideology

One could challenge me by saying that wherever there is thought there is, at least potentially, philosophy, and thus there is philosophy even in ideology, which is always thought, albeit historical and expressive. My response would be that although I admit that ideology is an attempt at philosophy, it is a completely failed attempt that winds up in an absolute betrayal of the essence of philosophical thought, in the sense that ideological thought is inauthentic and falsifying thought.

Certainly, at the origin of every theorization there is a speculative intent, and there are always ideas and concepts that constitute the conceptual apparatus of an ideology. I have even acknowledged that the end of ideologies would bring to completion the technicization of reason, and thus would imply the complete extinction of the cult of truth and the decline of ideas, ideals, and values essential to the meaning of life. In the ideological formulation, however, the primitive speculative intent dissolves in the substantial and exclusive historicity and pragmaticity attributed to every assertion. The conceptual apparatus of ideologies is composed of degraded ideas, empty concepts, and instrumentalized rationalizations. The end of ideologies implies the end of speculation only to the degree that ideology is closely connected with philosophy insofar as ideology represents the negative possibility of philosophy, and only in the sense that technical and pragmatic thought belongs to those impediments, mistakes, and deviations that make the way to truth indeed varied and adventurous, but above all rough, difficult, and even impossible. That notwithstanding, one might say that the primitive speculative intent at the origin of an ideology is still salvageable and redeemable; that with a proper treatment one could remedy the degradation and emptying-out of the idea that occurs in ideology; and that one could always revitalize the demand for truth to which in some way even error is connected, albeit negatively, because within the human condition truth is tied to error to such a point that the possibility of error cannot be eliminated without the elimination, pure and simple, of the search for truth.

However it may be, even if ideology is taken as an attempt at philosophy, it is a failed attempt, and thus it is, as I have said, inauthentic and falsifying thought. It never amounts to anything more than a forgery and parody of philosophy, namely, philosophy as a caricature and thus in a negative form. Due to its mimetic and parodying nature, it is nothing more than a substitute for philosophy, falsified and simulated philosophy, doctored-up and abusive philosophy, and thus, again, philosophy in a negative form. If it is philosophy, it is such not in a germinal and inchoative form, but rather in an attempted, and indeed bankrupt form. It is apocryphal and inauthentic philosophy, pseudo-philosophy, and thus, one more time, the negative form of philosophy.

5. *Weltanschauung*, Philosophy, Ideology

Philosophy in its inchoate form is not really ideology, but *Weltanschauung*, which already contains, germinally and potentially, all the fullness and richness that philosophical thought will reveal in a mature and developed awareness. *Weltanschauung* precedes the conscious and intentional exercise of thought, whereas ideology is its outcome. That means that a

Weltanschauung finds itself at the point where ontological relation and historical situation cross and become indissolubly connected, in the sense that the bond with truth concretizes and individualizes itself in a unique and personal interpretation, and the historical situation confirms itself in its own unrepeatability opening itself to an ontological dimension. This is what happens in "common sense," when it is not kindly softened in a form of quiet sensibleness but rather gathered, in a Vichian mode, in that convergence of singularity and similarity, individuality and communication, that indicates the fecund co-presence of personal dimension and ontological dimension.

The same thing occurs in "myth," when it is understood not merely as primitive and primordial, but rather and primarily as primigenial and originary, that is, as an original and surging gathering of the true that is indistinct and vague not because it is elementary and inchoate, but rather because it is fecund and pregnant, and in this sense is the common root of the highest human activities—art, philosophy, ethics, religion—that draw upon it without ever exhausting it, that develop from it without ever destroying it, and that, far from aiming to replace it, invoke its continual presence, which for them is the unique guarantee of constant nourishment and secure inspiration. This also happens in the "heart," when this term has its psychological, affective, emotive, and sentimental traits removed in a Pascalian fashion, alluding rather to that "faculty of the infinite" that contains hidden and latent aspects only because it is a total and global vision, and as such particularly enlightening and illuminating; faculty that escapes a discursive ratiocination only because it is beyond the distinction of the faculties, and thus in a position to nourish indefinitely every rational discourse; faculty that constitutes our self-consciousness only insofar as it is the originary possession of the infinite, and thus the direct relation with Being. In a word, it is the ontological dimension of the human beings and their personal access to truth.

Weltanschauung, understood in this way, not only possesses an inchoate, germinal, and potential richness, but also an originary, primigenial, and surging authenticity and genuineness. Philosophy is nothing else than a *Weltanschauung* intentionally and consciously translated into verbal and speculative terms. Conversely, ideology is coeval with philosophy and represents its negative and degenerate alternative. Whereas philosophy translates the personal interpretation of truth, namely, a *Weltanschauung*, into speculative terms, that is, whereas philosophy secures the bond that personally ties human beings to truth and confirms the ontological dimension of the entire human being, ideology is born precisely as the forgetting of Being, the obfuscation of truth, the rejection of the ontological relation, the betrayal of the originary bond. Ideology is not limited to being a reduced, watered-down, or degraded philosophy, but is the very negation of philosophy. Its essence is to arise as the surrogate for philosophy, for wherever ideology exists there can be no philosophy, and wherever there is philosophy there is no room for ideology. Philosophy and ideology are the two options for one decision, two possibilities for one choice. In its practice, ever since the beginning thought immediately finds itself faced with the dilemma: either to be a personal revelation of truth, a confirmation of the ontological dimension of the human being, and an affirmation of the truth-bearing nature of philosophy, or to be a simple expression of time, a complete instrumentalization of reason, and its reduction to technics, methodology, and ideology.

Faced with a *Weltanschauung*, the philosopher has the choice either to elevate it to philosophy or to pervert it into ideology. The choice depends on whether the originary ontological relation that the *Weltanschauung* contains is confirmed through the speculative nature of philosophical thought or disavowed through the complete technicization of ideological thought. Faced with a *Weltanschauung*, the philosopher is the "scholar" who, far from being cloaked in "arrogance," does nothing but recover through words and thought that which the simpler person already knows and that the common person can say only through life, demonstrating with proper evidence what Pascal profoundly states regarding "sciences whose two extremes touch," in the sense that "the great souls, having encountered all knowledge," return in a learned way to that ignorance pregnant with wisdom whence they came. Conversely, faced with the *Weltanschauung*, ideology seems to represent the attitude of the "half-scholar" Pascal mentions: "Those between the two extremes who have moved on from their natural ignorance but are unable to reach the other have a certain smattering of presumed science but act like know-it-alls. They turn the world upside down and judge everything poorly." And it is not coincidental that Dostoevsky condemns "half-science" in *Demons*, a book that one could surely consider to be the novel-tragedy of ideology, and that as such cannot be neglected by anyone who seriously considers the problem of ideology from the philosophical point of view: "Half-science has been especially distinguished for that—the most terrible scourge of mankind, worse than plague, hunger, or war, unknown till our century. Half-science is a despot such as has never been seen before. A despot with its own priests and slaves, a despot before whom everything has bowed down with a love and superstition unthinkable till now, before whom even science itself trembles and whom it shamefully caters to."

The philosopher, therefore, is the scholar who rediscovers what the ignoramus originally knows, and the ideologue is the half-scholar who destroys, betrays, and deteriorates it. Ideology is therefore betrayal and forgetting. It preserves nothing of truth, not even the need for it. To say that wherever there is thought, and thus even in ideology, there is philosophy is reckless optimism because it means that one does not understand that, in ideology, thought is employed *in order to deny* [*negare*] philosophy because ideology begins with the presupposition of *refusing* [*denegare*] Being and *disavowing* [*rinnegare*] truth. This is a point where the philosopher must abandon every irenic intention and cooperative spirit, because here we truly face *error*.

6. The Positive Reality of Evil and Error

Optimism and irenicism often lead us to emphasize only the positive traits of humanity, and indeed to claim that there is always positivity in the human being. In all times this has given rise to well-known theories aimed at making error and evil disappear, as with a roll of the dice, either because they would be dialectical moments necessary for truth and the good, or because they cannot sustain themselves, and should be in some way supported by truth and goodness, if only by taking on their appearance or assuming their intent because it does not seem seriously probable that human beings could consciously and intentionally want evil and error. At this point, one could begin a discussion on the reality of error and evil that would in itself require an endless treatment if it were to be sufficient, let alone exhaustive. I limit myself to the following remarks.

Regarding the possibility of eliminating error and evil by turning them into necessary dialectic moments of truth and good, we should observe, first of all, that the positive outcome that they can have is completely external to their character of falsehood and wickedness and is in no way either the result of some internal process or the coherence of a logic immanent to them. This is so much so that, in transcendentalistic conceptions, the possibility of deriving good from evil is not only completely outside human beings' abilities, but moreover is, in God, an absolutely eloquent demonstration of God's omnipotence. In the second place, we should observe that one cannot mistake as dialectic integration the fact that the human formulation of the true always contains the possibility of error and that the human practice of the good always presupposes the possibility of evil. This fact belongs to that situation of *insecuritas* [uncertainty], precariousness, and risk that comprises the essentially tragic nature of the human condition, which realizes the positive only within an act that contains the constant and effective possibility of the negative, to the point that the suppression of the possibility of evil would not be possible if not as the suppression of freedom itself, that is, as the suppression of the unique source through which human beings are capable of realizing the good and being worthy of praise.

Regarding the possibility of eliminating error and evil on the ground of the need, in which they find themselves, of being sustained by truth and the good, taking on their appearance or extorting consensus from the mind or consciousness, the following two observations will suffice. In the first place, that possibility belongs to the necessarily parodying and simulative character of error and evil, which are constitutively counterfeits and caricatures of truth and good, and precisely for this reason much more destructive and degenerate. Their disguise once again demonstrates their negativity because there is nothing more diabolical than denying the existence of the devil, and thus nothing more negative than exploiting good and truth as a mask and an alibi for evil and error, which employ this dissimulation in order better to insinuate themselves and make themselves acceptable, much in the same way that the Antichrist must assume the aspect of Christ and the power of darkness appears as the angel of light. In the second place, such a parodying character of error and evil still depends on the tragic character of the human condition, which is expressed in the ambiguous and contradictory nature of the human being, caught between opposites and strained between extremes, always prey to the torment that they impose on it, and nevertheless always tempted to confuse them and to disguise one as the other. Human nature is ambiguous in itself, able to hide the good under the appearance of evil and to camouflage evil with the features of good, and indeed to mix good and evil in the motivations of the very same act, which is therefore neither less good than evil nor less evil than good, according to the point of view. Human nature can even turn not only good into evil, thus degrading even the originarily authentic and generous impulses, but also evil into good, as when the overwhelming power of conversion reveals and announces itself right in the soul of the most obstinate sinner, or as when, speaking in Barth's terms, one finds ecstasy in the trivial.

7. The Irreparable Negativity of Ideology

With ideology, we find ourselves faced with error and evil, in all the stark reality of their negative force. Lacking everything else, the presence of ideology in our current age would be enough to convince us of the unavoidable reality of error and evil, and of their terrible efficiency in the human world. For the moment, let us put evil aside so that we may concentrate our attention on ideology as error. The temptation to deny error arises first of all from the need to take history into consideration, to the extent that for historicism and sociology, error does not exist because any cultural form is judged by the sole criterion of its correspondence to the moment and to the historical atmosphere that it inhabits and from which it emerges. Second, the temptation to deny error arises from the need to accentuate the positive nature of the human being, to the extent that from an optimistic point of view, error ends up having at most a material and objective existence (assuming one can say this), because subjectively it cannot be affirmed as anything other than truth, and rationally the fundamental human demand for truth would be enough to redeem it through a process of corrections and integrations. Thus error disappears, and at the most appears as something inadequate, anachronistic, partial, provisional, or whatever else it may be.

Certainly, nothing is more convenient and more comforting than to claim that error does not exist, to the extent that if a "consolatory and edificatory philosophy" truly exists, an object worthy of the ironic darts of today's critical and disenchanted spirit, it consists precisely in rationalistic optimism, and above all in that tendentiously and declaredly sociological historicism that is the more or less conscious base of the greater part of contemporary culture. But error does exist, and it is inauthentic thought, the thought that undertakes its activity for the very reason of denying itself as such. As defined above, such thought is purely expressive, historical, technical, and instrumental, and appears, among other things, in ideology. Allow me, therefore, to consider my way of conceiving the ontological dimension of the human being—as the originary bond between person and truth, and thus as the thinking that is both revelatory and expressive, ontological and historical—as the only way of taking history into account without neglecting the need to acknowledge the existence of error, or as the only way of admitting the reality of error without thereby forgetting the mutability and variety of historical situations, or as the only way of reconciling the plurality of interpretation with the distinction between true and false.

In fact, purely expressive, historical, technical, and instrumental thought is truly error in the most radical and profound sense. It is not error because it is a simple approximation, partial and provisional, of the truth, a pure attempt, more or less successful, to grasp and formulate it, a mere failure in the course of an investigation that is by its very nature precarious and uncertain. Nor is it error as a mitigation and weakening, a fracturing or dissipation of truth, almost already possessed, but now enfeebled, faded, or in the process of decomposition. Purely expressive, historical, technical, and instrumental thought is instead—frankly and resolutely—obfuscation and oblivion, forgetting and abandonment of truth, the distancing from it and the loathing of it. It is thought undertaken *as thought* in order to betray, deny, and abolish truth, in order precisely to replace it and declare its end and uselessness. One should not say that it is error only because it is no longer thought given that a purely historical, technical, and instrumental discourse does not seem worthy of the name of "thought." This move would reduce error to being a simple enfeebling of truth. Certainly, in its proper and complete meaning, the name "thought" can only be given to ontological and revelatory thought; yet thought that is only expressive and historical, technical and instrumental, is also thought, and moreover thought undertaken precisely with the goal of denying ontological and revelatory thought, denying truth to which the person is originarily tied, denying philosophy as the verbal and speculative recovery of that revelatory thought and originary bond.

Briefly, error and evil are not merely tentative approximations of truth and the good, or their simple degeneration and weakening; rather, they are respectively thought, albeit in a degenerate form, exercised precisely in order to refute truth; and freedom, albeit in a diminished form, exercised specifically in order to refute the good. They are the positive installation of a negative reality and the negative use of positive faculties; the efficiency of negative forces and the perversion of positive possibilities. In conclusion, they are the interweaving of positivity and negativity, so that both, rather than annul each other, bring each other strength, so that negativity, far from being incomplete and partial positivity, receives an ulterior charge of efficiency from positivity; and positivity, by overturning its own sign, serves only to transform negativity, in its weak and fearful state, into open and outright destructiveness.

Against the irenicism (and the eclecticism that logically follows) of rationalistic optimism, and against the technicism to which sociological historicism necessarily leads, I have proposed a dramatic position, and thus one more consonant with the tragic nature of the human condition:

Human beings have to reckon with the reality of evil and error and with the demoniacal destructiveness that follows from it. The uncertain and precarious situation in which human beings find themselves is not remedied by the impersonal event in which technical thought tests and corrects itself; rather, such a situation requires personal commitment, deliberate struggle, and knowing resolve, all of which lead to conquest and victory only through the constant risk for failure and defeat.

8. The Falsely Positive Aspects of Ideology and Their Denunciation

If things stand in these terms, there is no gain in looking for positive instances and indicators in ideologies. It is in fact clear that within the historical reality of human coexistence, good and evil are mixed, attempt and result intermingle, investigation and failure are confused, so that it is always possible, in the understanding mind of the historian, to see suggestions of good in the reality of evil and vice versa, as I have already pointed out. What I want to emphasize here is that the clarity of philosophical definitions is the only one that, due to its very precision void of confusions, is able to shed some light on the complexity of the human world. Thus, one will see that it is indeed true that in some way ideological thought affirms truth, to which it is tied through a relation, albeit negative; precisely for this reason, however, it confirms truth in the same way that even evil can be in some manner the testimony of the good, if in no other form than as a contrast. Above all, one will see that it is still optimism to bring the efficiency of ideologies back to truth and their force of attraction back to thought, as if wherever there is efficiency and appeal there necessarily ought to be something positive, true, and genuine. One should not believe that efficiency and seduction pertain only to the true and the good. Indeed, at second glance they belong precisely to technical and instrumental thought, which aims to be as successful and widespread as possible; whereas in contrast, what is rather suited to the true and the good are effectiveness and persuasion: that is, value, even when it is denied and disowned, and conviction, which is always strictly personal and irreplaceable.

An idea can be powerful even if it is not the word of truth, as the children of darkness are more cunning than the children of light. From this arises the greatest success, albeit transitory and momentary, of ideologies in comparison to genuine philosophy, which exercises its influence on individuals rather than on the crowds, on disinterested culture rather than on the technical and political world, on the long course of time rather than on the ephemeral incandescence of the moment. And as efficiency and appeal are the parody of effectiveness and conviction, likewise they derive from the dissimulating nature of ideological thought: not from truth, but from the counterfeiting of truth, not from thought but from the perversion of thought. Ideological thought is efficient and seductive especially because it fits with the times, it aims for success, and it is a completely explicated and potentially totalizing conception. These three traits, however, are nothing else than the counterfeiting of the three features of revelatory thought, which takes its own times into account not in order to suit them, but in order to turn them into a pathway toward truth, that is, an interpretation of truth that is always new and different. And it commits itself to a decision not so that it can choose the way to success, but so as to pay witness to truth. And it aims for totality not in order to transform it into the result of a complete explication, but so as to consider it as an inexhaustible source from which it gains its own contents.

One cannot say that the positive element of ideological thought is its rationality, albeit empty, or its universality, albeit apparent; that is, that character of rational coherence and technical experimentation necessarily conferred to it by its indispensable conceptual apparatus and its constitutive pragmatic intentionality. This empty and purely pragmatic rationality is not a positive element because it is indeed what renders ideological thought ever more mystifying, limiting its function to that of rationalizing a secret history and dissimulating a practical outcome. What matters is truth, not reason. Without truth, reason becomes pure expression or mere technics. That means that it remains a captive of the sterile antithesis between rationalism and irrationalism. In fact, if rationalism is the claim to the complete explication of discourse, ideology necessarily demands a rationalistic result, because understanding it means demystifying it, that is, declaring the unexpressed in it and thus canceling out its secret history by bringing it to complete explication. And if reason without truth results in a purely pragmatic utilization or in a merely technical exercise of thought, it will have an inevitably irrationalistic result, and this is precisely the case of ideology, which as the very expression of the times becomes the instrument of action.

Briefly, reason without truth, after having come close to the extreme rationalism of complete explication and of the self-correcting nature of thought, quickly results in irrationality because it is only historical and technical thought, wherein the critical nature of demystification and of experimentation is not enough to protect it from the powerful irrationalism of sociological historicism, of panpolitical praxism, and of radical empiricism.

Nor can one say that ideological thought has a revelatory nature in the sense that at least it reveals the time of which it is the expression. To admit that ideology can reveal or even just illuminate the time of which it is both portrait and awareness, product and instrument, means not to recognize the exclusively expressive and pragmatic, and thus non–truth-bearing, nature of ideology. First of all, of truth there is only revelation, and of time there is only expression—revelation can only be of truth in the same way that expression can only be of time. Nor can the terms be exchanged, because to speak of the revelation of time would mean considering it not as a pathway, which is the only thing it can be, but as origin, which certainly it is not; and to speak of the expression of truth would mean lowering it to a merely human or intra-human level, whether sociological or psychological or natural, with the result of turning metaphysics into an ontic form of pantheism or naturalism.

Furthermore, the truth about time can appear only in revelatory thought, that is, in the thought that expresses time precisely in the act that approaches truth. The truth *about* time occurs only if time itself becomes the pathway to truth. Merely expressive thought is necessarily misleading and mystifying. It expresses time only by hiding it; in fact, it has no other way of expressing time than by hiding it. This is not a matter of the concealing that necessarily belongs to revelation; when dealing with the inexhaustible, and thus with the unspoken, one must certainly say that there is no disclosure without latency, nor is there appearance that will not have an aspect of illumination meant to dissipate the darkness in the very act of emerging from it. Rather, the issue is here the fact that expression itself takes on the form of dissimulation, and that this very dissimulation acquires an aspect of expression—ideology expresses time only by falsifying it, and its expressivity appears only through an opportune demystification. Demystification can certainly have its beginning in an ideology adverse to the one in question, that combats it precisely by managing to denounce the implied in it; but it can find an adequate development only from a point of view superior to the level of ideologies and their mutual struggle. The completion of demystification arrives only through ontological thought, which abandons the limitations of demystification in favor of the depth of interpretation. A truly penetrating knowledge is attained only through interpretation; and where there is interpretation there is truth-bearing thought, ontological dimension, and bond between person and truth.

Neither pure and simple expression nor demystification can therefore be knowledge, understanding, and penetration of time, because expression is necessarily dissimulation and masking, whereas demystification is merely the denunciation of the irrationality of the secret and implied life, and is the attempt at reaching the totality of explication. Only interpretation can speak the truth about time; it can do it because it is a form of revelatory knowledge that deals with truth, that is, with the inexhaustibility of the origin and with the infinity of the implicit.

9. The Non-Ideological Character of Philosophy

The preceding objection also can be expressed in another way: Ideology is so far from being a solely negative reality that just as wherever there is thought there is philosophy, and thus there is philosophy even in ideology, so too does philosophy itself have an ideological character and aspect; and just as there is a revelatory moment in ideology, so too there is an ideological moment in philosophy. Briefly, if it is true that revelatory thought is always also expressive and historical, multiple and personal, situated and interpretative, one must also admit that philosophy, in the historicity that comes to it from the human condition of investigation, always has an unavoidable ideological aspect. The spirit of this objection, if I judge it correctly, is the following: No matter whether one considers not only the expressive character of philosophy, but also its ideological character, as something substantially positive that describes thought as such, or whether one considers not only the ideological character of philosophy, but also its expressive character, as something defective and lacking that it would be better if it were not so, in either case what is being pointed out is, first of all, that philosophy is not achieved as pure rationality, and second, that the ideological aspect of thought is identified without remainder with its expressive and historical aspect.

Now, I must say that such an objection neglects the central point of the position that I am proposing and sustaining, namely the affirmation of the originary bond between person and truth, of the inseparably revelatory and expressive character of philosophical thought, and of the indivisibly personal and ontological nature of truth-bearing discourse. From what I propose, it follows, in the first place, that philosophy, as always personal and thereby *also* historical and expressive along with being revelatory and ontological, does not in fact have the character of a pure rationality and an exclusive logicity. For this reason, my polemic against ideology is not at all carried out in the name of an "intellectualistic angelism" or according to the rationalistic myth of impersonal or depersonalized pure thought because I have taken into great account the demands of the historical situation and of living persons in the conception of this very philosophy by considering it as a personal revelation of the truth, revelation that depends on the way in which the individual persons freely take their own historical situation into view. From what I am proposing it follows, in the second place, that in no way can the terms *ideological* and *expressive* be considered synonymous, because expressivity, and thus historicity and multiplicity, also belong to philosophy, which is ontological and revelatory thought; they acquire an ideological significance only when they are isolated, emptied of truth, and deprived of their ontological dimension. Wherever the use of the terms *historical* and *expressive* may be appropriate, one can replace them with the term *ideological* only if one can exclude that the historicity and expressivity at stake are those that are freely assumed by the person as the pathway to truth, that is, that it is the historical situation in its ontological opening and in its revelatory possibility. Briefly, one can use the term *ideological* only after having ascertained that one is dealing with that form of historicity in which the person remains enclosed within his or her time, and with that form of expressivity in which thought is identified with the historical situation.

The distinction I propose between revelatory thought and expressive thought is, to speak of it in a more precise way, a distinction between thought that is *primarily* revelatory and thought that is *only* expressive: The first is *at one and the same time* ontological and personal, and thus clearly philosophical, whereas the second is *merely* historical and pragmatic, and thus ideological or technical. Revelatory thought cannot avoid being *also* expressive because of the originary solidarity between person and truth, according to which truth is accessible and can be formulated only through an irreplaceable personal relation. This implies that revelatory thought necessarily contains a historical and practical element yet not thereby a historical and praxistic element such as only non-ontological and non-revelatory thought could have in its feature of being solely temporal and openly pragmatic. In fact, there can be thinking that is *only* expressive, namely, thought that deliberately rejects truth and allows itself to be exhaustively qualified by historicity. In it, the historical and practical element is no longer the pathway to truth or the possible ontological opening, but is absolutized in itself thereby becoming openly historicist and praxistic, and thus typical of ideological and technical thought.

Various consequences follow from this position, two of which I briefly underscore here. The first consequence is that only in philosophical thought, that is, in thought that is in itself both ontological and personal, are the expressive and revelatory aspects indivisible and inseparable; conversely, ideological and technical thought follows precisely from an abusive separation of these two aspects, which is the result of an explicit rejection of the revelatory aspect. The second consequence is that the historical and practical, contextual and multiple, individual and social element is not negative in itself, because on the one hand, it can be positively assumed in an ontological dimension as the possible opening to truth, and thus as the point of departure for a personal interpretation of truth, which happens precisely in philosophical thought; and on the other hand, it becomes negative only if it appears as an unavoidable limitation or as an insurmountable closure, which occurs precisely in ideological thought that empties itself of truth only so it can fill itself with time, that frees itself from Being only in order to render itself master of the situation, that rejects the origin only in order to dissolve itself in the moment, and that, in the end, incapable of comprehending that nothing other than freedom can respond to originary stimulation, and incapable of understanding how much uncertainty and instability this conscious and responsible relation with Being contains, sees in truth nothing other than the extreme limit of constriction and oppression, and thus, by rebound, prefers the other extreme, namely, the ephemeral and the arbitrary.

10. The Concreteness of Authentic Philosophy

My polemic against ideology is therefore not carried out in the name of a rationalistic and impersonal philosophy, or a philosophy that is "angelistic" and forgetful of human life. This is not the case precisely because I can only conceive of philosophy as of thought that has one way alone of being revelatory and accessing truth: namely, by converting the historical situation into a way of approaching truth, by transforming the historical substance of the person in the revelatory light of truth, by imprinting an ontological opening and truth-bearing import on the very life of the person within his or her time and environment. This means, in opposition to ideology, to consider truth as accessible only within an interpretation that is necessarily always historical and personal because it involves whatever the person is, does, thinks, feels, says—the whole transformed into a revealing lens, a capturing antenna, a syntonic device. To grant the feature of interpretation to the originary bond between person and truth and to the ontological relation signifies precisely the following: to approach truth beginning from the concreteness of the historical situation and to make truth speak to the listening of time.

To ask philosophy to descend into time and embrace the rhythms of life is a useless and superfluous demand, I would even say, an offensive one. If a philosophy is worthy of its name, it is already within time and history, from history and time it has already accepted what it was able and obliged to accept, and within time and history it already acts and works in the way that is suited and proper to it. To say that philosophy needs ideology in order to make itself concrete in history and to place itself into human life is an assertion that does not take into account the fact that thought can only be revelatory if it is also expressive and historical, and that the insertion of philosophy within history and the historical qualification of philosophy do not require at all the absolutized historicity, expressivity, and practicity that characterize ideology. Philosophy is in itself already historical and living, personal and multiple, situated and active, expressive and working [*operante*]. Furthermore, only if philosophy is conceived rationally and angelistically as pure impersonal rationality does it then seem necessary, in order to make it concrete in time and insert it into life, to make it white hot in the fire of ideology, to conceive of ideology as "the palpitating form" of the historical existence of humanity, and to consider an "ideological structure" as unavoidable in human existence. This is because, by neither fulfilling its own function nor realizing its own essence, philosophy needs then to be replaced with a surrogate; that is, one needs to entrust philosophy's tasks to a mere caricature, briefly, one needs to resort to ideology, which ultimately means abandoning life to irrationality.

Personalization is not ideologization nor does historicity really belong to ideology, and thought can have a practical aspect without becoming ideology. In itself, philosophy that is worthy of the name is already personal, and thus multiple, historical, expressive, and working [*operante*]. Whoever entrusts ideology with the historical and practical qualification of philosophy by that very move shows an angelistic and rationalistic understanding of philosophy as of a distillate elaborated "in the paradise of pure rationality," as of only one possible philosophy, as of abstract speculations worthy of philosophers whom Vico would call "monastic" and "clerics of their own ideas." And so the antithesis of rationalism and irrationalism is not avoided because philosophy in its pure rationality and its definitive unicity is placed on the one side, whereas history, in its mutable multiplicity and mixed and murky complexity of life, is placed on the other. The potential Manicheism of this opposition, one stretched between nostalgia for ideal and desirable rationality and unicity, and regret over the real and undesirable multiplicity and irrationality, is not hidden; furthermore, the role of mediator is denied to philosophy—which alone would be able to unite the two poles by removing the presumptuous abstractness from the first and by freeing the second from an unjust devaluation—in order to confer such a function to ideology. Such ideology, having abdicated truth, is unable to resist the irrationality of "insuppressible motivations," and thus undeniably takes the side of an extreme irrationality, the inevitable backlash of a rationality hardened and accentuated beyond the just.

My polemic against ideology is therefore carried out in the name of the ontological and revelatory character that philosophical thought has and must have, since ideology not only falls short of such a character, but even arises precisely *as* its abdication. I do not at all intend to attack the historical aspect or the practical aspect in ideology, which are after all present also in philosophical thought, and not simply as compatible with the speculative nature of philosophy, but even as indispensable to it in the sense that without them the speculative nature of philosophy would no longer be such, but rather would fall into abstraction and vacuity. What I want to attack in ideology is the *absolutization* of the historical and practical element of thought, namely, the technicization of reason—or what I have called the historicization and pragmaticization of thought. My defense of philosophy against ideology is not the absurd defense of abstract reason against the concreteness of history and life; rather, it is the defense of ontological and revelatory thought against thought that is merely historical and instrumental, the defense of reason nourishing itself on the origin against reason that is only experimental and self-correcting, the defense of full thought against empty thought—ultimately, the defense of truth against technics.

The historical situation, far from being a fatal and inevitable limitation, is—I will repeat it once more—the only pathway one can utilize to access truth, since truth is accessible and formulatable only within an individual and concrete interpretation, and what impresses an interpretative stamp on knowledge is precisely its personality, its situatedness, and its historicity. Truth, therefore, does not let itself be grasped independently of time: Time offers it both access and residence, entrance and dwelling, figure and exercise. But there is trouble if time, encouraged by its own indispensable quality, grows overly proud, so to say, and crosses over the limits of its just rights. An absolutization of historicity would immediately follow, with the consequences I have revealed above bringing about repercussions for the very nature of thought, which deprived of its ontological import and its truth-bearing capacity, withdraws into expressivity and pragmaticity, becoming purely technical and fundamentally empirical.

11. The Difference Between the Historical Character and the Ideological Character of Thought

Historicity, situatedness, expressivity, practicity, and personality are not the same as ideology. And when one speaks of historical conditionality or of situatedness, or as I like to say, of the expressive character and the personality of philosophy, this does not at all imply that philosophy has in itself an ideological character. To speak of "social conditioning and of the ideological matrix of each of our discourses," as some say, mixes two different things: The social conditioning, or more broadly the historical conditioning, of all human activity can become, on the basis of a free personal decision, either a mere limit of existence or a real opening to Being. This depends on whether the person chooses *to be* history or *to have* history, to be identified with the situation or to turn it into an ontological means and an interpretative key. This historical conditionality is therefore not in itself the ideological matrix of *each* of our discourses; rather, depending on the character that one freely impresses on it, it can become either the expressive and interpretative character of revelatory and philosophical discourse or the purely historical and pragmatic character of instrumental and ideological discourse. The historical situation, taken in this way, is not an inevitable conditioning that would be better off not existing; rather, it is that historical gathering whose ontological opening one must freely recover. Then it becomes the sole revelatory organ that human beings can employ for gaining access to truth, which speaks only to those who know how to question it in person, and reveals itself only to those who know how to attune it to their own historical concreteness. Historical conditionality is therefore not disgraceful in itself, for that would mean despising the personal aspect of human activity; rather, pure absolutized historicity is the disgrace, which occurs when the situation is denied an ontological dimension and thought is denied a truth-bearing capacity. Historical and social, and thus personal conditioning is constitutive, essential, and positive. The ideological outcome, conversely, is only a possibility, but a negative and disgraceful one.

For these reasons, I cannot accept the idea that between philosophy and ideology "there is a relation not of opposition and mutual exclusion, but one of complementary inclusion and mutual integration," as some propose. The aspects that can be mutually integrated *within philosophical thought* are the expressive historical personal aspect and the revelatory truth-bearing ontological aspect. Indeed, in such a case, it is not even a matter of integration and complementarity, but of a real inseparability and indivisibility, so that one aspect finds its own configuration and the possibility of its own exercise only in the other. In fact, the expressive aspect of philosophical thought is inseparable from the revelatory aspect because what is expressed there is not the historical situation as such, but the very person who views her own situation as the historical opening to atemporal truth. And the revelatory aspect of philosophical thought is inseparable from the expressive aspect because there is never an objective manifestation of truth, but it is always a matter of gaining it within a historical perspective, that is, a personal interpretation. Conversely, ideology results from a cunning separation of these two aspects of thought, from a surreptitious dissociation of the expressive aspect so that it is separate and isolated.

One can therefore, in my view, neither affirm that "in humanity, philosophy will always have something ideological and ideology something philosophical," nor discount as completely incorrect the thesis that "ideology is not revelatory but only active, and that philosophy is not active but only revelatory." Certainly, philosophy *also* has an expressive and active, historical and practical character, but by the same token it does not have an ideological character, because ideology is the *absolutization* of the expressive historical active practical character of thought, and as such stands opposed to philosophy and has nothing philosophical about itself, if not the mere appearance of a forgery and caricature. Ideology, understood in this way, is not only undeniably opposed to philosophy, but is also the most arrogant and dangerous replacement for it. It craves its substitution, and is even capable of supplanting it in the minds less experienced and more sensible to the flashy and efficient aspects of thought.

It is true that "claiming that ideology can take the place of philosophy would be irrationalism"; but it is not "rationalism to separate ideology as if it did not have any function within philosophy": Rationalism would instead be to think that philosophical thought can have a revelatory character without having an expressive character, or can expand to its complete explication (as technical thought and with it also, at least indirectly, ideological thought claims to do), thereby forgetting the inexhaustible character of truth. Whoever neglects the originary bond between person and truth and the ontological dimension of existence finds oneself necessarily imprisoned, as we have seen, in the antithesis of rationalism and irrationalism, and bounces back and forth from one extreme to the other without ever managing to escape the opposition or overcome the dilemma.

12. The Unicity of Truth, and the Plurality, but not the Partiality, of Philosophies

It is very true that metaphysics always contains two opposed aspects, namely, the need to overcome ideology and the danger of falling into ideology, and that the dialectic of metaphysics consists precisely in avoiding both the relativism of ideologies—into which its historicity constantly risks making it fall—and the absolutism of a manifestation that claims to be exhaustive of Being, which would be impossible for human beings. In other words, one must recognize that in philosophical thought, the revelatory and historical aspects are inseparable, and that ideology arises from the forgetting of Being, from the suppression of the ontological dimension, from the depersonalization of human beings. Admitting that philosophy always has an expressive and historical character still does not imply, however, that "every historical form of metaphysics always has an ideological moment."

This conclusion is reached by those who begin with the presupposition that the multiplicity of forms in which philosophy presents itself historically is a fatal and inevitable (and moreover a disgraceful and lamentable) outcome of the human condition, and that the interpretative and thus multiple nature of human knowledge is a limitation that it would be desirable to remove; briefly, it is reached by those who preserve the nostalgia for a singular and definitive philosophy, and thus still maintain an ontic conception of Being and an objective conception of truth. To say that there is never *the one* metaphysics but that there are only ever *many* metaphysics, and that none of these, which are only ever particular and historical, exhausts what is supra-temporal in its unicity, means conceiving the relation between the expressive and the revelatory as the relation between the temporal and the supra-temporal, which to me is impossible. One cannot say that the expressive stands in relation to the revelatory as the temporal stands in relation to the supra-temporal, first of all because revelation is not possible without expression, so that that which is revelatory is always also expressive and historical, and second because the revelatory is not supra-temporal in itself, but is rather a historical and temporal revelation of that truth that is supra-temporal in itself yet always present in historical manifestations.

It is truth, and not philosophy or metaphysics that is one, inexhaustible, and supra-temporal. As human knowledge and thus interpretative of truth, philosophy is in itself, constitutively and essentially, multiple and temporal, plural and historical, or perhaps more aptly, always individual and personal. This is so not because of a defect, but due to its nature. Philosophies worthy of the name are not historical, particular, and multiple configurations of the one exclusive and unreachable philosophy, which as such neither exists nor can exist, either historically or supra-temporally, just as by definition there cannot be only one interpretation because interpretation implies the always new and different personality of its subject and the unfathomable infinity of its object. Philosophies are instead always new and different formulations of inexhaustible truth, and therefore *at one and the same time* revelatory and expressive, truth-bearing and historical; they are not ideological simply due to the fact that they are historical. What is entrusted to individual philosophies worthy of the name, even though it always transcends them in its inexhaustibility, is not the one presumed philosophy—as if it wished to compensate for its very unattainability by realizing itself in particular incarnations—but Being, truth itself, which provokes and solicits all philosophies. It commits itself and entrusts itself to all of them, yet it privileges or prefers none, and in none of them does it affix or exhaust itself.

I do not believe that historicity, situatedness, and expressivity lead necessarily to ideology due to the character of particularity and partiality that seems to inhere essentially in ideological knowledge. There are those who maintain that social and historical conditioning, and thus the ideological character of every human discourse, imply the necessarily inadequate and partial character of all our truths, and who, through an appeal to transcendence coherently configured in terms of negative ontology, seek not only a guarantee against the absolutization of ideologies, but also a remedy for the skeptical relativism that seems to derive from that recognition. I do not believe, however, that one can speak of a necessarily partial and inadequate character of all of our truths, either formally or substantially.

One cannot speak of it formally because it is impossible to establish a comparison between two things as different as truth and our formulation of truth. One could establish a comparison between one formulation of truth and another, and such a comparison happens every time a philosophical and speculative discussion occurs; but a comparison between truth and a formulation of truth would be a real *metabasis eis allo genos* [change into some other kind] and as such, absurd. One cannot speak of it substantially either, because to reveal truth means neither knowing it all as in a complete apparition that follows the lifting of a sort of Maia's veil, nor grasping its simple parts whose progressive integration one would hope for or whose fatal inadequacy one would lament. Truth is not a totality made in such a way that the thought that reveals it can be considered compromised or diminished because it does not say truth in its entirety, and the formulation of truth is not made in such a way that it should be considered inadequate and partial because it does not attain a complete explication. On the one hand, the ideal of philosophical thought is not the complete enunciation of a reality that can be more or less resembled: It is not a matter of defining the truth once and for all, but of grasping it as truth, and thus as inexhaustible, so that the absence of that complete explication, which an affirmation of truth is not meant to give, cannot be attributed to partiality or inadequacy. On the other hand, the nature of truth is to be inexhaustible, and thus more soliciting than satisfying, more origin than object, more orientation than discovery: To grasp it in its inexhaustibility means really to grasp it all, and it is precisely for this reason that the tiniest glimmer of truth is already extremely diffusive.

In short, any assertion of truth can be neither inadequate nor partial because truth is either grasped or not, and if one grasps it, one grasps it all. To grasp all of it does not mean to be able to enunciate it in a complete and definitive explication, which would rather imply that one has not really grasped it at all. Conversely, it means to begin a discourse that continually regerminates from its own source, that incessantly reproblematizes its own questions, that always alludes to something other and more than that which it states explicitly. To grasp it all means to grasp it in its inexhaustibility, and this gives rise to the essentially unending, diffusive, and ulterior character of philosophical discourse, which is far from being ideological, partial, and inadequate because its ontological dimension and its truth-bearing matrix make it part of the inexhaustible richness of its source and capable of conferring an enticing and opening character to every limitation.

There is no need, then, for a guarantee against the skeptical relativism that would follow from the always partial and inadequate character of the human formulation of truth, because such a character does not exist. The nature of the human formulation of truth, far from requiring a "negative ontology"—which is forced to insist on the ineffability of truth in order to justify the presumed partiality of all of our truths—instead demands an "ontology of the inexhaustible" in order to explain the incessant, diffusive, and ulterior aspect of truth-bearing and philosophical discourse.

13. The Problem of Negative Ontology: Ineffability or Inexhaustibility

When I state my opposition to negative ontology, it is not because I do not acknowledge a meaning of discourse beyond discourse, a unity of discourse that cannot be spoken, a presence that is effective [*efficace*] even though it is and remains unenunciated. Rather, I maintain that the way in which truth resides in the word is precisely this presence that is the source of continual and unending discourse and is the unending diffusion of ulterior significations. First of all, the presence of truth in the word is not the presence of the object of discourse, but of its origin: It resides there not as explicated, but as implicit; not as the object of an (albeit ideal) complete explication, but as the stimulus for an unending explication. But then again, it is precisely the word in its explicitness, which therefore is charged with a broader ulteriority and a richer resonance, that is the bearer of this inexhaustible source of discourses and meanings. One can truly say that the explicitness of the word does not coincide with the explication of truth, but is rather the support for the outward radiation of the implicit, the sustainer of the ulteriority of the inexhaustible, and the core of the meaning of discourse beyond discourse.

I do not want to eliminate the concepts of "indirect" and "allusive," which inhere necessarily in the revelation of truth, namely in that inseparability of disclosure and latency that accompanies the manifestation of what is hidden, just as the light breaks through the darkness whence it appears. I wish instead to avoid the concepts of cipher, symbol, and allegory to the degree that they are the organs of a myth that presents itself as conscious and intentional, and that for that very reason is false and artificial. Such concepts, as well as those of inadequacy and partiality, are in my opinion directly opposed to the concepts of the revelatory character of thought and the inexhaustibility of truth.

The positive and profound sense of so-called negative ontology is not the ineffability of truth, or the fatal inadequacy of the word, or the inevitably symbolic and allegorical character of philosophical discourse, but the inexhaustibility of truth, the presence of the implicit in the word, and, if anything, the allusive and mythic character of philosophical discourse. The ineffable, the inadequate, and the symbolic—these are ambiguous and insufficient concepts when applied to truth and to its formulation: The ineffability of truth is not yet the fertile reserve of an inexhaustible secret that has come to be revealed; the inadequacy and partiality of the word is not yet the unending and diffuse abundance of the implicit; the symbolic nature of philosophical discourse is not yet the ulteriority of truth-bearing thought. This is so, first of all, because these concepts are at their root negative, so much so that when faced with a radically ineffable truth *all* words are *equally* inadequate and partial, and *all* discourses are *equally* allegorical and symbolic, so that every possible distinction is gone, even the distinction between true and false; and second, this is so because these concepts are produced through a pure and simple reversal because it is clear that the affirmation of the inevitability and definitiveness of silence is an evident sign of the undeclared nostalgia for complete explication.

Yet again the only recourse is to the concept of interpretation because only interpretation manages to unite seamlessly the opposing demands more often betrayed than expressed on the one side by negative ontology and on the other by the rationalistic conception of explication. In fact, interpretation presents itself as the possession of an infinite: on the one hand a true possession, and thus one that captures and penetrates; and on the other hand the possession of an infinite, and thus necessarily multiple, even if such multiplicity does not indicate inadequacy and incompleteness. It is possession, yet of an infinite, and thus such possession is continually open to development yet not partial, ulterior yet not allegorical, mythical yet not symbolic.

For a modern formulation of the ontology of the inexhaustible, I could find no confirmation more fecund and influential than Schelling's late speculation, which appears in many texts, but in a particularly suggestive way in the 1821 *Erlangen Lectures*. There, among many uncertainties and hesitations, among the many flashes of brilliance left aside without any development, among the many apparently fecund yet substantially sterile proposals, arises the demand to transform the concept of the indefinable and the ineffable into that of the originary and the inexhaustible. On the one hand, the transcending of every definition reaches an essentiality and a purity that perhaps no negative theologian had ever reached before, and on the other hand, the infinity of the origin is brought out from precisely the pure absence of every definition, namely, from the very impossibility that the indefinable is defined by its indefinability. On the one hand,

Heidegger's ontological difference is anticipated in a truly remarkable way, and on the other hand, the discourse is continued beyond Heidegger, I would say almost reopened after the impasse to which Heidegger has involuntarily but harmfully led us. In essence, Schelling wants to avoid both mystical negative ontology and also Hegelian explicated ontology, both the definition of Being through its inaccessibility, namely the total cessation of the word and of thought, the *alogia pantele kai anoesia* mentioned by Dionysius, as well as the complete unfolding of Being, namely, the resulting identity of Being and thought. To such an end, Schelling proposes a dialectic that neither ends with not knowing nor blooms into absolute knowledge, and for which knowing as not-knowing shows Being as its reverse, and thus indicates Being without resolving it in itself. He therefore pushes thought down a path so radical that it can do nothing but strike against its reversal and remember its originary content, without being able to stop either at the object, or at God as entity, or at the unknowable, or at the indefinable, but at least indicating and unfolding the inexhaustibility of its own ground.

Everyone can see, from this brief outline, what a wealth of suggestions and confirmations could be derived from Schelling when he is considered not only as a post-Hegelian thinker, which he was in reality even if this is often and willingly forgotten, but also as a post-Heideggerian thinker, which he could become today even though some, driven by very specific interests, have tried to defame him as a typical "destroyer of reason." I would like to take advantage of this occasion to underline the surprising modernity and timeliness of this thinker who demonstrates an admirable talent and a prodigious vigor even in his later work, so unjustly slandered first by the Hegelian tradition and later by the Marxist tradition. If the originality of Kierkegaard and Marx in comparison with Hegel is the vindication of Being as opposed to thought, Schelling deserves equal recognition because indeed he had already enacted such a vindication within the idealistic realm well before them, and in particularly effective terms. If the virtue and merit of Kierkegaard and Nietzsche are the consideration of the tragic nature of the human condition, they find an ally in Schelling, who against Hegelian optimism had already underlined the problematic and dramatic nature of existence by proposing a philosophy of freedom. If one of the demands of contemporary thought is the rejection of totality, one should not forget that Schelling had already done so when he realized that what Hegel places at the end should have been placed at the beginning, and that the unity that follows duality can only take the form of a totality, which is ultimately abstract and utterly lacking when compared to the inexhaustible richness of the originary unity. If another concern of philosophy today is the analysis of human activities, which is proposed not only by the phenomenological school but also by cultural anthropology, one should think of the many suggestions and clarifications that could readily be found on this topic in Schelling's "positive philosophy"; and the list could easily go on.

14. Revelatory Thought Is the One Mediator between Truth and Time: The Necessity of Philosophy between Religion and Politics

Just for a moment, I wish to return to the question of negative ontology in order to make a final clarification. The claim of the ineffability of truth would, among other things, result in the abolition of metaphysics in favor of particular and specialized philosophical discourses. That would go against the elementary observation that particular philosophical discourses can be made either in a purely technical and empirical way, and thus lose their philosophical character, or in a properly philosophical way, which clearly requires a metaphysical discourse—that is, that type of ontology that, only if it preserves the traits of inexhaustibility and of ulteriority that we have examined, explains how a discourse remains at the philosophical level without falling into pure technics. This observation can present itself again regarding a way of setting up the relations between ideology and religion that unfortunately has its supporters.

There are those who assign ideologies to the historical and social field of politics and reserve the meta-cultural permanence of absolute values to the pure interiority of religious faith. Thus the human field remains divided between politics and religion, leaving no room for philosophy. The danger arises that, through the mere act of not leaving to philosophy the place that it is due, the first two overreach the confines of their own fields and, within human life, claim to perform functions beyond those that are rightly theirs; and that philosophy, deprived of all meaning, indeed deposed of its reign and its legitimate function, no longer offers to religion and politics the support and control that, while placing philosophy in its proper position of dominance, also prevented their unjust claims and absurd transgressions. I believe, instead, that there absolutely needs to be room for philosophy between the fields of politics and religion. There needs to be room for ontological thought and truth-bearing discourse, and this precisely so that religion, pushed into the realm of pure interiority, may not emphasize its "meta-cultural" character to the point of losing itself in the smoky haze of the ineffable, in a new degenerate form of "negative theology"; and so that politics, devoted to the mere historicity and pragmaticity of ideologies, may not be abandoned to the pure and hard battle of pragmatic choices, of unconscious as well as declared interests, of the mere "particular," that as such is not at all open to dialogue but decidedly closed in on itself, and that communicates with the others only through violence and war.

On the one hand, only what is truly meta-cultural is gradually embodied in diverse cultural and historical forms without ever identifying itself with them; rather, it sustains and promotes them, expressing them autonomously and generating them from its own infinite potentiality, and finding in them not only its only site, but also its unique way of manifesting itself, indeed its unique way of living, since it has no other life than those very forms in which it is embodied and resides time after time. One can even say that the meta-cultural character of a reality of this sort does not at all result from a purely negative transcendence, from a sort of inaccessibility that floats above the events of history, from a state of permanent inconfigurability and of continual resistance to formulation, but precisely from the possibility of embodying itself in always newer and more diverse forms, of inserting itself in the world of history with a presence always renewed and relevant, of drawing from its own internal space the voice and timbre that are most effective within the specific historical moment and that make themselves most heard in the historical now. The possibility of escape is simply the other face of such a possibility of embodiment, the other side of the coin, since the force employed to break from a historical form that has become a purely superficial garment and more of an impediment and obstacle than a present and living reality, has the same nature as that employed in embodiment; indeed it is absolutely the same. This force shines much more in embodiment than in escape, more in the assumption of a new form than in the demise of the old one, more in the invention of the aspect in which to shows itself, the figure through which to appear, the voice with which to speak, than in the abandonment of the older aspect, figure, and voice. In short, what follows is that the meta-historicity of a reality appears less from its power to transcend its own historical forms than from its power to be embodied in ever newer historical forms.

Here too I wish to cite Schelling, when he says that in a reality of this sort, the positive does not amount to being outside of every form (certainly, in order to be able to enclose itself in a form it must be outside of every form since, as Plotinus said, only the unformed has a form, whereas the unforming is formless: *to eidos en to morphothenti, to de morphosan amorphon*) but rather to the ability to be enclosed in a form, namely, the freedom to be or not to be enclosed in a form: "*Um sich in eine Gestalt einschliessen zu können, muss es freilich ausser aller Gestalt sein, aber nicht dieses, das ausser aller Gestalt, das unfasslich-Sein ist das Positive an ihm, sondern, dass es sich in eine Gestalt einschliessen, dass es sich fasslich machen kann, also dass es frei ist, sich in eine Gestalt einzuschliessen und nicht einzuschliessen.*"

Now, the incarnation of the meta-cultural reality of religious faith can be made only by ontological thought, namely, by revelatory thought, whether it presents itself in the explicit speculative form of philosophy or whether it works in its truth-bearing function within a moral attitude. Only revelatory thought can serve as mediator, and avoid both the violent oppression of the religious element by the practical attitude, and also the withdrawal of the religious element into a hazy and ineffectual supra-historical distance. In fact, on the one side, revelatory thought behaves in such a way that the historical forms in which religious faith is embodied result not from an external imposition on the part of the historical situation, as if time were something to be endured rather than interpreted, something more passively received that actively adopted, but rather from an invention in which that philosophical search for the truth that is inevitably stimulated by the religious possession of truth is realized only through an interpretation of the needs of time and a deepening of the historical situation; on the other side, precisely in its capacity to grant an ontological opening to the historical situation, revelatory thought is able to unfold the infinite potentiality of a supra-historical substance in a concrete and historical way.

On the other hand, the particular, taken in itself, is closed in on itself and incapable of dialogue and communication. Relinquishing the political field to ideologies means considering it as the domain of the "particular," in which thought has no other function than to rationalize pragmatic choices, to justify the interests of groups, or to monopolize truth for its own advantage. In conclusion, it means identifying political reality with the threshing-floor that makes us fierce; it is in fact useless to expect from ideological thought, which by its nature has abdicated truth, the capacity to release the particular from its own enclosure, to ensure or even only to wish for the compossibility of perspectives, to establish not the reality of a reciprocal dialogue but maybe just its possibility, to guarantee or to foretell their mutual compatibility or even their agreement. In order to be able to accomplish all of this, ideological discourse should become philosophical, whereas historical and pragmatic thought ought to become revelatory and truth-bearing. That clearly requires a level superior to that of ideology: a level, in short, where the particular, rising up to the level of the person, actually becomes open, engaged in dialogue, and integratable with others. I say the particular and not ideology, which as such keeps the particulars closed within their own particularity, which unmasks the particularity of others, but without unmasking its own (ideological thought is in fact incapable of connecting particularization with integration), and which hurls each one against all others in a state of permanent struggle without any hope for peace other than mere compromise. Without revelatory thought, and with only ideological thought, politics is left to the more or less declared battle among interests, the pure play of forces, the substantial pragmaticity of choices: In a word, the bond between morals and politics is severed, a bond that is as precarious, uncertain, and unstable as possible, but that it would be inhuman to want to eliminate entirely.

In conclusion, without the intervention of revelatory thought, and without the intervention of a more or less developed philosophy, the division of the human world between religion and politics would also carry a separation between the two camps so radical and so profound that it would obstruct every communication. This could take no other existential form than the simultaneous reduction of morals to politics and the abolition of philosophy in religion. Without philosophy, politics would fall into the irrationality of the human all too human and religion would involve itself in the irrationality of an all-too-real *Schwärmerei*; one would then observe those monstrous juxtapositions, of which history provides no paucity of examples, of "divine kingdom" and "state of nature." Whoever overlooks philosophy only to admit religion on the one side, and science and ideology on the other, risks falling into a mix of fideism and technicism, for which, on the one hand, religion distances itself to the point of losing not only its capacity to operate in history, but also its real importance within human spirituality, and on the other hand, the historical world is abandoned to the irrational, with no hope for salvation other than mere technology. It goes without saying that in such a perspective it would become impossible to distinguish, in the course of history, the moments and perspectives when religion, more than embody itself in a cultural form, has compromised itself with the overly human reality of the times and thus has damaged its very nature of religion beyond repair, from those moments and perspectives that are its real incarnations in which, in the act of extracting them from out of its own virtuality and of inspiring them from the inside, it has taken form and figure, presence and effectiveness [*efficacia*], dwelling [*sede*] and reality.

Without philosophy and without revelatory thought there can be no dialogue and less than ever the "dialogical integration and articulation of ideologies," as is vainly hoped. In order for there to be dialogue, two things are needed: truth and alterity. That, yet again, is possible only through the concept of interpretation because on the one hand, interpretation is by its nature multiple and infinite, since there is never interpretation without plurality or without alterity, and on the other hand, interpretation is always the interpretation of truth as well as of truth there is nothing but interpretation, given the infinite and inexhaustible character of truth. In order for there to be dialogue, neither sympathy nor ideas are enough, because sympathy tends to dissolve in generic benevolence, in itself incapable of grounding respect for the person, and ideas may be mere historical products devoid of truth and thus incapable of establishing a common plane of understanding. Dialogue requires what I have elsewhere called a real "exercise of alterity," as well as the presence of truth in the plurality of interpretations.

There is no dialogue based on ideologies. What sort of respect do ideologies deserve? None, because they are inauthentic and falsifying thought. What level of reciprocal understanding do they create? None, because they rather divide and separate. Only truth carries a uniting force. We need to return to respect for the person, which above all is a tribute to the great truth that consists in the affirmation that the possession of truth is always personal. Dialogue is made possible by the originary bond of person and truth that stands at the base of revelatory and ontological thought, and that makes indivisible and united the respect that one owes the person and the respect that one owes truth. These very two terms begin in fact through mutual respect, the person by constituting his or her own dignity and task through the listening to truth, and truth by giving itself over to nothing but freedom and interpretation, which in themselves are always personal.

15. The Rational Effectiveness of Philosophy, not of Ideology: Theory and Praxis

The conception of philosophical thought that I proposed includes the characteristics of historicity and practicity in human thinking, such that these do not endanger the revelatory capacity of thought worthy of the name, but in fact maintain it. To such an end, it is necessary that historicity and practicity should not become absolutized, as happens in historicist thought and pragmatic thought that characterize ideology. The task of revelatory thought is to rediscover truth from the point of view of our time without distorting it through unwarranted historicizations, and to render truth acceptable to our time without thereby demeaning it through inappropriate exploitations. That requires, clearly, an appeal to freedom, and thus a commitment, a decision, a taking of a stance, a deliberate and active will, which have nothing to do with pessimistic renunciation, with egoistic escape, with narcissistic contemplation. But that also implies the devaluation, in fact the repudiation of ideology, where the exaggeration of the historical and practical aspect of thought reaches such a display of history and praxis, of technicistic historicism and panpolitical praxism, that it obscures the much more discrete and reserved, but also much more profound and arduous, commitment of revelatory thought.

In light of these considerations, I would like to tackle a final question, namely, to remove the impression, aroused perhaps in some reader, that my definition of revelatory thought, with the subsequent devaluation of ideology, should carry an attitude of political indifference. Some seem to believe that the absence of ideology makes a political commitment impossible. It is natural that to them the battle against ideology seems an exhortation to political disengagement, and the exaltation of revelatory thought seems the defense of abstract, academic, and scholastic philosophy. In reality, I believe that the demand that motivates them to sustain the political necessity of ideology is the extremely important demand not to hand the historical, social, and political world over to irrationality. In that, I not only agree with them, fully sharing this demand, but indeed I believe that I am even ahead of them because from this very demand arises the definition of revelatory thought that I proposed as distinct from merely expressive thought. The fact is that I do not believe that the most secure means of releasing the historical, social, and political field from irrationality is that of entrusting it to ideology because ideological thought, having *ab initio* abdicated truth, is not only an exceedingly fragile barrier against the invasion of the irrational, but cannot even claim to stand up to it or contain it, being itself nothing other than the same irrationality covered up and disguised, and thus much more deceptive and dangerous.

I am doubtful that the little conceptual aspects that ideology contains would be sufficient to serve as a rational guide in social and political reality and to propose valid programs of action in the human world in general, when it is clear that ideology, with its self-confident historical adaptability and its pragmatic and technical mastery, does nothing other than rationalize and justify preexisting situations or render preestablished projects more efficient. The rationality of ideology is very indirect, in the same way that the respect hypocrisy pays to virtue is indirect, or the recognition that the tyrant grants to the force of persuasion in order to render his or her coercive actions more efficient is indirect. In this way, ideology is nothing other than an alibi for politics that operates immorally or professes to be amoral, or a technics more or less aware and more or less purified of political struggle and the exercise of power. This conclusion is inevitable even for someone who, rightly wanting to avoid as absurd "an attitude of absolute scientific neutrality in the face of every ideological vision," is then led to flatten truth onto ideology by dispensing the latter from judgments of truth or falsity, thus affirming that ideological discourse—not descriptive, but persuasive and directive; not scientific, but practical and value-bearing—must be considered as more or less reasonable or plausible in relation to ends that are considered as final. It is clear in fact that this plausibility, reasonableness, and persuasiveness demonstrate precisely the instrumentality and technicity of ideological discourse because the fixing of goals, toward which ideology is directed, is recognized as external to ideology and preliminary to it.

Doubting the rational effectiveness of ideology in the world of history and action and in the social and political realm does not entail the denial of the practical bearing of thought or of the theoretical weight of action. Rather, it entails the awareness that the relations between theory and praxis are much more complex than the concept of ideology allows us to see. It is on the proving grounds of political reality that the concept of ideology shows its insufficiency, as appears for example in the patent inadequacy of the Marxist concept of the interaction between superstructure and base, and of the spiritualistic concept of the mediation between the abstractness of the universal and the concreteness of the situation. In fact, a living and effective presence of reason in history is represented neither by the presence of a conceptual apparatus that becomes the tool of action insofar as it has been the expression of the situation, nor by the presence of a conception that is ultimately nothing other than a compromise between the Republic of Plato and the dregs of Romulus. That can happen when ideology results either from a deliberate abdication of truth by thought or from the artificial derivation of a practical political scheme from a presupposed philosophical conception. Things happen much differently when the political commitment is contained within a moral commitment, and the moral commitment is seen in all of its ontological import: then the commitment, with all of its "practicity," is in direct relation with "truth" in an originary unity-distinction of theory and praxis. On the one hand, a philosophy of politics and a philosophy of morals become then possible without the necessity of thereby "deriving" morality and politics from a presupposed philosophy; and, on the other hand, a morality and politics are possible that, even without referring to a specific philosophy, have a "truth value" and a decidedly revelatory character—that is, on the one side is a concrete and committed philosophy that does not directly dictate norms to the politicians, and on the other side are a politics and a morality so impregnated with truth that they could in no way be reduced to pragmatic and instrumentalizing technics.

16. The Inevitability of Moral, not Ideological, Commitment

In order to clarify this point, I conclude with some clarifications that seem appropriate for everything discussed so far. In the first place, from what we have seen it follows that an ideological commitment is not at all necessary. Moral commitment, not ideological commitment, is what is really necessary, regardless of whether it is an ethico-religious commitment or an ethico-political commitment. Now, neither an ethico-religious commitment nor an ethico-political commitment need ideology: what is necessary in religious decision and life on the one side and in political choice and action on the other side is truth, not "ideas," revelatory and ontological thought, not technical and instrumental thought, the testimony of Being, not the mere familiarity with beings.

Some assert that the "sociality of humanity inevitably takes on an ideological structure," that "ideology is the palpitating form of human coexistence," that in the social, political, and juridical realm, ideological commitment is inevitable to the degree that it is "vain and dangerous to believe to be immune to ideological coefficients": in the end, one hears from many sides of the inevitability of ideological commitment. Now, I certainly recognize the unavoidability of commitment, but I do not understand why the commitment must necessarily be ideological. Certainly, from a Marxist or neo-enlightenment point of view, namely from the point of view of those for whom there is no other form of thought than historical and pragmatic reason or technical and experimental reason, not only the taking of a political stance but also a philosophical theory and a religious faith are an ideological commitment. It is certainly not in this way, however, that ideological commitment is spoken of by those who, motivated by a demand for truth, cannot avoid distinguishing between authentic thought and inauthentic thought. In fact, the inevitability of ideological commitment ends up being configured as something much more simple and "human all too human," that is, the fact that "one cannot avoid being committed again and again to the realization of practical interests."

And so what is it that, frankly and without hesitation, we ask of thought? To express these interests in a rational discourse, and to "rationalize" them, justify them, and make them efficient in the search for one's own satisfaction and success? This is precisely the function and the aim of ideological discourse, that is, of inauthentic thought, of thought that ultimately identifies with its own historical situation and that is instrumentalized by practical action. Or do we ask of thought that it confer to the historical situation, of which these interests are a part, a wider dimension and broader perspective, in which they are not only expressed, but even judged, not only satisfied, but even redeemed, not only made efficient, but also formed for civil coexistence? These are, on the contrary, the function and aim of philosophical discourse, which ignores all practical commitments void of the participation of truth.

When one speaks of the inevitability of ideological commitment though, one perhaps uses the term *ideology* to indicate every type of thought, or maybe simply to give thought as such a greater practical emphasis. Why, then, are we overly worried about avoiding the absolutization of ideology, to the point of asserting that "the possibility of a dialogue with others is conditioned by this intentional effort not to absolutize it," and of considering the reference to transcendence as the guarantee against an absolutization of that sort? If every thought is ideological, then even this demand for dialogue, for avoiding absolutization, or for transcendence, is ideology. Or instead it is not, and then one cannot say that every commitment is inevitably ideological.

Some will perhaps justify the necessity of ideological commitment through the impotence of the human spirit, in the sense that human beings, by virtue of their condition, are faced with the tragic alternative: either to maintain the value of a purity as infertile as it is unreachable, or instead to seek its realization through the intervention of non-axiological factors. The realization of value would require an inevitable "contamination," and this "humiliation" is ideology, which would then become the "necessary tool for the realization of value in society and in history." With that, one already recognizes that ideological thought is inauthentic thought, because one holds that the mediating function between the

Republic of Plato and the dregs of Romulus cannot be entrusted to anything but a form of thought that is in itself much closer to the bestial tendencies of human beings than to truth, whereas entrusting it to revelatory thought as close to truth would be nothing but utopianism and angelism.

Now, apart from the fact that acting in the historical world does not in fact imply a "contamination," and that human thought is contaminated and humiliated only if it commits itself to endeavors marked by the renunciation of truth, we must recognize that a conception of that type is a form of "realism" that although the exact opposite of "perfectionism," nonetheless carries with it, even with the sign overturned, all of its inconveniences, in the sense that a real distinction between value and its absence remains impossible, given that history is all equally decadence, error, and evil. It is very true that in order to act in history, the "idea" requires, in a Hegelian sense, "passion"; but, that does not in fact imply that thought should betray its originary ontological root and its primitive truth-bearing import in order to be technicized as a mere instrument for action. Just as the practice of virtue cannot be derived from that indirect respect for virtue that is hypocrisy, except by a leap, so too from a thought that has preliminarily abdicated truth one cannot derive a need for truth, a request for judgment, a moral yearning, a concern for justice, but only a series of practical accommodations, technical expediencies, and empirical compromises.

From revelatory thought, in its being full with the inexhaustibility of truth, there gushes forth an ability far more ductile and inventive, much richer and unforeseeable, than the apparent fecundity of technical and pragmatic thought, which is so tied to the situation that it remains its prisoner, and is such a servant of action that it cannot inspire it. Conversely, revelatory thought, with surging naturalness and spontaneity, finds by itself the modes of its realization, drawing new possibilities from itself, providing itself with the means to render the universal concrete. No matter how humble, base, decadent, and wild the condition of human beings might be, the ontological dimension of human activity and the revelatory nature of human thought will never prevent the ignition, in such a human condition, of a fire of truth and rationality or the realization of a more valid morality, or a more civil coexistence. What characterizes the relation with Being and revelatory thought is not the unattainability of an abstract and ideal reason, but rather the fecundity of concrete proposals, the inventive fertility of acts that are not forgetful of truth and Being simply for the reason of their own being adherent to the real situation. That which characterizes technics and ideological thought is not its adherence to the situation and the awareness of the field of reality within which to employ the ductile inventiveness of thought, but rather the dissipating process of an experimental and pragmatic rationality, so confined to the situation that it cannot even rise enough above it as to inspire, or guide, or control it.

17. The Philosopher and Politics

In the second place, it must be noted that on the one hand, the criteria for political choices are not immediately furnished by philosophy, which must first of all try to be philosophy and nothing else; and on the other hand, that if philosophy and politics do not have an immediate connection, this does not mean that they are separated *toto coelo*, to the point that the rationality of thought takes flight into the limbo of the abstract and that social and political reality sinks into the quicksand of irrationality. The relation between philosophy and politics is not direct, but emerges from a profound and originary solidarity of theory and praxis, which precedes the very distinction between thought and action, theoretical life and practical life, cognitive world and active world. If the relation were direct and followed after the distinction of theory and praxis, there could be nothing between philosophy and politics but an absurd mutual subordination of one over the other, or a monstrous combination of the two. These possibilities have been present quite often in the history of thought and action, and have been quick to enact their ruinous influence. But if the relation is indirect, and dictated from the distant (yet not for this reason less effective) inspiration of an originary solidarity of theory and praxis, then between philosophy and politics, in their proper and necessary distinction, there becomes possible a fecund and mutually advantageous collaboration.

The philosopher is neither the abstract and "monastic" thinker of the ivory tower nor the one who is both philosopher and politician at the same time. To say that philosophers must not be abstracted from society and uprooted from history does not mean that they must engage in politics because it is not possible to be a philosopher and politician at the same time except through a contingent and accidental personal union. The philosopher must do philosophy and nothing else, and right there one finds a civil task and political relevance. The task of the philosopher is not that of active politics, but of reminding us that the dregs of Romulus must not make us forget the Republic of Plato; that historical reality must not be absolutized such that it is lost in the forgetfulness of Being and in the betrayal of truth; that all the practical schemes and all projects of action have an ethical character, and that any action without a moral dimension is unthinkable; that ideas are truly ideas only if they are not instrumentalized; that there is a relation with Being to which we must remain faithful, both in thought and in action; that technics can never be an end in itself and that experimentation is not self-grounded; that the dialogue that grounds coexistence is never possible without truth. Whereas the philosopher's task is to *remind us* of all of this, the task of *realizing it* in history and within social reality belongs to the politician. This does not mean that the philosopher assigns the norm to the politician, because the philosopher does not invent all this. Rather, the philosopher recalls it, and reminds everyone that each one of us must remember it, because the revelatory nature of thought is not the exclusive domain of philosophical thought, but inheres in every thought worthy of the name, and the purely theoretical and speculative character of thought is only one of its aspects and specifications.

The task of the philosopher in the recollection of all these things is all the more important since human beings might have forgotten all of this, given that they are all lost in the forgetting of Being and in the betrayal of truth, and all drowned in the mere expressivity and pragmaticity of technical thought. Then usefully does the philosopher remind human beings of them. Even the most simple and common person would be able to remember them, however, as long as one remains faithful to the originary bond that ties the person to truth and to the essential ontological dimension of one's own humanity. In this sense philosophers, in order to have political relevance, have no need to engage in ideology. It is enough that they are *truly* philosophers, because merely by doing genuine philosophy they are battling ideologies implicitly, and thereby are taking an explicit political position. The philosophers' mode of engaging in political debate is precisely by their taking up a position against ideologies in the name of genuine philosophy; and precisely by their refusing to engage their philosophy *directly* in the political struggle, which would lower it to ideology, the very thing philosophers must not do if they wish to remain faithful to the genuine essence of thought.

The political import of the philosopher's position consists in the very care used to separate ideology from philosophy: by seeing in ideology the betrayal of thought in the name of action, and thus the same reality of the dregs of Romulus and of the petty state of the everyday; and, by indicating in philosophy the appeal to the ontological relation and to the bond with truth implicit in action itself, and thus a thought that despite being exquisitely speculative does not become abstract, academic, and evasive. The political import of the philosopher's position consists therefore in this: The philosopher wants to be the caretaker of truth even in action, not the knight of action without truth; the philosopher fears not that action destroys contemplation, but that action will forget Being, since action mindful of Being, beyond confirming itself in its own being as action, also has the value of truth, and thus menaces only contemplation that is sterile and inert, solipsistic and narcissistic, but not the profound and radical contemplation that is the memory of truth, realizable not only in speculative thought, but in every human activity. In conclusion, the distinction that is dear to the philosopher's heart is not the distinction between thought and action—as if thought could only belong to philosophers and they would feel threatened by every uprising of action, almost as if action were an indiscrete and inopportune disruption of the speculative calm—but the distinction between remaining faithful to truth and betraying it, between lending an ear to Being and ignoring it, whether this occurs in thought or in action.

18. The Inadequacy of the Mutual Subordination of Philosophy and Politics

If things stand in these terms, one can accept neither that the philosopher claims to be able as such to dictate laws to politicians, nor that the philosopher accepts the subjection of philosophy to actual politics. In today's society, two diverse modalities of the relation between the intellectual and the politician seem to take shape and thus characterize themselves in a rather rigid and extreme way. On the one side, the politician as executor of the intellectual, and this is the relation desired by the neo-enlightenment thinkers; and on the other side, the intellectual as the instrument of the politician, and this is the relation practiced by the communists.

In reality, even the neo-enlightenment thinkers, like the communists, are in a certain way supporters of historicism and panpoliticism, as they value thought only insofar as it has an importance more cultural than speculative and already contains an immanent and essential political outcome; but their attitude of support is archaic, even pre-Marxist, in the sense of a radically anti-metaphysical reason, and nevertheless regulative and exemplary. If it is true, as Del Noce has expertly pointed out, that the current sociologists are, like the ideologues of the consulate, the recovery of the Enlightenment after the failure of the revolution and the substitution of the political revolution with the scientific revolution, it must be said that today's true neo-enlightenment is represented by sociology, as it replaces metaphysics with science and traces itself back directly to the eighteenth-century Enlightenment, leaving Marxism completely outside of its own genesis.

There are various consequences that follow: First of all, there is the poverty of neo-enlightenment thinking in comparison to Marxism, which is enriched by the Romantic experience, even though it pushed it away, and by its evidently metaphysical origin, even though it has been rejected. In the second place, there is the sterility of the anti-Marxist attitudes of neo-enlightenment, which can neither offer an alternative to Marxism, as it does not share any problem with it, nor represent its overcoming, as it does not include the experience of Marxism within its own genesis. Finally, there is the hybrid and absurd nature of collaboration or a convergence or an alliance between neo-enlightenment thinkers and Marxists, who might find something in common only on the condition that each denies their own position. In conclusion, in neo-enlightenment thinking the relation between thought and action, in spite of every apparent divergence, appears ultimately in the exact terms of the eighteenth-century Enlightenment: theory provides the norm for practice, and does so in its derived distinction, artificial separation, and presumed precedence in respect to practice—in the sense that it is not truth, but "philosophy" that prescribes laws to action, which is in itself blind and irrational.

On the opposite side, it is very true that the deep meaning of Marxist thinking is the identity of theory and praxis, thought and action, philosophy and politics, since one arrives at such an identity precisely from the need to define the nature of philosophy after the advent of historicism, from the recognized impossibility of conceiving philosophy purely as thought, and from the resulting necessity to realize philosophy by overcoming it without eliminating it, that is, by making it consist of action itself, in an integral praxism, in which philosophy is all the more affirmed as philosophy the more it is identified with action, and action is all the more active and practical the more it is seen as philosophy itself finally realized. That is the originarily metaphysical nature of Marxism, which arises as a philosophy of history. From here derives the profound inadequacy of those interpretations of Marxism one could qualify as watered-down, namely, the methodological interpretation, or the ideological one, or the sociological one, or the empiricist one, which were or are very popular.

What occurs in Marxism, however, is that the identity of theory and praxis is posited as final rather than as originary, and the functions of truth, substantially negated, are attributed to philosophy, even if pragmatically conceived. Thus, the identity of theory and praxis assumes the aspect of the servitude of theory to praxis, with the subsequent substitution of instrumentalism for praxism. The negation of originary truth confers to the "realization" of philosophy the aspect of practical suppression rather than the aspect of theoretical overcoming, namely the form of its complete subordination to politics rather than the form of its complete identification with politics. The result is the conception of the intellectual as an instrument of the politician, a conception that in reality represents more the practice of communism than Marx's genuine convictions.

In this way, therefore, we find them in society today, with characteristics by now unmistakable: on the one side the intellectuals, who understand their own task as the claim to give laws to the politicians, and on the other side the politicians who, in their realism, place the intellectuals in their own service; on the one hand, the idea of philosophy as the guide for politics and on the other hand, the idea of philosophy as the instrument of politics. These two conceptions share the fact of presupposing the separation of thought and action as a point of departure, caring little about reaching an anterior sphere whence the derived distinction could attain its explanation as well as its norm. It is clear that thought and action, once they are considered in their separation and in a by now rigidified specification, cannot be placed in direct relation lest it be through a reciprocal subordination. If an *originary* identity of theory and praxis is left out of consideration, then their distinction becomes a real opposition, which can be mediated only through the degradation of one of the terms in respect to the other. On the one side, the idea that thought precedes action, and on the other, the idea that action precedes thought. Thus, on the one hand, practice is lowered to the pure and simple "application" of theory, that is, a form of fanaticism; and on the other hand, theory is lowered to the mere instrument of practice, that is, a form of cynicism.

In fact Enlightenment thinking, by taking practice to be a pure and simple application of a presupposed theory, makes theory into an abstract and implacable reason, which in every case needs to correspond to a riotous and recalcitrant reality. Lacking the moral inventiveness that knows how to understand and interpret the individual case and render the law effectively and benignly operative within it, that knows how felicitously to configure the norm in a way that adheres to the concrete situation while remaining imperative and binding, reason that is simply presupposed and imposed on practice becomes a norm only through the pitiless face of rigorism, the inflexible severity of moralism, and the squalid ferocity of fanaticism. And panpoliticism, by dissolving thought into action, not only deprives action of any truth-granting criterion, but even authorizes the instrumentalization of theory to practice by professing the radically and definitively ideological nature of every form of thought. This leads inevitably to cynicism, because one does not limit oneself to the claim proper to *Realpolitik* that politics is completely independent from morality, but indeed one goes so far as saying that there is no other form of morality than politics.

Those two conceptions also have in common the fact that they confuse truth with philosophy. Or better, they eliminate truth and demand from philosophy that which only truth can give. It is for this reason that they either—deceiving themselves—exalt philosophy as the direct guide for action and politics, or—being disappointed—lower it to being an instrument of politics and action. Enlightenment thinking forgets that it is truth, and not philosophy, that gives laws to practice and politics. This means that not only the practitioner and the politician, but also the philosopher must make themselves docile and wise listeners to truth. If the philosopher has something to say to the politician and to the person who must act, it happens only to the extent that the philosopher reminds them of what they know or should know already by themselves, but perhaps have forgotten, and it can be helpful if someone reminds them of it. It would be enough, however, if they were to remain faithful to the originary ontological import of humanity itself in order to remember it, and to ensure that the presence of Being and truth have authentic value in their activity. Enlightenment thinking, however, does not confer to philosophy the task of recalling truth, being this a task that everyone shares, but rather the task of legislating human activity. This fact feeds, with a scornfully and ruthlessly aristocratic spirit, the presumptuousness of human reason and the arrogance of philosophers.

In its turn Marxism, taken between the inauspicious decision to eliminate every truth from thought and the just need to grasp the profound link between theory and praxis, on the one hand wants to destroy philosophy as something purely thought, and on the other hand wants to replace it with a praxis in which philosophy is realized. In that move, it forgets that philosophy can only be something thought because it is the translation into verbal and speculative terms of the revelatory and ontological thought that is originarily present in every human activity, provided that it is not erased by an act of rebellion or betrayal, and that what one should try to reach is not so much the realization of philosophy in praxis, but rather the authentic presence of truth that is also found in praxis.

19. The Originarity of Practice

The relation between philosophy and politics is therefore not as simple as the simplistic approaches to the relation between theory and practice make it seem. Certainly, on the one side there is philosophy, and even the philosophy of politics, and on the other side there is actual politics, which presupposes schemes for action and practical projects. But neither does the philosophy of politics have the task of directly defining those schemes for action, as if it were a matter of "deriving" practice from a theory or of "applying" a theory to some practice; nor do those practical schemes represent the result of a philosophy subdued to politics, of a practice that generates from itself its own theory. Now, philosophy translates into reflexive, verbal, speculative terms the revelatory and ontological thought that can be present in any human activity. And, if they are not reduced to ideological, merely technical and instrumental thought, those schemes of action and practical projects are charged with truth. To bring such a charge to clear awareness and to explicit reflection, that is, to translate it into speculative terms, is the task and nature of the philosophy of politics. And it is in this sense and with these limits that philosophy can be of benefit to politics.

With that I move directly to the third point left to examine. If philosophy is nothing other than the *verbal* and *speculative* translation of revelatory and ontological thought, the task is to vindicate the revelatory and ontological character that every human activity, even practical action, has in itself. Ultimately, it is a matter of enacting that vindication—neither "good-sensical" nor simplistic but rather fully human—of the common sense I have already mentioned. Revelatory and ontological thought can in fact be attained by everyone, even if not in its philosophical formulation; what is extremely difficult, however, is to remain faithful to it and not lose it in the forgetfulness of Being and in the technicization of thought. Human beings find themselves faced with a choice: Either everything is reduced to technics, even philosophy, or everything has a revelatory import, even practical action.

In the case we are examining, it is a matter of highlighting the charge of truth inherent in action, that is, of affirming what could be called the *originarity* of practice. In order to place itself in relation to truth, practice does not require the mediation of philosophy, because it possesses its truth in an originary way, and thus in itself it can find and vindicate it. One should not confuse the revelatory aspect of ontological thought with the speculative aspect of philosophical thought, even if the latter fails to be properly speculative when it is not originarily revelatory. In the final analysis, what counts the most is the revelatory nature of thought, namely, truth, rather than its speculative nature, namely philosophy. One should not fall into theoreticism, as if the relation with Being were merely cognitive. Practice in such a case would be nothing but a simple derivation, application, and consequence of a presupposed theory, and truth would vanish in the face of an absurd, oppressive, and arrogant absolutization of philosophy. There is truth also in action as such, and that is what one should recover and reaffirm. Certainly, the awareness that one can have of it and the explicit treatment of it that one can undertake is philosophical discourse in the truest sense; but such a discourse could not be achieved without the affirmed originarity of practice. And from the point of view of such an originarity, it no longer matters whether philosophical discourse is anterior or posterior to action because that anteriority would not lower practice to a mere application of a presupposed theory, nor would that posteriority confer a simply ideological character to theory, the revelatory nature being by now assured, for practical action as well as philosophical discourse.

The originarity of action is confirmed by the fact that in the historical world, practical action has the power to modify the conditions in which revelatory thought operates. Naturally, such fact does not at all place truth in question, but only regards our means of access to it in its mutation and renewal. If there were not such an originarity to practice, the proclaimed historical conditionality of thought would be a purely irrational and negative fact, conceived as something that would be better off not existing at all: whence the pernicious consequences of a persistent, albeit unknowing and hidden, nostalgia for the unique, definitive, immobile, and completely explicated metaphysics, a nostalgia that carries with itself naturally the devaluation of the historical world, seen as an annoying and troublesome cover rather than as a possible opening, and as irremediable and disgraceful decadence rather than as the site of our choices.

I conclude with a fourth and final observation. It is evident that, in the end, anyone can use the terms in the manner one wants, but one must also accept the risks that come with an arbitrary and careless use. The term *ideology* is used by many in a way for which the traditional word "morality" or "ethics" would be best suited, as the concretion of the universal in the particular; and others consider ideology as the mediation between the Republic of Plato and the dregs of Romulus, and thus as essential to whomever would act in the world, forgetting that precisely in this mediating function lies the very ethical inspiration of all individual actions and the very moral inventiveness within concrete situations. To use the term *ideology* in this sense, to indicate operations in which the remembering of Being and the loyalty to truth are decisive, may mean an unconscious or implied will to detach politics from morality, and morality from truth, and this would be extremely disgraceful.

Let the term *ideology* be used then to name the plans of action and practical projects in which interpretation of time and revelation of truth are joined in such a decisive way, in which the historical dimension and the ontological dimension can work together in such a fruitful way, and that could attest so positively to the originarity of action. Proceeding in this way, however, we expose ourselves to the risk of historicism, namely, of treating even revelatory thought as solely expressive thought by claiming to demystify and historicize it, and to the risk of sociologism, namely, of supporting in a very loose and careless way the current confusion of truth and technics, indeed the current substitution of truth with technics. Certainly, the risk of ideology, and thus of mystification and instrumentalization, is constant, and no critical caution with respect to this, exercised on itself and on others, is ever enough. But if these plans of action and practical projects have a value, they have it not as conceptualizations of the historical conditions or technicizations of practical action, but as conceptualizations, however provisional, of the ontological import of action, and as testimonials, however fleeting, of faithfulness to Being.

Notes

This chapter was written as the conclusion to the discussion that followed my presentation on the same topic at the conference held at the Centro di Studi Filosofici di Gallarate, dedicated to the theme *Ideology and Philosophy*. In these pages, there remain traces of the discussions to which I was responding, as appears from citations left without explicit reference. In particular, they concern discussions with Lotz, Gironella, Muñoz, Alonso, Lazzarini, Prini, Bagolini, Piemontese, Rigobello, Giannini, Nicoletti, and so on.

Page 17: On Vico's *"Lesbic rule," one recalls the passage from De nostri temporis studiorum ratione: "Non ex ista recta mentis regula, quae rigida est, hominum facta aestimari possunt; sed illa Lesbiorum flexili, quae non ad se corpora dirigit, sed se ad corpora inflectit, spectari debent*" (Opere, I 91). ["It is therefore impossible to assess human affairs by the inflexible standard of abstract right; we must rather gauge them by the pliant Lesbic rule, which does not conform bodies to itself, but adjusts itself to their contours." Vico, *On the Study Methods of Our Time*, translated by Elio Gianturco (Ithaca, NY: Cornell University Press), 34.]

Pages 118–119: On the meaning of the term *idea* in Dostoevsky, one can turn to the concise commentary written by F. Stepun, *Dostojewski: Welschau und Weltanschauung* (Heidelberg: Pfeffer, 1950), 38–54.

Page 123: The citation from Pascal is thought 327 of the Brunschvicg edition: "Les sciences ont deux extémités qui se touchent. La première est la pure ignorance naturelle où arrivent les grandes âmes, qui, ayant parcourutout ce que les hommes peuvent savoir, trouvent qu'ils ne savent rien, et se recontrent en cette même ignorance d'où ils étaient partis; mais c'est une ignorance savante qui se connâit. Ceux d'entre eux, qui sont sortis de l'ignorance naturelle, et n'ont pu arriver à l'autre, ont quelque teinture de cette science suffisante, et font les entendus. Ceux-là troublent le monde, et jugent mal de tout." The citation from Dostoevsky's *Demons* is taken from the translation by Richard Pevear and Larisa Volokhonsky (Vintage, 1995).

Page 143: The expression from Pseudo-Dionysius is taken from *Migne*, P.G. 1033 C.

Page 143: As was noted, the critique of Schelling as the "destroyer of reason" is from Lukács, *The Destruction of Reason* (Merlin Press, 1980). The rage with which Lukács denigrates Schelling is proof that from his point of view the true adversary is Schelling himself; and *pour cause*, given that the post-Hegelian Schelling is, in the critiques given of Hegel, an otherwise valid alternative to Kierkegaard, and perhaps an even better one: an alternative much more valid as one clearly sees that he contains, and thus absorbs and negates, the other possibility of the dissolution of Hegelianism, namely the line of Feuerbach-Marx.

Page 146: The citation is from Plotinus, *Enneads*, VI, vii 17, "The form is in the object shaped, but the shaper had none." In fact for Plotinus, on the one hand, "true reality must neither be formed nor be form," such that "the primal existent, the first, is without form" (*dei . . . to ontos . . . me memorphosthai mede eidos einai. Aneideon ara to protos kai proton*: ibid., 33); on the other hand, "the principle is without form not in the sense that it is lacking form, but in the sense that it is the source of every form" (*Arche de to aneideon, ou to morphes deomenon, all'aph' hou pasa morphe*: ibid. 32), such that "the form is the trace of the unformed" (*to gar ichnos tou amorphou morphe*: ibid., 33).

The citation from Schelling is taken from the *Erlangen Lectures* (V 13) and means: "In order to be able to take on a form, it must surely stand outside of every form, but its positive aspect does not consist in that, in its being outside of every form, in its being incomprehensible, but rather in its being able to take on a form, in its being able to be understood, namely, in being free to take on or to reject a form." The fact is that indefinability cannot be taken as a definition of the principle because this only has a simply negative character, as "mere independence in respect to every external determination" ("*blosse Unabhangigkeit von ausserer Bestimmung*"); the indefinability can be its definition only when it assumes a positive meaning, as "the freedom to take on a form" ("*die Freiheit sich in eine Gestalt einzuschliessen*"). In the end, one can always refer back to the eighth section of the sixth Ennead of Plotinus.

Page 148: I developed the concept of an "exercise of alterity," which is essential to dialogue, in the essay "The Knowledge of Ohers" (1953), included in *Esistenza e persona*, second and third editions. I extended this concept in the theory of an "exercise of kindredness" as essential to every understanding, and thus to every conversation and communication, in *Estetica: teoria della formatività*, pp. 210–212 of the second edition, and *passim* in my other books on aesthetics. Inherent in the same conception of interpretation, seen as central and originary, is the necessity, for every form of dialogue—of persons with persons, of persons with things, of persons with works—to invent revelatory points of view, not as abstract points of view, but as glimpses of living persons, on par with a dramaturge, indeed of "placing oneself in the shoes" of that very interlocutor real or ideal, which is precisely an exercise of alterity and of kindredness. See also earlier in the work, pp. 79–80.

Pages 156–157: The citation from Del Noce refers to his suggestive contribution to the discussion on *Ideology and philosophy*, published in the Acts of the conference, cited, with the title *Intorno alle origini del concetto di ideologia*, pp. 75–86.

Part III

Truth and Philosophy

5

The Necessity of Philosophy

1. Science and Religion Claim to Supplant Philosophy

Today, philosophy is clearly undergoing a crisis. The present culture seems to want neither to preserve any of its functions nor to assign it any place. Other forms of knowledge and types of activity partition the *regnum hominis* [the human domain] among themselves, and even vie for it. Although they battle with one another in order to rise to a dominant position, they all agree that there is no task for philosophy. In the current mindset, philosophy has nothing to say any longer because the field is dominated by the increasingly invasive presence of science, art, politics, and religion.

Science above all seems to impose itself on contemporary individuals who, enamored with its continually surprising results, tend to see it as the exemplary form of knowledge, if not even its only valid form. Fascinated more by the spectacle of technical applications than by the truly inventive moment of scientific thought, contemporary human beings tend to devalue every form of knowledge that does not possess the traits of science, namely, the delimitation of its field of research, the functionality [*operatività*] of its concepts, the self-correcting nature of the reason it employs, and the intersubjective validity of its conclusions. The same scientists become more open to the temptation of hubris inherent in technological progress than to the lesson of humility implicit in the inventive and cognitive moment of science, and for that reason tend to absolutize scientific knowledge, judging the other forms of knowledge according to the criteria of science, and thus illegitimately demanding from them what they cannot, do not want, and should not provide. And so philosophy is forced to adopt the traits and procedures of science, preferring to divide itself into particular areas of research rather than bringing all human existence under question, agreeing to be despersonalized in an objective yet also continually revisable validity, and neglecting criteria for truth other than the functionality of concepts and the self-corrective ability of reason. If it did not act this way, philosophy would have to resign itself to being considered fanciful and useless: beautiful, perhaps, and suggestive if viewed as an artistic dream, but hybrid and superfluous if taken as a form of knowledge, unless it agrees to be reduced to philosophy of science, namely, to the critical and methodological awareness that scientific thought has of itself.

From another perspective, religion today, in the minds of many, claims a presence so incontrovertible and intense that it renders the presence of philosophy superfluous. Today religion is intent on recovering the purity of its eternal content beyond every historical incarnation, in order to find there the inspiration for new incarnations more consonant with the current times. One finds on the one hand, the refusal to unite religion with the various philosophies that have arisen in the history of Western thought; and, on the other hand, a gathering within pure interiority of the individual who has taken the genuinely religious leap of faith, the source for valid suggestions regarding the construction of a new, religiously inspired culture. On the one side arises the temptation of a form of fideism scarcely concerned with the grounds of credibility of faith and scarcely mindful of the reasonableness of religious assent, and intended instead to emphasize the audacity of faith; and, on the other side arises the mistrust toward every agreement between religious faith and a determinate philosophy, in the sense that the one who made the leap of faith is no longer interested in the sort of truth offered by philosophy. Today, therefore, it seems that when the field is controlled by religion, there is no longer any place for philosophy, because now everything has been decided, and the contribution of philosophy, whether a preparation or a confirmation, is useless: With every optional and decisive characteristic taken from philosophy, no other task remains for philosophy than the neutral and descriptive interrogation of religious assent and refusal.

2. Art and Politics Claim to Subrogate Philosophy

As if the invasiveness of science and religion were not enough, today there is an artificial exaggeration of art and politics, which claim to replace philosophy by taking over its many functions. This fits in well with one of the primary characteristics of contemporary culture, which is essentially a culture of surrogates. One need only take a look around to confirm it: In every field, a specific activity is replaced by an inferior or different activity that, forced to take the place of the original with diminished and inadequate powers, corrupts its primary intent. Thus, for example, ethics becomes the surrogate for religion and absolutizes autonomous and sufficient human reason, with the result that human reason, proud of its own absolute nature, ends up either with the suspension of guilt and thus with universal justification, or with the establishment of an abstract moralism that is uselessly intransigent and constricted. Or reason establishes itself as the surrogate for truth, with the result that, by forgetting the originary relation with Being that is the sole source of content and criterion, it becomes boundless and uncertain, and so unstable in the precariousness of its conclusions that it also loses the last power one might be willing to grant it, namely self-corrective ability. Or still, tolerance becomes the surrogate for charity, and forgets that faith in one's own ideas and the recognition of the ideas of others are indivisible, just as the cult of truth and the love for one's neighbor are indivisible, with the result that in the forgetting of truth one also loses the basis for the respect of other persons. And finally, technics becomes, in every field, the surrogate for excellence: in art, where the deft manipulation of artistic means gives the appearance of art without giving the substance of it; in science, where the technical moment is emphasized over the cognitive and creative moment; in ethics, where the technics of behaviors replaces the inventive process through which the originary moral appeal translates itself into norms; and in philosophy itself, reduced to a procedural rationality of techniques variously adapted to specific fields of inquiry.

In such a climate, it is not strange that philosophy finds surrogates in art and in politics; and it is not strange especially because that is where the philosophical vicissitudes of the past one hundred and fifty years have taken us. When, with Hegel, philosophy achieved a sort of idealization of the whole reality and of pure self-contemplation, the only way left for philosophy to realize itself in the world was to deny itself in concrete reality and overturn itself into nonphilosophy. Hence, the nonphilosophy of Marx, which is politics; the non-philosophy of Kierkegaard, which is faith; the nonphilosophy of Nietzsche, which is will to power; the nonphilosophy of a certain aestheticism, which is art. So it happened that art and politics, the typical forms of nonphilosophy, became the surrogate for philosophy. And, in fact, art has claimed to become a total attitude of humanity by claiming for itself not only the fullness of ethical commitment that belongs to a decisive choice or a radical protest, but also that trait of total and exclusive knowledge that only philosophy, or even only religion, can desire. Furthermore, politics has become inseparable from ideology, so much so that today one cannot take a political position without being aligned with a particular ideology, and one cannot find a political conflict that does not take the form of an ideological struggle. And certainly there is no need to recall that ideology is precisely one of the most common surrogates for philosophy.

3. Philosophy, by Marking the Limits of Science, Keeps It Within Its Nature

Under the threat of being supplanted by science and religion, and of being replaced by art and politics, philosophy undergoes a crisis. Precisely in this very state of extreme confusion, philosophy can, however, find the appropriate ground for its fecund revival. Under these conditions, philosophy is necessary more than ever. It has not only the task, but also the ability to restore every activity to its own field, and the proper function to every activity. Faced with the exorbitant claims of science and religion, and the absurd transgressions of art and politics, philosophy can find its own task in the safekeeping of the limits beyond which those activities deteriorate and degenerate, and within which they can be instead realized in their genuine nature.

First of all, philosophy is capable of demonstrating that between science and philosophy there is not, strictly, any possible conflict, because the limit that constitutes science in its sphere and that institutes it in its validity is precisely that which also marks the realm and validity of philosophy. Not that science goes up to a certain point, and beyond it philosophy begins, as if one were dealing with two successive degrees of the same knowledge, and as if science and philosophy divided up objects of inquiry, some fitting only for science and others fitting only for philosophy. *Everything* can be the object of philosophy, including science itself, whereas science proceeds *from itself* to find its own limits or even to construct its proper object. So it is rather a matter of two different forms of knowledge, situated on different levels, between which there is no possible encounter, and thus no possible conflict. If there is a conflict between science and philosophy, it is because one of them has fallen short of its specific task and infringes on the field of the other, and because the philosopher and the scientist, forgetful that they can simply listen to each other, claim each to interfere instead in the field of the other.

That happens first of all when philosophers exchange the right—which they have—to philosophize about science and to take the scientific method seriously, for the right—which they lack—to meddle in scientific questions, either by prescribing to scientists the method to follow and by directing their operations, or by incorporating the results of science into their own knowledge and by utilizing such results for their own goals. Philosophers can certainly give a definition of science and form a theory of the scientific method, but they can do so only insofar as science itself instructs the philosophers regarding its own method and procedures. Although they meditate *on* science and speak *about* science, philosophers have nothing to say *within* science, nor can they claim to have a say in the course of scientific research. If they do it, they cease to do philosophy and practice nothing more than bad science.

The conflict can also arise when scientists exchange the right—which they have—to establish the method fit for the object of their research, for the right—which they lack—to establish what would be the only valid form of knowledge. Scientists certainly have the incontestable right to declare that scientific knowledge is the only one appropriate to the objects of their own research. But they cannot extend and absolutize scientific knowledge to the point of claiming that it is the only form of knowledge possible. If they do that, they cease to do science, because the proposition "there is no other form of knowledge than scientific knowledge" is not a scientific proposition, but rather a philosophical proposition, which forms the ground of scientism. They are thus doing philosophy, but do so without knowing it, namely, they do a philosophy that is acritical and lacks self-awareness, or in other words, bad philosophy.

Science that absolutizes itself by claiming to supplant philosophy thus fails completely to meet its aims because it not only fails to deny philosophy, but it even manages to deny itself as science. It therefore follows that just as scientism does not destroy philosophy because, however indirectly and incoherently, it affirms it, likewise denying scientism does not mean killing science, but recognizing it within the limits that belong to it and within which it is sovereign. Without philosophy, science exceeds its proper sphere and degenerates into scientism: Only philosophy can protect it from this transgression and preserve it as science.

4. Only Philosophy Guarantees the Reciprocal Independence of Philosophy and Religion

In the same way, religion that wants to supplant philosophy is perverted and loses its being religion, within which only philosophy can restore and maintain it. In fact, the religious possession of truth is of such a nature that not only does it neither extinguishes nor excludes the philosophical investigation of truth, but rather it permits and consents to, and indeed even implies and provokes it. Faith is, in itself, ambiguous because it can be considered, from a religious point of view, as being turned toward God, and from a philosophical point of view, as being turned toward the world. In the first perspective, it is the gift of God; in the second, it is a human act; in the first, it is fullness, faith, abandon, and in the second, it is choice, audacity, leap; in the first, I will not say it is a *certainty*—because such a scientific term does not suit a *hope*, like faith—but surely it is a *possession*; and in the second, I will not say it is a *doubt*—because a word allied to skepticism does not fit such a courageous *leap*—but certainly it is a *wager*. Here is why that which *religiously* is a *possession* can *philosophically* be an *investigation*: through faith, human beings can reach the truth and revel in it with trusting abandon in a fullness of knowledge and life that no other form of knowledge can ensure; yet, they do this through a choice that cannot be made once and for all, in a definitive and secure way, and that must instead be repeated in every instant, with an intrepid struggle and continual triumph over doubt. Faith, paradoxically, unites *securitas* [security] and *insecuritas* [insecurity], the fullness of possession and the need for confirmation, the tranquility of success and the precariousness of the wager, the serenity of the discovery and the anxiety of the search. Philosophy, reclaimed and even awoken in its independence by religion itself, inserts itself in such dialectic.

There are religious spirits who accentuate the fullness and tranquility of the possession to such an extent that they no longer feel the need for philosophy, because in them faith continually self-regenerates with primordial and impetuous vehemence. There are spirits no less religious, in whom the very possession becomes, due to its inherent need for reconfirmation, the stimulus for research, and the more profound their religiosity the more intensely they feel the need for philosophy. The experience of the first ones is a demonstration not of the superfluity of philosophy when compared with religion, but rather of their reciprocal independence. This is also confirmed by the experience of the second ones, who far from considering philosophy as dependent on religion conceive of it rather as the clarification of a particularly evocative existential situation, which is faith. And it is on this reciprocal independence—confirmed all the more by the existence of philosophical spirits who do not feel the need for religion, and who thus, more than deny it as superfluous or inferior, simply ignore it—that the convergence and collaboration of philosophy and religion can ground itself, which keeps religion from being corrupted by its attempt to supplant philosophy.

But in order to defend itself from the invasiveness of religion, philosophy has no need to make a similar invasion into religion by claiming to absorb it into itself as an inferior and mythical form of philosophy that is good for simple people and for less-evolved civilizations, and destined to be resolved and dissolved completely in philosophy. This rationalistic philosophy, which does not recognize the leap of faith, finds itself ill-equipped when faced with the religion that, by considering the pathway of philosophy disastrous, declares philosophy's superfluity. This philosophy even risks handing over its domain to such religion, to the detriment not only of philosophy, no longer recognized in its rights, but also of religion itself, extended beyond its proper limits.

This all appears with particular clarity in the spiritual drama of contemporary human beings, who are well aware of the failure of the Enlightenment—namely, of that form of rationalism that claimed to overcome religion—but are no longer able to believe in what the Enlightenment has destroyed. Caught between the nostalgia for ancient faith and the present impossibility of adhering to it, equally unsatisfied with religion and with its negation, both desirous and incapable of believing, contemporary human beings wander from one experience to the next, and on the one hand they defile every faith by corroding it with doubt, whereas on the other hand they impress the character of faith onto the very profession of rationalism. And they move from the current rationalistic and sophisticated replacements for faith, such as aestheticism, moralism, and political praxism, to the contemporary postulatory and confessional affirmations of rationalism, such as atheism, nihilism, and anti-religion. All of these possibilities are equated on the same level and are, at the same time, both rational conclusions (of a reason without truth) and acts of faith (of a faith without truth), or better, both cerebral choices and arbitrary ratiocinations. They are the confused adventures of contemporary human beings, who are unable to perceive the connection between possession and investigation, fullness and anxiety, faith and daring, and for that very reason they are restless, unhappy, uncertain, and unsatisfied.

5. The Degeneration of Art and Politics Without Philosophy

It would be easy to show, finally, how the art and politics that claim to replace philosophy are not only unsuccessful in their intentions, but result in the loss of their own nature: Art degenerates into aestheticism, and politics into panpoliticism. Art wanted to set itself up as an absolute by claiming to resolve all human values—speculative, practical, and religious—within itself. In this way, it has corrupted even artistic value, weakening it into ever more feeble and small manifestations. The occurrence of aestheticism in the contemporary world is telling: Once it becomes the absolute value that absorbs in itself all other values, art, which has claimed to be the only one capable of welcoming the fullness of life, can afford emptying itself out, and so emptied, it can claim to impose itself over life itself. And here, having become pure play, mere technique, simple experimentation, extreme specialization, art almost returns to its infancy but without the support of myth and magic, which in primitive societies fill those empty artistic manifestations with meaning.

No less telling is the occurrence by which politics has wanted to replace philosophy by turning it into political revolution, as happened with Marxism, or into an instrument of political action, as happened in sociologism. Through this process, philosophy and politics have their natures completely perverted: Philosophy loses its specific speculative nature; politics grows monstrously to overextend itself into all human activities, in a panpolitical vision that is extremely squalid for human beings, for whom no other activity would remain but revolution, no other persuasion but struggle, no other communication but ideological conflict. Only if philosophy avoids being replaced by art and politics will the latter remain truly themselves, restored to those limits that not only define them, but also maintain them in their proper and irreplaceable function.

In conclusion, the independence of philosophy is demanded by science, religion, art, and politics because only if philosophy remains irreducible to them can these four activities realize their proper nature and be rescued from the degeneration that ensues from their illegitimate claims. Only in virtue of the effective presence of philosophy is science truly science and not scientism, is religion truly religion and not fideism, is art truly art and not aestheticism, and is politics truly politics and not panpoliticism. Philosophy therefore retrieves its irreplaceable function in its restoring such various activities to their own tasks, rescuing them from the contemporary tendency to their absolutization, and thus protecting them from the danger of error and perversion.

6. Due to Excessive Critique, Philosophy Declares Its Own End

At this point, however, one can reasonably doubt whether philosophy is able to bring about order with respect to various human activities, because today we find ourselves confronted with a new and paradoxical fact: Philosophy *itself* declares its own end. Philosophy has lost its naïveté: It has enacted such a radical self-critique that its own very existence is placed in question. This all began with Kant's critique, when philosophy realized that it could not claim to submit human knowledge to critique without submitting itself to critique. It did not then hesitate to face the problem of its own possibility, and understood that in order to undertake such a critique it would have to become aware of its own conditions. Having set out on this path, philosophy no longer stopped and carried the critique to its fullest rigor and its ultimate consequences.

One of the first conditions of philosophy is that it makes use, and cannot not make use of *thought*. It was idealism that became aware of this condition: metaphysics, as the mirroring and total vision of reality, was challenged and forever destroyed because it is unthinkable that philosophy could face its object and grasp it in its external totality in the same way that common thought understands the objects of experience in front of it. It was a critical moment: It seemed that the object of philosophy would dissolve in an affirmation of universal subjectivism. Yet philosophy, sharpened by critique, managed to recover the totality of its object and the absolute nature of its knowledge in a new form, one that was compatible with the new demands. The result was Hegel's conception of philosophy as the self-consciousness of reality at the end of its development.

A new awareness was not far behind: the *historical conditionality* of philosophy. This was the work of historicism, from Hegel to Croce, from Marx to Dilthey. The conception of a definitive and supra-temporal philosophy, one that would always and for everyone be valid as the one truth, was appropriately destroyed, as this was in extreme contrast to the pluralism of cultures, points of view, and philosophies that prevails in human affairs. This was also a critical moment, because it seemed that philosophy itself would have to vanish in a form of radical relativism. But, even here, philosophy found a way to rise above the storms and to protect its own absolute validity through the very recognition of the multiplicity and temporality of philosophies.

A further step was taken by existentialism, which from Kierkegaard to Heidegger, from Nietzsche to Jaspers, gave philosophy an awareness of its own *personal conditionality*. It seemed that everything would dissolve in pure biographism, destined to signal the death of philosophy itself: the reduction of thought to lived life, the exceptional character of individual experience, and incommunicability among persons. In the end, however, only the idea of pure contemplative nature and the objective communicability of philosophy were destroyed; and it was a good thing, because philosophy is not a science, translatable into completely depersonalized propositions, and instead involves a strictly personal commitment in which it is very possible to find the foundations of interpersonal communication.

Now, the condition of which contemporary philosophy has become aware poses a problem more difficult to overcome, and seems to compromise totally the very possibility of philosophy. This condition is in fact *language*, namely the language *with* which philosophy ought to speak of its proper object, indeed of itself, indeed *of* the same language *with* which it speaks. This time, philosophy finds itself involved in an endless process whose result risks being the conclusiveness of silence, the very end of discourse, the death of philosophy itself. Critique has become crisis: Philosophy has pushed itself into a situation that seems to have no exit. In order to become aware of its own conditions and in order to secure itself in its own possibility, philosophy turned narcissistically back upon itself: It forced itself to speak only about itself, and its discourse has become so extenuated and rarefied that it has ended up exhausting itself in the becoming aware of its own impossibility. Briefly, philosophy is so critical that it becomes empty: It has no other object than itself, nor any result other than its own destruction.

To this, one can add another condition whose awareness crops up in contemporary philosophy: the *plurality of the fields of experience*. Experience—one knows—is open, inconclusive, unforeseeable, subdivided in an innumerable plurality of camps and, within it, our thought works to resolve the determinate questions that, ever new and different, slowly come to light. Well, now it is claimed that philosophy is none other than this operative thought rendered self-aware, thought to the second power, almost a double consciousness or a reflection in the second degree, internal to the individual fields of experience and intent on methodically confronting their specific problems. Philosophy in this way splits into particular discourses, becoming philosophy of art or of science or of religion or of morality or of politics and so on. And in each field it intends to present itself as methodology, experimentation capable of self-correction and self-check, agile and supple functionality apt to individual fields of experience, in close contact with empirical data, reluctant to make generalizations, devoted to technical and precise solutions. Now, the "second power" consists in the fact that this thought, at the very moment in which it operates within a field of experience, is aware of itself, that is, it takes itself and only itself as an object: It is self-transparent rationality insofar as it is technically operative; ultimately, it is empty thought. That explains how it cannot resist the invasion of the so-called social sciences [*scienze umane*] that present themselves so full of real content; that is, it is ready to surrender to sociology, psychology, cultural anthropology, ethnology, the history of culture, and so on. In this way too philosophy is on its way to complete abdication.

7. The Crisis of Philosophy as the Renunciation of Truth

The situation, therefore, seems to be the following. On the one hand, critique becomes so destructive that it compels philosophy, now forced to speak only of itself, to annihilate itself. On the other hand, the concreteness of experience, offering itself to a thought that aims only to exercise its own experimentation, becomes so dispersive that it annihilates philosophy in particular discourses. On the one side, the excess of critique results in the impossibility of philosophy as autonomous knowledge: The generality of philosophical discourse is so empty that philosophy, falling prey to a self-critique always more refined and debilitating, loses its very existence. On the other side, the charm of concreteness leads philosophy to abdicate its place to the social sciences: The particularity of philosophical discourses is so specialized that philosophy itself, ever more imprisoned within the fields of experience in which it works, renounces its own independence.

And so, today, philosophy finds itself faced with this alternative: either engage in a general discourse, and then speak about nothing other than itself so that it is only philosophy of philosophy and its discourse is empty, or better, its only content is the declaration of its own end; or, aim to be a full discourse, one that might speak of something, but then is dispersed in particular discourses that are no longer philosophical because the reflection that operates within them is not philosophy, but sociology or psychology or anthropology and so on. In both cases, philosophy seems to be over, either due to the impossibility of a general and autonomous philosophical discourse or due to the degeneration of particular and concrete philosophical discourses.

It is once again a critical moment, in fact a truly dramatic one, for philosophy. In this situation, it is too easy, or I would say simplistic, to declare the end of philosophy. Nor do I want to call comical the spectacle of philosophers who clamor to declare the death of philosophy or to reduce the task of philosophy to the demonstration of its own uselessness. Certainly, some idols will have to be destroyed once and for all by the present crisis, and even this negative part will be a victory; but, above all, there will arise from it the possibility of a recovery still more solid and secure than before, and this is the work to which all of us can and must contribute, philosophers and nonphilosophers alike.

Above all, one needs to realize that the present crisis consists in the fact that *philosophy has renounced truth.* In fact, the negative character of the alternative described above resides in an impoverished conception of philosophy: philosophy that consents to be *solely* philosophy of philosophy, or *solely* philosophy of science or of religion or of morality or of politics and so on, is *no longer* philosophy, is *not even* philosophy. In order to be philosophy, philosophy must not only speak of itself and of a realm of experience, but *while* it speaks of itself and of this realm it must *also* say something else much more radical and originary: something that, while it grounds philosophy in its very possibility, furnishes it with the criteria through which it can perform its own reflection within experience. Thought can truly be to the second power only if it is full, profound, and radical: only if it is the thought of truth. Only in this way can it illuminate experience by giving it a truly critical conscience, and reside in individual realms neither to the point of remaining their prisoner nor to that of subduing itself to them as their mere instrument, but by working as their guide and control, correction and verification, norm and direction. Only in this way can it open the exactitude of technical solutions to universality, and present itself not as a specialized reflection or a merely particular discourse, but rather as the whole of philosophy concentrated on a point.

Two consequences follow from this: On the one hand, one must consider the idea that truth is the "object" of philosophy to be definitively—and happily—destroyed; on the other hand, one must restore truth to philosophy in a new way, keeping in mind that philosophy must operate within multiple fields of experience and in relation to determinate questions. In the end, the problem to which we must respond is the following: whether philosophical discourse, due to the fact that it does not have truth as its object, ought to be deprived of truth; and whether philosophical discourse, due to the fact that it dedicates itself to specific realms and determinate problems, ought to accept that it is solely technical.

8. The Choice between Truth and Technics

Here is, in summary form, the response I advance. In the first place, if truth cannot be the object of philosophy, this does not mean that philosophy lacks truth. Truth is not the object, but the origin of philosophical discourse, and philosophical discourse is not the enunciation, but the site of truth. Philosophy does not speak directly *of* truth, which is not an object of argument, of which one might say *de veritate* [on truth], and *of* which and *about* which one could speak: Truth is the impulse, and not the outcome of discourse, and thus it escapes from it in the very act that nourishes it and founds it. An objective discourse *about* truth is not only not philosophical, but is by definition impossible in the sense that truth vanishes in the very act through which it is taken up as the *object* of a discourse, and that of which and about which one can speak is no longer truth: rather, truth is present *in* discourse, to solicit it and constitute its inexhaustible reserve. Truth certainly allows itself to be possessed by philosophy, but not in an absolute or definitive enunciation, valid for everyone and for all time as the true one: instead, it is philosophy's task to give it a personal interpretation and to venture its formulation at its own risk and peril, with the awareness that it is not interpretation that exhausts and monopolizes truth, but truth that gives itself to interpretation and unceasingly renews it.

Moreover, in the second place, philosophical discourse is not reduced to purely technical discourse simply due to the fact that it faces and resolves specific questions in particular realms of experience. *Technical* discourse clings rigorously to the particularity of its objects; when, after opportune planning, convenient experimentation, and adequate operations, the individual problem is resolved, the discourse is exhausted, and there is nothing left to say. Things happen very differently in philosophical discourse, which is *problematic*, and therefore such that once opened it never ceases and regerminates continually, so that of everything that it addresses, even the most definite, there always remains something to say. That happens because philosophical discourse, while speaking of its *object*, which is definite, refers to the *origin*, which is inexhaustible. When it faces a specific question, philosophical discourse does not limit itself to accompany such treatment with self-awareness; rather, it makes this self-awareness the site of an ulterior possession, which grants it fecundity as well as flexibility, depth as well as adherence to the concrete, inexhaustibility as well as the capacity for solution. The discourse is philosophical if it also reveals Being while speaking of beings, if it also speaks the truth while speaking of things, and if it shows the existential bond that ties human beings to Being and the person to truth while attending to individual fields of experience and particular questions.

Therefore, let us not say that philosophy is dead: The impossibility of its speaking *of* truth is solely the sign that truth is something much more originary than the object of a discourse. Philosophy can possess truth in a profound and I would even say surging way, and it always holds it present, also and above all when, in particular discourses, it addresses determinate questions and definite objects. This indeed is a point where philosophy demonstrates with the greatest evidence its decisive importance in today's world, orienting us before the great choice facing each of us today: *the choice between truth and technics.* Particular discourses are not univocal, because any one thing can be spoken of in a way that is either *solely technical* or *truly philosophical*, depending on whether one keeps solely to the determinacy of the problem and of the object, or instead confronts it with the sense of an ulteriority more vast and profound. Regarding even the smallest thing, human beings are faced with a decisive choice about which they cannot remain neutral and must choose. This is the choice between thought that is revelatory, even when it speaks of the most minimal datum of experience, and the discourse that is empirical, even when it refers to truth; the choice between philosophical discourse, which in speaking of any one thing always says also something else, and technical discourse, which only speaks about one thing; the choice between remaining faithful to Being and dominating beings, remembering truth and limiting oneself to experience, recovering the origin and closing oneself within the moment.

9. Philosophy as Consciousness of the Ontological Relation and the Problem of Philosophical Language

If one asks in what way philosophy can attain and possess truth, one will see that it cannot do it in the form of *knowledge* because truth is not the final object of a total vision, but only in the form of *consciousness.* This is not consciousness in the Hegelian sense, as consciousness of the already completed reality, but, if anything, in the way Schelling conceived of it: consciousness not of that which is last, but of that which is first, not of a history brought to its end, but of an unexhausted origin, not of the presumed totality of human spirit, but of its infinite, originary potentiality. Philosophy is nothing other than the becoming conscious, through thought and language, of the relation with Being and the truth that human beings *are*, and that human beings *live*, in agreement and in refusal, in any one of their activities. In this sense, philosophy allows us to know nothing more than what we already know; perhaps, however, we have forgotten it, and conveniently philosophy reminds us of it; and this is one of its great merits, that only in philosophy, and not in other activities, can human beings become critically conscious of that which they are. Philosophy translates into speculative terms that which even the simplest human beings already know. This means that even if the philosophical form belongs to few, its content belongs to all. Thus, the concept of philosophy as methodology and reflection to the second power is uselessly and excessively aristocratic, and there is a greater difference between philosophical thought and technical thought than there is between philosophy and common sense. Actually, methodology and technics, when they intend to pose as the only possible philosophy, are forms of "semi-science," of the forgetting of truth; they are, in their presumptuousness, much more ignorant than the ignorance laden with knowledge that is asserted and developed in philosophy.

Certainly, being capable of saying with words and thought that which average human beings can say only with life is not easy, and the claim of the greatest part of contemporary philosophy, namely that we must begin with an analysis of language, is more than justified. What *philosophical language* should be when philosophy is a speculative and verbal recovery of the originary can be found in what I have already said: First of all, language must be such that it possesses truth without thereby reducing it to an object of discourse; and second, it must be such that it only speaks of its own objects while also speaking truth. In the end, one needs on the one hand, a language that possesses without exhausting, and thus can contain the infinity of the implicit without ever being resolved in the "everything said"; and on the other hand, a language that is not restricted to signifying only that of which its speaks, but that *also* always says something ulterior *while* speaking of something definite.

The evidence of philosophy is not that of science, which says all that it needs to say, and thus, says it all. Philosophy does not leave "everything said," to which there corresponds a "quickly understood," so that the information is transmitted, and the communication exhausted without true dialogue; rather, in philosophy the word has always something to say because from its very explicitness a new eloquence surges forth without respite, which always makes it speak by sustaining a true dialogue as unceasing questioning, continual conversation, and infinite interpretation. That does not mean that the philosophical word is indefinite and imprecise, because its rigor consists precisely in knowing how to unite, indissolubly, *evidence* and *profundity*; nor does it mean that it is solely metaphor or allegory—as if sign and meaning were two series so heterogeneous that they could be connected only by the substitutability of the cipher—because fortunately the word does not need to be a symbol in order to become profound. The densest pregnancy of the philosophical word is given by the truth that it possesses, and that is not a simple unspoken yet to be deciphered, but an implied inexhaustible that should be made to speak.

10. The Effectiveness of Philosophy as Recovery of Truth

Understood in this way, philosophy can take decisive action in the current world, and to some extent this has already happened. We still need to say that philosophy, and it alone, lays the foundation for a true *dialogue* between human beings, because its discourse is at once personal and revelatory, namely, it institutes a multiplicity of individual and unrepeatable interpretations of the true, and at the same time holds them together in an unceasing reciprocal communication based on the uniting force of truth. Strictly speaking, there is no dialogue in science because the communication is impersonal; nor in religion, because dialogue is absorbed in something much more profound, namely love; nor in art, because there is true conversation only with the work; nor in politics, because, as long as ideologies dominate, there is only struggle or compromise, fanaticism and factiousness. Philosophy, however, creates dialogue because, in the very act in which it endlessly multiplies the personal interpretations of truth, it unites all of them in the common awareness of possessing truth without exhausting it but rather nourishing themselves on it continually.

Finally, we must still say that, by recovering truth in such an originary way, philosophy not only asserts itself in its own possibility, but also demonstrates its ability to point out to various human activities that from which they can draw fullness of content and vigor. We can now understand completely why the mere presence of philosophy is enough to restore any one of the activities to its genuine nature: Philosophy succeeds in doing this only because it does much more, that is, it guarantees that the *presence of Being and of truth* matters authentically in all human activities, regenerating them continually and saving them from dissolving into technicism, into specialization, into the void. Philosophy keeps the effective presence of truth alive, of that truth "that is great and conquers everything": *megale he aletheia kai huperischuei.*

Notes

Page 182: The Greek citation is taken from the Septuagint, and more precisely from a passage in the first book of Ezra that has no equivalent either in the Hebrew Bible or in the Vulgate (IV 41). But it is frequently cited: Schopenhauer, for example, added it as the motto for *The Two Fundamental Problems of Ethics* (1841). Even Shaftesbury mentions it in *Sensus communis* (IV 3), but in Latin: "*magna est veritas et praevalebit*." And Schopenhauer does the same in Chapter XX of the second volume of *The World as Will and Representation*: "*magna est vis veritatis et praevalebit*" (*Sämtliche Werke*, ed. Hübscher, III, 313).

6

Philosophy and Common Sense

1. Examples of Relations between Common Sense and Philosophy

The entire history of philosophy is crossed by the problem of the relations between philosophical thought and common sense, along with the most diverse solutions that have been proposed for them. Not only does philosophy often distance itself from common sense, but also deliberately challenges it with theories that seem paradoxical, such as the denial of movement and multiplicity, or the affirmation of the immateriality of the world and the ideality of space. Nor less infrequent are the cases when philosophy has wanted to begin with common sense and remain faithful to it, or at least reconcile with it after its temporary abandonment. Common sense has been considered, on the one hand, as the origin of total skepticism, as apparent in the long refutations by moralists of all ages who enumerate the most bizarre and insane foolishness found in public affairs; and, on the other hand, as the source of sure and certain knowledge against the absurdities of custom and the sophisms of speculation. Reserving true knowledge for philosophy, ancient classical thought looked with suspicion on the ideas of the many, considering them simple opinions, whereas a notable part of Hellenistic and Roman philosophy was dedicated to a revaluation of the apparent and the customary that form the broad realm of common sense.

Of the many possible ways to configure the relations between philosophy and common sense, two strike me as particularly significant. Nicholas of Cusa, who introduces the idiot, namely, the layman, to instruct the orator as well as the philosopher, because wisdom is not found "*in arte oratoria aut in voluminibus magnis*" [in the oratory art or in big books] but screams out in the piazzas, "*foris clama in plateis*"; and Hegel, who claims the most absolute opposition between genuine philosophy and *gesunder Menschenverstand*, namely, the ordinary common sense that is worthy of derision because of its inanity. Cusa's attitude found full support over the centuries because it was a just vindication of pure philosophy against the empty, bookish wisdom of the scholastics and rhetoricians. *Common sense* itself[1] took vengeance on Hegel's contemptuous words, however, and disseminated the tendentious idea, in Anglo-Saxon countries—an idea that today is also becoming more widespread in Italy—that German philosophy is something extravagant, just as Schopenhauer told us: "In England, when one wants to explain something very abstract, or practically incomprehensible, one says 'It is like German metaphysics.'"

Today, the two most typical positions on this problem are in my opinion represented by analytic philosophy and the phenomenological school. That analytic philosophy ends up being a sort of revaluation of common sense seems clear to me ever since it has chosen ordinary language as its field of analysis after renouncing its search for a perfect logical language; and renouncing the search for the meaning of words, it aims at a mere description of their effective use. In such a way, by taking words from their metaphysical use back to their everyday use philosophical reflection aims to dissolve rather than resolve philosophical problems that would only emerge through the confused and improper use of words, and that likewise would belong to what Wittgenstein expressively calls "bumps that the understanding has got by running its head against the limits of language." Merely by being a simple description of ordinary language, analytic philosophy finally achieves the very suppression of philosophy to the advantage of daily life and common sense. Conversely, phenomenology directly opposes common sense because it considers the most rigorous absence of presuppositions to be essential to philosophy: The philosophers must relinquish all of their habitual convictions, must suspend their assent to all that seems obvious to common sense by a simple acquiescence; that is, philosophers must suspend the prejudgment inevitably present in the "natural attitude" toward the world, in the commonplace, and in the everyday. To adopt Husserl's meaningful expression, only if one "brackets" the world can philosophy become reflection that is truly critical.

2. The Ambiguity of Common Sense, Held between a Demand for Universality and a Destiny of Historicity

The question, "What is common sense?" is anything but obvious. One should note that even those who believe that all human beings possess

1. Trans. Note: In English in Pareyson's original.

an equal capacity for reason do not avoid irony when talking about good sense [*buon senso*] or common sense [*senso comune*]. Thus it happens that Descartes, precisely where he states that by nature reason is equal in everyone, namely that "*le bon sens est la chose du monde la mieux partagée*," observes that "everyone thinks himself so well-endowed with it that even those who are the hardest to please in everything else do not usually desire more of it than they possess"; this confirms that "it is not enough to have a good mind; the main thing is to apply it well." Kant says that "it is indeed a great gift of God to possess right or (as they now call it) plain common sense. But this common sense must be shown in action by well-considered and reasonable thoughts and words, not by appealing to it as an oracle when no rational justification for one's position can be advanced." The polite irony of Descartes and Kant suffices to warn us that good sense, if it even exists, in fact means nothing outside of what one makes of it; and because this use always occurs in a historical circumstance, it follows that the concept of common sense threatens to disintegrate and dissolve under even the most superficial of inspections.

Common sense has, without a doubt, an ambiguous and fleeting reality, a very imprecise and unstable realm, a very uncertain and frail definition; therefore, one could never think of making it an organ of philosophical thought. On the one hand, as good sense, namely, as the faculty of judging correctly, it would like to coincide with the very universality of reason; but, on the other hand, as the common heritage of ideas, judgments, and beliefs, it can only coincide with the collective consciousness of a historically determined group or period. It thus finds itself divided between the demand for universality and a destiny of historicity, and it is not easy to find a parallelogram that compels these two diverse forces into a singular direction that is positive and constructive. Depending on whether one stresses the demand for universality or the destiny of historicity in common sense, then one ends up giving either a rationalistic or historicist interpretation of it; both interpretations end up rendering impossible even posing the problem of the relations between common sense and philosophy.

On the one side, if the call to good sense consists in the recommendation to free ourselves from the encrustations of culture and tradition in order to achieve the authentic human vision of reality, one could then easily object first, that even good sense is no less historically conditioned than the historical prejudices from which it should be purified and second, that the unique and genuine conception of reality, which would constitute pure philosophy, does not exist because a person cannot be separated from a historical situation, and in the best case such a conception is simply the product of a mystification that absolutizes as eternal what is merely temporal. On the other side, if one accepts the interpretation offered by historicism in order to escape the abstract nature of the rationalistic position, one will become incapable of identifying any difference between the most elaborate philosophy and the most limited prejudice, as both are the product of time: philosophers and the common persons would be equally determined, each in their own way, to express a historical situation, and no conception could claim to be truer than any other, as there is no other criterion of judgment than its adherence to the time in which such a conception is born, and in the best case, thought would have no other function than to grant each historical epoch the possibility of self-establishment and self-awareness.

All of the difficulties that emerge in the recourse to common sense derive from its duplicitous and vertiginous nature, divided between the universal and the historical, between the individual and the supra-personal, between the theoretical and the practical.

Thus the historicity of common sense may be considered not only as a destiny, but even as a limit, against which the universality of good sense would rightly rebel. Such is the situation related so well by Alessandro Manzoni who, when speaking of the foolish but general belief in spreaders of plagues, comments: "Good sense still existed, but it was concealed for fear of common sense." In contrast, it may happen that the demand for universality advanced by good sense is revealed to be nothing more than a pretense and a presumption, because the same fate of historicity that encumbers common sense afflicts also good sense. Such is the case for all that seems evident but is merely obvious, made such by a passive and unreflective acceptance, as when habit changes that which is historical into something natural. This gives rise to the astute observation by many French moralists, that is, that what seems to be nature is often nothing more than history: "A different custom will give us other natural principles."

Furthermore, the call to good sense may be considered an arbitrary exercise of reason, against which a valid support would be a tradition sustained by an enduring consensus: It is the case of the polemic of the traditionalists against the Enlightenment thinkers, intended to recognize true universality not in reason individually exercised but in tradition communally accepted. Conversely, it may happen that the generality of common sense, far from coinciding with the universality of reason, is reduced to the mediocrity of a random public voice or to the anonymity of mass opinion: These are the cases denounced by Shaftesbury, when he contemplates the possibility that "they can poll an indifferent number out of a mob [. . .] to attest a story of a witch upon a broomstick . . . ," and by Kant, when he notes that "seen clearly, [common sense] is but an appeal to the opinion of the multitude": "of whose applause the philosopher is ashamed, while the popular charlatan glories and boasts in it."

Finally, the appeal to common sense is the most evident example of the uncertainty between a theoretical conception that requires from thought that it provide first and fundamental principles on which to construct a speculative system of philosophy, and a practical conception that requires that reason provide criteria according to which individual, social, and political life should be ordered, perhaps by crumbling them into maxims of practical wisdom such as those provided by sentences and proverbs.

3. The Inanity and Presumptuousness of Common Sense Taken Separately from Philosophy

In this great confusion, when one wants to make common sense the point of departure for philosophical thought, perhaps by relying on the incontestable fact that philosophy deals with things that are of interest to everyone, one runs the risk not only of opening the way to the most conventional clichés, but also of elevating the most uncontrolled prejudices to the level of philosophical assertions; not only of recognizing everyone's right to interject in matters of philosophy, but also of denying philosophy the need for competence that is nonetheless required of every other form of knowledge.

From this point of view, the analogy between common sense and improvisation is noteworthy. In improvisation, that is, right there where through extemporaneous conditions originality should take control, the need to confront unforeseen situations often imposes resorting to memory and convention and accepting the most comfortable and easiest solutions; thus, one runs the risk of assembling a collection of worn-out ideas, automatic associations, jaded formulas, and stale reminiscences. Analogously, the recourse to common sense in matters of philosophy, that is, the very desire to reach the greatest depth in matters of the deepest human interest, risks weakening itself in the gathering of simple and obvious thoughts, of superficial and simplistic judgments, of predictable and foreseeable discourses: common persons never believe they are more original and independent than when they offer a couple of hackneyed ideas or relate the last thing they heard, above all today when the techniques of subtle persuasion have reached great perfection and efficacy, such that it seems to everyone that these thoughts spring impetuously from the mind, when in fact they only rise mechanically from memory.

This is the reason why the greatest philosophers, despite their recognition of the very broad human interest of philosophy, have never allowed common sense to serve as the organ or the verification of philosophical thought. Kant observes polemically that "to appeal to common sense is one of the subtle discoveries of modern times, by means of which the most superficial ranter can safely enter the lists with the most thorough thinker and hold his own." We need to convince ourselves, he says, that every faculty has its specific field: Common sense serves experience, as the chisel serves to carve wood; yet, as one needs an awl for the incision, thus for speculation one requires critical reason. Otherwise the doors of philosophy are open even to the judgment of incompetents. This is what Fichte wants to avoid when, by lamenting that according to common opinion "philosophizing is as automatic as eating and drinking, and that everyone who simply possesses the faculty of speech has a voice concerning philosophical matters," he notes that making recourse to common sense in philosophy is like "when philosophical propositions and expressions which can only be understood and judged within a scientific-philosophical system are brought before the court of unscientific understanding and misunderstanding"; and he wishes that "a fair-minded and unprejudiced man will just as dispassionately refrain from talking about philosophy as he refrains from talking about trigonometry or algebra if he has not learned these sciences."

Even more drastically, Hegel notes that "philosophy is philosophy only as it is diametrically opposed to good sense in its limitation." "In the case of all other sciences, arts, skills, and crafts, everyone is convinced that a complex and laborious program of learning and practice is necessary for competence. Yet, when it comes to philosophy, there seems to be a currently prevailing prejudice to the effect that, although not everyone who has eyes and fingers, and is given leather and last, is at once in the position to make shoes, everyone nevertheless immediately understands how to philosophize, and how to evaluate philosophy, since he possesses the criterion for doing so in his natural reason—as if he did not likewise possess the measure for a shoe on his own foot . . . sound common sense that has never labored over, or informed itself regarding other knowledge or genuine philosophy; and we are assured that these are quite as good substitutes [while] it offers at its very best only a rhetoric of trivial truths . . . [and] . . . it is not difficult to grasp such vague and misleading truths, or even to show that the mind in believing them is also aware of their very opposite . . . with more the presumption of being able to consider philosophy as a collection of 'sophistries' and 'visionary dreams.'" Hegel concludes by saying that "true thoughts and scientific insight are only to be won through the labor of the Notion. Only the Notion can produce the universality of knowledge which is neither common vagueness nor the inadequacy of ordinary common sense, but a fully developed, perfected cognition."

4. The Impossibility of Surrendering Philosophy to Common Sense

I would not have lingered so long in very authoritative quotations were I not convinced that the idea, which is rather widespread today, that the sciences constitute the only form of knowledge translates into a decisive devaluation of philosophy, not only in the sense that philosophy, due to the fact that on the surface it does not possess the rigor belonging to the sciences, is not even considered to be a form of knowledge, but even in the sense that, precisely for this reason, it is completely surrendered to common sense, that is, to the everyday speaking of all people.

Philosophers, precisely because they are philosophers, avoid interjecting *in* science and at most, instructed by scientists themselves, reflect *on* scientific methodology. Conversely, it sometimes happens that scientists have something to say about matters of philosophy: either in the sense that they—illegitimately—reduce the philosophy of science to the awareness of its own method that they must have as scientists, or in the sense that they believe they can speak of it by means of that simple common sense that they themselves have carefully expunged from the context of their own research, or in the sense that philosophy strikes them as nothing more than idle talk. This last claim could however be made only on the base of the proposition that there is no knowledge other than scientific knowledge; this proposition, one should note, is not scientific, but philosophical.

It is worth lingering for a moment to entertain some considerations. First of all, philosophy, even when it is reduced to philosophy of science, implies a further reflection, one that brings the concept of science and scientific methodology into a context that not only is no longer the domain of science, but also presupposes at least implicitly the accomplishment and comprehensiveness of philosophy. Moreover, it is not fair that such scrupulous teachers of method in their own field could advance common sense as a reason for interfering without method in other fields. And finally, it is not surprising that certain scientists, after having thereby done philosophy with little effort and on the cheap, become even more convinced of the idea that there is no other form of knowledge than the scientific one, and consider philosophy to be poetry or rhetoric, or even to be unfounded daydreaming and ultimately useless. No one is more admirable than the scientists who are also philosophers, and it seems that today we have a need for these complete and superior figures. But they must do philosophy as philosophers, not as scientists. This, however, they cannot do without failing their duty towards science itself; and much less can they do it with simple common sense, which they could only do by denying the very concept of philosophy.

5. The Rigor of Philosophical Knowledge

Now, that is not to say that philosophy is not a form of knowledge, or that it lacks its own rigor. Certainly, neither its knowledge nor its rigor is that of science due to the profound difference that separates scientific truth from philosophical truth. I know of no better way to express such difference than with Jaspers' suggestive reflections on the diverse cases of Galileo Galilei and Giordano Bruno. Scientific truth is impersonal and demonstrable: It would thus be absurd to want to die for it. Galileo did not have difficulty recanting what he said: His retraction did not compromise the truth he held, which could survive and be asserted without him. Conversely, philosophical truth is personal and decisive: Affirming it means that one is ready to die for it. Bruno believed that he could not recant what he said: His retraction would have compromised a truth that could not exist without him. Galileo's truth would not have become truer with his death; but, Bruno's death was the only possible demonstration of his truth.

All of that does not mean that philosophy is arbitrary, imprecise, preachy, and thus indebted to the unpredictable play of emotions, to the emphatic rhetoric of persuasion, to the hasty observations of good sense, and ultimately to the ordinary language of common sense. Philosophy is a form of *knowledge*, it has a *universal* character, and possesses its own *rigor*. The fact that such knowledge, universality, and rigor are not those of science is not its defect, but an essential condition for its normal exercise.

Its *knowledge* is such because it is the possession of truth; but, because truth is accessible only through a historical path and only mediated through a personal relation, it is a knowledge that refracts into a plurality of perspectives, it can never be formulated in an absolute and definitive enunciation, and it cannot accept the unicity of the proposition as a criterion for the distinction between true and false. Its *universality* is the universality of truth, which speaks to everyone, but to each one in one's own way, and thus is always present within an individual interpretation, which by its own right is communicable only personally and historically, and thus through a new plurality, indeed infinity, of interpretations in an unceasing dialogue through which every revelation is what it is as the promise of new revelations.

Nothing is tougher than its *rigor*, which consists in a problematization that stops at nothing, because philosophy submits everything to question, first of all itself. It is not philosophy if it is not also philosophy of philosophy, to the point that it cannot begin but with a justification of its own point of view and a foundation for its own possibility; it can not continue without interrogating itself ceaselessly on the legitimacy of its own operations and without becoming critically aware of everything that is implicit in its necessary self-awareness; and it cannot complete its work without recalling that which solicits, supports, and seals its perpetual and obstinate questioning, and without revealing that its word is the site of a meaning much more expansive than that enunciated by its very explicitness.

It is precisely this unflinching and constant problematization that distinguishes philosophy from common sense, which in its immediacy does not pose questions. Thus philosophers see a problem there, rather than an organ; they see a duty, that is, a dedication to rigorous deepening and reflective recovery, rather than a right granting everyone indistinctly the ability to speak in matters of philosophy. In the end, philosophy places common sense under question, as it questions the rest, and not just radically, but also globally—the whole human experience and all human activities.

6. Philosophy as the Problematization of Experience and of Common Sense Itself

Experience and philosophy clearly are distinct despite being closely joined, and it helps clarifying the point of contact between the one and the other, avoiding both their separation and their conflation, that is, as if to say, avoiding philosophy that is empty verbiage as much as philosophy that is raw empiricism. Philosophy has both a speculative and a concrete nature, and the one guarantees the other, in the sense that it would not be philosophy, but mere empirical endeavor, if it did not raise itself above experience as pure speculation intended to give reason to it, and it would not be true speculation, but a verbal game, if it did not return to experience in its concreteness in order to draw from it content and stimulation for its own problematic. The reference to experience not only avoids a suppression of the speculative feature of philosophical reflection, but is in fact the necessary condition for it. Reflection, however, does not reach the level of philosophical speculation unless it transcends experience with a radical and global problematization, intended to discover primary and irreducible presences there and to recover inexhaustible and originary possibilities in them.

That means, first of all, that philosophy is not confined to experience, neither as the methodology of various human activities, as a form of refined empiricism wishes, nor even as the investigation of the various cultural forms of human life, as the anthropological and sociological disciplines wish it to do. Certainly, methodology is indispensable for a proper and proficient exercise of various activities, and the study of the various cultures does say something about human beings as such. Yet philosophy cannot be reduced within these limits, because a reflection that supervises the functionality of concepts and corrects the exercise of reason, without however establishing the operational goals, ends up resulting in thought that is purely technical and instrumental; and an investigation of human cultural forms, even if it leads to an intensification of the experience that human beings have of themselves and the world, is at its root nothing other than a reduplication of meanings through reflection. In both cases, thought is nothing other than the movement through which experience folds upon itself without the radical and total problematization that is desired by philosophy.

It also cannot be said, however, that philosophy stands above experience so as to give it norms and prescribe it ends, and so as to presume to take on a leading role with respect to various activities, as Enlightenment rationalism would like philosophy to do. By identifying not only reason, but even truth with philosophy, Enlightenment thinking, rather than confining itself to recognize that philosophers have the task, fully human, and for them particularly demanding, *of recollecting* truth and *pointing to* Being, reserves for the philosopher the very task of legislating within human activities. This excessively aristocratic spirit unfortunately feeds not only the arrogance of philosophers, but also the presumption of reason. Philosophy is not able to establish and impose the norm for the various human activities; rather, it discovers it, more or less operative or latent, within experience itself, and its task is to liberate that norm from the darkness in which human forgetfulness and negligence have wrapped it, and to present it to everyone's personal obedience and responsible performance.

Should one then say that philosophy stands neither within nor above experience, but concludes it, in the sense of "arriving late" to a reality that unfolds without her, adding to things already done, with neither the possibility nor the task of intervening there, as the various forms of historicism ultimately maintain? Certainly, it is quite true that philosophy comes at the end, like "the owl of Minerva, which flies at dusk," according to Hegel's famous and suggestive image. Yet, it supervenes experience neither so as to absorb it in itself, nor to limit itself to a reflection of it; rather, as I was saying, in order to problematize it from its root and in its entirety and to recover in it the first and originary possibility. Philosophy arrives at the end precisely in order to be able to grasp with more agility what is first. In this sense, far from being a conclusion, it is rather the recovery of the origin—not the closing of the reflective consciousness, but the freshness of the morning of the world.

According to the historicist perspective, instead, in the belated awareness that it furnishes for history, philosophy either resolves all reality into thought, as with Hegel, or reduces thought to the simple expression of history, as with Marx. How difficult admitting such conceptions is appears clearly from the fact that, in both cases—whether philosophy is elevated to the level of a supreme and absolute ratification of the real, that is, to a complete justification of history, or whether it is degraded to the level of a mere ideology, that is, to a superstructure that limits itself to express and reflect a determinate historical moment—the result is the same: namely, only violence remains as the sole possible philosophical rebuttal. In fact, in order to reopen the closed Hegelian system there is no other real possibility than revolution, and in order to refute a determinate ideology that reflects a given historical situation there is no other way than changing through action the very historical situation of which that particular ideology is the expression.

It might seem that philosophy, intended as total and radical problematization, has no other possibility than a renewed transcendentalism, intent on defining the possibility, the value, and the meaning of various human activities, dedicated to maintaining each one of them within its proper camp and its genuine nature, and capable of pointing out their formal and indubitable structures. Philosophy would not live up to its very own problematizing nature if it were to stop here, though. We need to go deeper, and point out, to various human activities, the source from which they can draw fullness of content and of vigor. The impulse of the problematization would in fact not even arise were it not fed by an originary solidarity with truth that impresses it with a continual desire for deepening and recovery; and thought would content itself with being the internal reflection of individual human activities, destined to be empty, technical, and neutral, were it not to have an ontological dimension by which human beings, albeit unable to exit from the situation, are not only not reduced to it, but end up qualifying it as situation only insofar as they elaborate and modify it.

7. Common Sense as the Object of Philosophy Is the Originary Ontological Relation

This is precisely the point where common sense, if considered in its profound and genuine nature, not only offers a valid and secure support to philosophy, but also persuades philosophy to be reconciled with it and rediscover its fertile pregnancy and decisive importance. In fact, if philosophical thought becomes too decisively distanced from common sense, one will not be able to avoid asking: Does philosophy not deal with things of interest to everyone? And can one truly believe that truth is the exclusive privilege of some individual, and that the only way to possess it is through philosophical reflection? If, conversely, common sense becomes too violently ensnared in the sphere of vulgar opinions and inane prejudices, one would have to ask: Is not the profound similarity that ties all human beings together, and of which the plurality of cultures is more of a realization than a denial, also a sign of their originary solidarity with the truth that is everyone's solely because it belongs to no one in particular? And are there not modes of possessing the truth that are more effective, even if they lack the speculative character of philosophical thought?

To these questions, this same common sense can suggest a valid response when it is correctly understood as an originary presence of Being and of truth at the base of every human activity: this is a presence that human beings can live in consensus or in refusal, and that philosophy has the difficult task of translating into verbal and speculative terms. This is what Vico recalls when he makes the entire human world depend on common sense, taken as the founder of concrete human communities and as the historical incarnation of truth, and thus as the sign of the originary ontological opening of human beings and of the revelatory character of their thought.

In the act of presenting Vico as the great theorizer of common sense, allow me to pay special homage to the greatest of Italian philosophers, pointing out in him, the last of the humanists and the first of the romantics, the living denial of the clichés common in our culture, namely, that the modern world would stand on the declared continuity of humanism, reformation, and enlightenment. He in fact shows that between humanism and romanticism there runs a direct continuity, whose study could be extremely fecund for the solution of many of today's problems, and whose development could purify these two great movements of modern culture from the negative sides that have until now compromised their destiny. This could be done by separating the pure humanistic meditation from the overvaluation of the word that so heavily burdened the European and especially Italian civilization with a load of unbearable rhetoric or arid philology, and by warning that romanticism, if correctly denuded of the *Schwärmerei* that has given it more damage than impetus, has not yet closed its cycle and would have much to say even today, despite the denigration that Hegel has made in the academies and Marx has made in the town squares.

In common sense, Vico sees on the one side not the abstract universality of reason present in all human beings, but the concrete universality of a historical community held together by consensus and by the participation of individuals in the same social life; and on the other side, in it he sees not the identity of a system of speculatively communicable thought, but the multiple and historical incarnation of the *vis veri*, considered above all as forming energy and effective in the "vulgar wisdom" of "the mind of nations," that is, in civil prudence, much earlier than in the reflective and conscious wisdom of the philosophers. If one freely welcomes Vico's suggestion, one can identify in common sense, properly developed by philosophy, the way to confront some of the most urgent problems facing the world today.

8. The Inseparability of Universality and Historicity in Common Sense

First, let me address the problem of the relations between universality and historicity. It is clear that if universality is that of a totally complete and explicated system of ideas, and if historicity is that of a circumscribed situation that fatally encloses human beings within time, then universality and historicity will never be reconcilable, and an abyss will always divide truth, understood as the one possible philosophy that is so ideal that it is lost in the smoky fog of fantasy, and situation, meant as the unavoidable obstacle to the achievement of the true, so impassible an obstacle that the situation itself appears as the only properly human truth.

Common sense, however, is neither a stable patrimony, in whose possession all participate in a form of integrated and peaceful association, nor a reserve of explicit ideas and transmissible norms on which one could easily model one's thoughts and actions; nevertheless, common sense consists in a reference to a unique and solid center that does not dissipate but rather is renewed in the historical process, and that does not shatter but rather is multiplied in the plurality of voices that are inspired by it. Understood in this manner, common sense manifests within human beings their originary ontological opening, that is, the essentially ontological character of all human activities which achieve their authenticity only through a happy convergence of the vigor of Being in human acting and of the listening to Being on the side of humans.

It is in virtue of this ontological dimension that truth is not an assurance of possession as much as an appeal to recovery, not a reserve on which one draws as much as a call to which one gives a response; and the human formulations of truth hit the target even when they are multiplied in a plurality of interpretations, and even when they resolutely escape a unique and definitive enunciation.

Only in the ontological opening of the human beings, therefore, do universality and historicity present themselves as inseparably conjoined, because then the situation is viewed as the only pathway to truth, and truth is seen as the energy that operates within the very formulation that is proposed of it; and both encounter each other in the constitutive plurality of interpretation, which thus reveals its richness, namely, the richness that belongs to us and to truth. Interpretation is multiple only because it contains, at the same time, the plurality of persons who know how to configure it and the infinity of truth that manifests itself there. In virtue of this concept of interpretation, historicity and plurality can be recognized to the manifestations of common sense, and such manifestations avoid being reduced to prejudices that one should bracket and to vulgar opinions of no philosophical value.

That truth is not the object but the origin of thought is not its degradation because solely in this fashion can one ensure its effective presence in the human world, namely, the infinity that can easily bring together all perspectives, however diverse they may be. That human beings cannot approach truth but from a historical situation is not a defect because solely in this manner can they possess truth in a shared and irreplaceable way. That the interpretation of truth can never be the only one, but is in itself multiple, is not its disadvantage or the sign of its deplorably approximate character because solely in this way can it hope to be grasping [of the truth]. I want to insist neither on the diffusive inexhaustibility of truth nor on its interiority to the human mind, which would still be a form of objective or intimistic *metaphysics*, nor solely on the inventive and tentative processes of investigation, which would still be a transcendentalist *phenomenology* or an empiricist *analysis*, but rather on the fact that truth offers itself only within the personal and historical formulation that it is given—what is properly an *ontology* of the inexhaustible.

9. Only Truth Unites Without Depersonalizing

In the second place, there is the problem of the relations between the person and that which rules over it. The appeal to common sense is the warning that without the recognition of a supra-personal limit, freedom is transformed into presumption and personalism degenerates into narcissism; at the same time, it is the awareness that this limit must not negate personality. Now, it is clear that common sense would lead to an oppression of the person if its object were a cultural patrimony or a content of thought, things that could only be shared by everyone through an abasement and common vulgarization, that is, only through a reduction to the level of the masses, to anonymity, and to depersonalization.

One can think of fleeing this danger by renouncing the content and resorting to form, that is, by entrusting common sense to reason itself in its exercise. But even this formal reason does not belong to the realm of persons, because it is solely technical and instrumental thought, deprived of criteria and ends. It is the reason *ployable à tous sens* [bendable in every direction] mentioned by Pascal, which possesses not the truth in itself but, at most, the capacity for coherence and the sanction of a success. Now, what kind of community and similarity can be instituted by this technical reason, in itself indifferent to the person, even if personally exercised? And what sort of respect should a person grant to this mere technical instrument, which is useful for the success of experiments in which one risks, at most, a momentary failure, but one does not decide responsibly for oneself? Subjecting the person to this impersonal and depersonalizing reason entails a tyranny even greater than that exercised by an authority indifferent to consensus or exercised by the mass' uncontrolled rule.

What can unite without depersonalizing is therefore something more originary and profound; such is, again, the fundamental ontological opening of the human being. The person is in fact constituted by the relation with Being, a relation that is essentially (albeit active and revelatory) listening to truth. Only truth rules over the person without oppression of such a person, because truth only gives itself to a conscious act of freedom without thereby authorizing the unforeseeable whims of an arbitrary originality, as those who support freedom but forget Being seem to believe.

On this point, allow me to add the following clarifications. First of all, *commonality* [comunanza] means neither empirical universalization nor rationality in action, that is, neither depersonalizing standardization nor rational impersonality. In its genuine significance, common sense is not the reign of the anonymous, the standardized, and the vulgar: True common sense is *similarity*, not a leveling out; it is not depersonalization, but the commonality instituted among persons. The *common* is common among similars, that is, among persons: It is situated at the level of personality and not of the masses, where there is no true community because there is no individuality. True *community* [comunità] is similarity: deepening of personality and singularity, not their negation.

Human similarity is founded precisely by the commonality of common sense as ontological relation, which is common par excellence: Nothing is more *common* than it because it deals with the relation with Being that human beings *are*. The commonality is the reference to the one truth on the part of similar persons, who not only recognize their similarity but also consider it to be founded by that *common reference*. This is confirmed by the fact that such humanity and similarity is a *task* much more than a *nature*, in the same way that truth and Being are origin more than objective reality or definite form. As there is no truth outside of the interpretation it is given, so there is no humanity outside of the performance that every one of us gives of it; and as truth is not reduced to an arbitrary and subjective self-styled interpretation, but is the judge of the interpretation in which it resides, so too humanity is not reduced to historical human beings and to their process of becoming, but is the judge of the realization in which humanity time after time takes form and reality.

Against depersonalization and impersonality, one needs to reclaim the person and the individual. In so doing, however, one does not at all compromise *common sense*, which in itself brings community together without depersonalizing, unites without standardizing, and belongs to everyone without being abased. Precisely by appealing to common sense—and only by appealing to it, as to the ontological opening that qualifies everyone originarily—one can discover the reason behind the *respect for everyone*, even for the aged and the ignorant, based on something more than mere humanitarianism or rhetoric that is for the most part sentimental. The humble and the ignorant are oppressed by the rationality of the Enlightenment, which, by asserting that reason is found equally in everyone, seems to be an affirmation of freedom and equality; in reality, however, it is the domination by pure intelligence and the predominance of the intellectual, as one sees in the sort of philosophical persecution such as the continual resort to irony, the ludicrous, and mockery, the typical weapons of scholars and intellectuals. In the end, it is a hierarchy of pure intelligence, which is the most questionable aristocracy since it inevitably translates into a sort of tyranny exercised by intellectuals and technocrats. This "cruelty," typical of the Enlightenment, has not found a better way to reform itself than through the tearful and sentimental humanitarianism of philanthropy, or the sickly sweet and rhetorical ethics of sympathy. It is not surprising, therefore, that the tragic nature of the human situation eludes this attitude that, by separating so clearly the heart and the intellect, divides itself between derision and tears, between mockery and weeping, between irony and sentimentality.

Fortunately, the appeal to common sense brings everything back into balance: Just as it brings about respect toward the humble and the ignorant, so too it scales down the cult of originality and the elephantiasis of personality. That is always something opportune, given that it may happen that even personalism, forgetting that what constitutes freedom as freedom is truth, winds up in the narcissism of self-adoration or in the arbitrariness of vitalism, as revealed in some outcomes of intimistic spiritualism and inferior forms of existentialism, forgetful as they are of the ontological relation that alone can successfully teach an attitude as difficult as humility, which is always ready to degenerate into depression, or to reverse itself into pride, or to fool itself into hypocrisy.

10. The Identity of Theory and Praxis Can Only Be Originary

In the third place, there is the problem of the relation between theory and praxis. Common sense testifies that, as regards truth, cognitive activity is not privileged in comparison with practical activity because even action has its own originary ontological dimension that permits it to draw a norm directly from its depths without the mediation of reflective thought and much less of philosophy, because it would otherwise have to accept the blatant absurdity that an ethical genius is necessarily a thinker and that the existence of an ignorant saint is impossible. This means that the level of the ontological relation precedes the distinction between theory and praxis, and that the fundamental and most important distinction is always the decisive choice between remaining faithful to truth or betraying it, between listening attentively to Being or forgetting it, whether that occurs in thought or in action.

This is of great importance because of its possible political consequences, above all today when the unity of theory and praxis is postulated from many perspectives and one speaks of the relations between the intellectual and the politician. In fact, if one leaves aside the originary identity of theory and praxis as is included in the ontological relation, the distinction between the one and the other tends to solidify into an opposition, one that can be mediated only through a reciprocal subordination. One then ends up on the one side, with the idea that thought precedes action and on the other side, with the idea that action precedes thought: in the first case, the practical is reduced to the pure and simple "application" of a presupposed theory; and in the second case, theory is degraded to the mere instrument of praxis. Here is the origin of two attitudes that in today's society become ever more distinct and ever more unmistakable: on one side the intellectuals, who think of their task as of the claim to give laws to the politicians; and on the other side the politicians, who realistically subjugate the intellectuals as their own instruments. Both forget that, in every field, everyone's task is to assert the presence of truth in all human activity.

11. The Profound Collaboration of Common Sense and Philosophy

What, then, are the relations between common sense and philosophy? We have seen first the misery of common sense: its simplistic features, its bonhomie, its lack of problems, its insipidness, and its presumption. What results is the impossibility of conceiving common sense as the organ of philosophy, which rises above it with a resolute superiority, if only for the fact that philosophy turns common sense into one of its problems. But as soon as common sense is submitted to that radical problematization that is philosophy, it suddenly reveals itself as the true and profound "object" of philosophy—as that ontological dimension that belongs to all human activities, and that is the task of philosophy to translate into verbal and speculative terms.

It is therefore a matter of enacting a vindication of common sense that is not "good-sensical," but rather fully human, because the ontological thought that stands at the base of human activities is attainable by everyone, even if not in its philosophical formulation, and even if the much easier and more simplistic technical thought tends to forget its presence and to tread on its potential vigor.

The conclusion is that common sense without philosophy may degenerate, becoming a simple commonplace, whereas with philosophy it can strengthen itself, manifesting its genuine and profound nature of being the intermediary between truth and time, of being the source of unity for thought and action, and of being the originary ontological opening of human beings. One can say, then, that common sense and philosophical thought encounter each other and conspire together, that the one cannot stand without the other, and that the highest philosophical thought reconfirms the most profound common sense. There is a need, as Pascal says, for the two extremes to touch each other: philosophers, having traversed what is to be known, return in an educated manner to that ignorance so deprived of knowing whence they began. The essential point is not to stop halfway, that is, at the semi-science that is gaining ever increasing popularity because it fits the process of standardization that characterizes our time. Once again, we return to Pascal: "Those between the two extremes who have moved on from their natural ignorance but are unable to reach the other have a certain smattering of presumed science but act like know-it-alls. They judge everything poorly and turn the world upside down."

Notes

Pages 185–186: The citations from Nicholas of Cusa are taken from *Idiotae Libri;* Hegel's citations come from the Preface to *The Phenomenology of Spirit*; and Schopenhauer's from the essay "On University Philosophy" contained in the first volume of the *Parerga und Paralipomena* (*Sämtliche Werke*, ed. Hübscher, V 174). The expression from Wittgenstein, as is commonly known, is found in section 119 of the *Philosophical Investigations* (English translation by G.E.M. Anscombe, P.M.S. Hacker and Joachim Schute. Oxford: Blackwell Publishing, 2009).

Page 187: The citations from Descartes and Kant are the celebrated passages from the beginning of the *Discourse on Method* (Descartes, *Discourse on the Method*, trans. by Robert Stoothoff, from *The Philosophical Writings of Descartes, Vol. I.* [Cambridge: Cambridge University Press, 1985], 111) and from the *Preface* to the *Prolegomena* (Immanuel Kant, *Prolegomena to Any Future Metaphysics*, translated by Carus. [New York: The Library of Liberal Arts, 1950], 7).

Page 188: From Alessandro Manzoni, I cited a passage from chapter XXXII of *I Promessi Sposi: The Betrothed*, translated by Bruce Penman (New York: The Penguin Group, 1984), 316; and the idea that "*une différente coutume nous donnera d'autres principes naturels*" is from Pascal (*Pensées* 92), but reflects the thought of all French moralists beginning with Montaigne.

Page 189: The citation from Shaftesbury is taken from *Sensus Communis* (IV, 3), and the one from Kant again from the *Preface* to the *Prolegomena* (IV, 259).

Pages 190–191: Kant is cited again from the *Preface to the Prolegomena* (IV 259–260); Fichte is cited from *A Crystal Clear Report to the General Public Concerning the Actual Essence of the Newest Philosophy*, in *Philosophy of German Idealism*, ed. Ernst Behler (New York: Continuum, 1987), 40–41; from Hegel is the harsh polemic contained in the *Introduction* to the *Phenomenology of Spirit*, translated by A.V. Miller (Oxford: Oxford University Press, 1977), 41–43.

Page 92: Jaspers' theory on the difference between philosophical truth and scientific truth is found in *La mia filosofia*, (Turin: Einaudi, 1947), 110–111; *Von der Warheit* (Munich: Piper, 1947), 651; *Der philosophische Glaube* (Munich: Piper, 1948), 11. On this, see my *Esistenza e persona*, 1950, cit., 58–59, and the suggestive reflections by Xavier Tilliette, *La vérité de Galilée, la vérité de Giordano Bruno,* in *L'infaillibilité*, edited by E. Castelli (Paris: Aubier, 1970), 257–270.

Page 199: As for the difference between the interiority of truth to the mind and the inseparability of truth from interpretation, I refer the reader back to page 88, and to the corresponding note. The expression from Pascal, on reason that "is bendable in every direction," is taken from *Pensées* 274.

On page 203 I return to the thought from Pascal (327) already cited on page 123.

Bibliography

Pareyson's Works Translated in English

"The Unity of Philosophy," *Cross Currents* 4 (1953): 57–69.

"Pointless Suffering in *The Brothers Karamazov*," *Cross Currents* 37, 2–3 (1987): 271–286.

Existence, Interpretation, Freedom: Selected Writings. Edited by Paolo Diego Bubbio. Translated by Anna Mattei. Aurora, CO: The Davies Group, Publishers, 2009.

Articles, Book Chapters, and Reviews on Pareyson in English

Benso, Silvia. "On Luigi Pareyson: A Master in Italian Hermeneutics." *Philosophy Today* 49, 4 (Winter 2005): 381–390.

Bredin, H. T. "The Aesthetics of Luigi Pareyson." *British Journal of Aesthetics* 6 (1966): 193–203.

———. "Review of *L'esperienza artistica. Saggi di storia dell'estetica*." *British Journal of Aesthetics* 16 (1976): 87–90.

Brown, M. E. "On Luigi Pareyson's 'L'estetica di Kant.'" *Journal of Aesthetics and Art Criticism* 29 (1971): 403–410.

Carravetta, Peter. "Introduction to the Hermeneutics of Luigi Pareyson." *Differentia* 3/4 (1989): 217–241.

Franke, William. "Existentialism: An Atheistic Or a Christian Philosophy?" in *Analecta Husserliana: The Yearbook of Phenomenological Research Volume CIII: Phenomenology and Existentialism Book One: New Waves of Philosophical Inspirations*. Dordrecht: Springer Science + Business Media, 2009.

Harris, Henry Silton. "Review of *Fichte. Il sistema della libertà*." *Journal of the History of Philosophy* 18 (1980): 97–98.

Kretsch, Robert Winston. "Review of *L'estetica e i suoi problemi*." *Journal of Aesthetics and Art Criticism* 21 (1962): 104–105.

Lazea, Dan. "The Ontological Personalism of Luigi Pareyson: From Existentialism to the Ontology of Liberty." *Appraisal: A Journal of Constructive and Post-Critical Philosophy and Interdisciplinary Studies* 6, 1 (2006): 7–16.

Lippman, Edward Arthur. "Review of *Estetica. Teoria della formatività*." *Journal of Philosophy* 52 (1955): 791–796.

Munro, Thomas. "Review of I problemi dell'estetica." *Journal of Aesthetics and Art Criticism* 26 (1968): 396–397.

———. "Review of *L'esperienza artistica. Saggi di storia dell'estetica*." *Journal of Aesthetics and Art Criticism* 33 (1975): 464–465.

———. "Review of *L'interpretazione dell'opera d'arte*." *Journal of Philosophy* 15 (1956): 255–256.

———. "Review of *L'interpretazione dell'opera d'arte*." *Journal of Philosophy* 53 (1956): 814–819.

———. "Review of *Teoria dell'arte. saggi di estetica*." *Journal of Aesthetics and Art Criticism* 25 (1966): 219–220.

———. "Review of *Verità e interpretazione*." *Journal of Aesthetics and Art Criticism* 30 (1972): 570.

———. "Review of *Verità e interpretazione*." *Journal of the History of Philosophy* 70 (1973): 132–133.

Pareyson, Luigi. "Review of *Existence, Interpretation, Freedom: Selected Writings*." *Appraisal: A Journal of Constructive and Post-Critical Philosophy and Interdisciplinary Studies* 8, 2 (2010): 52–53.

Romanell, Patrick. "Review of *Estetica. Teoria della formatività*." *Philosophy and Phenomenological Research* 16 (1956): 572–573.

Savile, Anthony. "Review of *I problemi d'estetica*." *British Journal of Aesthetics* 7 (1967): 389–390.

Schaper, Eva. "Review of *L'estetica di Kant*." *British Journal of Aesthetics* 9 (1969): 198–199.

———. "Review of *L'estetica e i suoi problemi*." British Journal of Aesthetics 3 (1963): 77.

Sepper, Dennis L. "After Fascism, After the War: Thresholds of Thinking in Contemporary Italian Philosophy." *American Catholic Philosophical Quarterly* 80, 4 (2006): 603–619.

Valgenti, Robert T. "The Primacy of Interpretation in Luigi Pareyson's Hermeneutics of Common Sense: A Response to D. Di Cesare's 'U-Topias of Understanding.'" *Philosophy Today* 49, 4 (Winter 2005): 333–341.

———. "The Tradition of Tradition in Hermeneutics" in *Consequences of Hermeneutics*, eds. Jeff Malpas and Santiago Zabala (Evanston, IL: Northwestern University Press, 2010), 66–80.

Vattimo, Gianni. "Pareyson: From Aesthetics to Ontology" in *Art's Claim to Truth*, ed. Santiago Zabala (New York: Columbia University Press, 2008), 77–89.

Index

absolutization, xxxvii, 44, 135–137, 139, 152, 161, 174
aesthetics xii, xxv–xxvii, xxix, 5, 9–10, 44, 59, 77, 164, 169, 173–174
alienation, 94, 97, 102
alterity xxiii, 55, 68, 107, 148, 164
  See also othering
anxiety, 172–173
atemporal, the, 5
  See also under Being; truth
Augustine, Saint, 75, 78, 109

Barth, Karl, xix, 125
Being
  atemporality of, 38
  decision for, 43, 91–92
  faithfulness to 42, 92, 162, 180
  forgetting of xxxvi, 16, 42, 44, 92, 96–97, 104, 123, 138, 155–156, 160, 200
  freedom of, xxxii, 43–44
  gift of, 92
  ineffability of, xxxii, 23–24, 141 142
  inexhaustibility of, xxv, xxxi–xxxiii, 24, 37–38, 40, 42, 76, 138
  interpretations of, xxxvi, 38–40, 74
  listening to 41, 198, 200
  opening to, 14, 97, 136
  and philosophy, 138–139
  presence of 35–38, 52, 159, 182, 196
  relation with, xxii, xxiv–xxv, xxxiii, xxxvi, 5, 14, 47, 62, 88, 92, 122, 133, 153, 155, 161, 169, 180, 200
  revelation of, xxv, xxxi, xxxv, xxxviii, 38, 43, 73, 179 (*see also under* thought)
  and testimony, 89–92, 151
  ulteriority of, 37–39, 100, 144
  See also ontology; truth
Bergson, Henri, 27
Bible, the, 100, 111, 183, 203
Bloch, Ernst, 108–109
Bonhoeffer, Dietrich, xii–xiii
Bruno, Giordano, 192, 204

Christianity, xii–xiv, xxi, 8, 119–120, 125
commitment
  to Being, 42, 106
  ideological (problem of), 151–154
  moral, 150–154, 169
  personal, xxvii, xxxv, 73, 128, 176
  to truth, xix, 149
common sense, vi, xxxvi–xxxviii, 97–98, 122, 160, 181, 185–203
community, xxxiv, xxxvii, 8, 34, 74, 88, 197, 199–201
critique, xxx, 33, 109, 163
  excessive, 174–177
  See also under ideology
Croce, Benedetto, xxi–xxii, 120, 175

Cusano, Nicola, 27

Descartes, Renè, 187, 204
  cogito of, xxvii
Del Noce, Augusto, 10, 156, 164
demythification, 21, 24–25
demystification, 18, 20, 25, 77, 95–96, 97, 101–102, 110, 129–131
depersonalization, 51, 62, 73, 138, 199–200
Destutt de Tracy, A., 82–83
Dilthey, Wilhelm, 8, 175
discourse
  explicit, 17, 95–96, 99, 129
  expressive, 17, 82, 86, 93, 95
  ideological, 86, 94, 136, 139, 147, 150, 152
  instrumental, 17, 26, 136, 150
  philosophical, 5, 21, 23, 86, 136, 140–142, 144, 152, 161, 177–180
  semantic and cryptic, 18–20
  technical, 26, 127, 179–180
  totality of, 20, 65, 67
dogmatism, xviii, xxxi, xxxiv–xxxvi, 58, 83
Dostoevsky, Fyodor Mikhailovich, 118–119, 123, 163
  Brothers Karamazov, the, 118
  Demons, 118, 123, 163

effectiveness
  of historical thought, 4, 26, 34, 81
  of philosophy, 148–151, 182
empiricism, xxxii, 31–33, 130, 194
Engels, Friedrich, 107
Enlightenment, the, xxxv, 93, 120, 157–159, 173, 188, 194, 197, 201
Epicurus, 110
error, xxxiv, 22, 36, 50, 72–73, 77–78, 85, 89, 103, 121, 124–128, 157, 174
ethics, 5, 122, 162, 169, 183, 201
existentialism, xx,–xxii, 8, 175, 201

faith, religious, 144, 146, 151, 168
false consciousness, 93–96, 101
  See also masking
fanaticism, xviii, xxxviii, 3, 8, 26, 59, 158-159, 182
Feuerbach, Ludwig, xxii, 163
Fichte, Johann Gottlieb, 8, 190, 204
fideism, 3, 147, 168, 174
formativity (theory of), xii, xxvi, xxix, 96
formulation(s) of truth, xix, xxxii, 15, 21, 23, 39–40, 42, 52–78, 92, 100, 125, 139–142, 179, 198
  historical, xxxiii, 16, 39, 42, 52–55, 57–60, 62–63, 73, 109, 199
  multiplicity of, xiii, xix, 16, 39, 53–60; 66, 88
  personal, xix, xxxii–xxxiv, 25, 44, 55, 62–63, 69–70, 74, 88, 107, 109, 199
  See also interpretation
freedom, xxi–xxii, xxiv–xxv, xxvii, xxxii–xxxiii, xxxv, 16, 37, 43–44, 64–65 67, 72, 74, 97, 110, 117, 119, 125, 127, 133, 143, 146, 148–149, 164, 199–201
  and Being, 25–27
  ontology of, xii, xv, xviii
  originary, xxix, 14, 91–92
  of revelatory thought, 25–27

Gadamer, Hans-Georg, xvii, xxxiv, 10
Galilei, Galileo, 192
God, xii, xiv, 11, 44, 118, 124, 143, 172, 187
good sense, 160, 187–188, 190, 192
Guzzo, Augusto, xix, xxi, 44

Habermas, Jürgen, 108–109
Hegel, Georg Wilhelm Friedrich, xxi, xxii, xxv, 8–9, 143, 153, 163, 169, 175, 180, 185–186, 190–191, 195, 197, 204

Heidegger, Martin, xiii–xiv, xvii, xix, xxii, xxiii, xxvi, 5–6, 8, 27–28, 35, 44–45, 57, 72, 77, 100, 143, 175
Heraclitus, 27
hermeneutics, xi–xii, xv, xvii, xxv, xxxiv, xxxvii–xxxviii, 47, 50, 52, 54–55, 65, 69
historical conditionality, 8, 82, 136, 161, 175
historical forms, xxxii, 5–6, 31, 33–34, 37–43, 52–55, 57, 138, 145–146
historical situation. *See* situation
historical substance, xxiv, 15, 61–62, 73, 133, 146
historicism, xxiv–xxv, xxxii, xxxv, 4–5, 13–15, 17, 31–33, 48, 73, 87, 119, 149, 156–157, 162, 175, 188, 195
  integral, 13, 25, 31
  sociological, 91, 94, 101–103, 110, 126–127, 130
historicity
  in common sense, 188, 197–199
  destiny of, 186–189
  in ideology, 81–86, 89, 93–97, 101–102, 121, 131–136, 138–139, 145, 149
  of interpretation, xxxiii, xxxviii, 37–38, 48–52, 56, 58–59, 106, 135, 198
  of philosophical thought, 135, 148
  of values, 33–35
history, xxxii–xxxiii, 13, 17, 25, 48–49, 54, 58, 72–75, 84–85, 96, 102, 106, 126, 134, 136, 145–155, 177, 180, 188, 195
  of Being, xiii, xxv, 37–38, 40
  of ideology, 81, 83, 93
  of metaphysics, xxv, xxxii
  permanent values in, 32–37, 43
  of philosophy, xxix, 14, 45, 100, 168, 185
  philosophy of, 157
  secret, 95, 129
Hölderlin, Friedrich, xiii–xiv
human condition, 121, 125, 127, 131, 138, 143, 153
humanism, xiv, 26, 44, 197
Husserl, Edmund, xxiv, 186

ideology, 4, 81, 152, 155, 161–162, 195
  critique of, xxv, xxxiv–xxxv, 103, 107
  as distinct from philosophy, 81–89, 93–107, 115–124, 131–139, 147–151, 155, 169–170
  meaning of, 113–115
  negativity of, 126–131
implied, the, 19–20, 67–68, 95–96, 130, 182
  distinct from the implicit, 76–77
  explication of, 98–101
import
  ontological, 36, 41, 51, 73, 90–92, 95, 136, 151, 159 (*see also* ontology)
  political, 155–156
  truth-bearing, 133, 153
ineffable, the, 23–24, 71, 76, 101, 142, 145
  distinct from the inexhaustible, 23–24, 141–144
  See also under Being, truth
inexhaustible, the, 20, 130, 141
  ontology of, 23–24, 101, 141–142, 199
  origin, 66, 75, 130–131, 179
  See also under Being; truth
interpretation
  constitution of, 69–71
  individual, xxxiii–xxxiv, 23, 66, 88, 193
  personal, 4, 16, 21, 87, 91, 107, 122, 133, 137, 179, 182
  personality of, 49, 71–75
  of truth, xxxii, xxxiv, 16, 39–40, 43, 47, 52, 55–56, 67, 69, 74, 97, 103, 122, 129, 133, 148, 199 (*see also* formulation(s) of truth)
  See also revelatory thought; truth

instrumentalism, 83–84, 158
  See also praxis(m)
instrumentalization. *See under* discourse; reason; thought
interval
  between explicit and implicit, 17, 20, 93, 95
  between said and unsaid, 18–19, 65, 98
  between truth and person, 62
irrationalism, 24–25, 76, 129–130, 135, 137–138

Jaspers, Karl, xix, xxi–xxii, 8, 175, 192, 204
John, Saint (the Evangelist), 28

Kant, Immanuel, xxiii, 175, 187, 189, 190, 204
Kierkegaard, Søren, xix, xxii, 36, 45, 143, 163, 169, 175
kindredness, xxxiv, 10, 34–35, 41–42, 44, 74, 164

Lesbic rule, 117, 162–163
logos. *See* word, the
Lukàcs Georgy, 163

Mannheim, Karl, 82, 84, 108, 110
Manzoni, Alessandro, 188, 204
Marcel, Gabriel, xxii, 44
Marx, Karl, xxi, 82–84, 89, 94–95, 97, 102–103, 107–110, 143, 150–151, 156–159, 163 169, 175, 195, 197
Marxism. *See* Marx, Karl
masking, 14, 18, 56–57, 93–98, 107, 115, 131
  See also false consciousness
materialism, historical, 101–103
metaphysics, xxii, xxv–xxvi, xxxi–xxxii, xxxv, 84, 87–88, 107, 130, 138–139, 144, 157, 161, 175, 186, 199
Milton, John, 73, 78
Montaigne, Michel de, 204
myth, 21, 24, 67, 75, 97–98, 104, 122, 132, 141–142, 173–174

Napoleon, 83
neo-enlightenment, xxi, 151, 156–157
Nietzsche, Friedrich, xi, xxxii, 5, 31, 93, 99, 110–111, 143, 169, 175
  See also will to power

ontological opening, xxv, 15, 58, 62, 87, 132–133, 136, 146, 197–198, 200–201, 203
ontological relation, xxiv, 5, 43, 47, 90–91, 96, 107, 122–123, 134, 155, 180, 196, 200–202
ontology, xii, xv, xviii, xxii, xxiv, xxvi, xxxii, 5, 23–24, 28, 35, 44, 47, 76, 100–101, 139, 141–144, 199
  negative, 5, 28, 76, 100, 139, 141–144
origin, the 14, 24, 27, 40–42, 45, 179–180, 185
  history as, 48, 95
  as inexhaustible, 20, 66, 75, 131, 180
  See also under Being; truth
originarity
  of Being, 36
  of interpretation, 47–77
  of practice, 160–162
  of tradition, 40–42
originary bond, 16, 90, 96, 117, 122, 126–127, 131, 134, 138, 148, 155
originary solidarity. *See under* solidarity
othering, 55–57
  See also alterity

panpoliticism, 3, 83, 156, 159, 173–174
pantheism, 84–85, 130
Pareto, Vilfredo, 94, 107, 110

Pareyson, Luigi (works of)
"Angoscia o Rischio?," xx
Esistenza e persona, xxi–xxiii, 3, 7–9, 110, 164, 204
Estetica: teoria della formatività, xxv–xxix, 9, 44, 77, 164
Fichte, 8
Iniziativa e libertà, xx
Karl Jaspers, xxin, 8
Ontologia della libertà: il male e la sofferenza, xv, xxivn
Studi sull'esistenzialismo, xix, xxi, xxiii
"The Unity of Philosophy," xxix–xxxi, 8
Parmenides, 5, 28
Pascal, Blaise, 57, 78, 122–123, 163, 199, 203–205
Paul, Saint, 28
person, the (*la persona*), xix, xxi–xxv, xxvii, xxxiii, 14–17, 21, 42, 47, 49, 51–52, 62, 64, 67, 71–74, 86–88, 116, 132–136, 148, 155, 159, 179, 199–200
personalism, xvii, xxii 5, 8, 27, 77, 88, 109, 199, 201
personality, xxix, xxx, xxxiii, 48–52, 62, 68, 71–72, 88–89, 107, 119, 135–136, 139, 199–201
personalization, 51, 62, 73, 134, 138, 199–200
phenomenology, 186, 199
philosopher, the, xx, xxx–xxxi, xxxvi, 74, 100, 123–124, 154–156, 169, 170–171, 185 189, 194, 197
philosophy
authentic, 133–136
and common sense, 185–197
crisis of, 177–178
end of, 174–177
as the guardian of truth, 104–107
and ideology (*see under* ideology)
of the implicit, 77, 98
language of, 180–182
necessity of, 144–148
noble risk of, xxi, 6, 10
of philosophy, xxxvi, 107, 177, 178, 193
plurality of, 138–141
of politics, 151, 160
as problematizing, 193–196
effectiveness of, 148–151, 182
rigor of, 192–193
unity of, xxix–xxx, 5, 8, 101
Plato, xxi, 6, 10, 28, 150, 153–154, 162
Phaedo, xxi, 10
The Republic, 150, 153–154, 162
Plotinus, xvii, 27, 146, 163–164
poetry, 98, 192
politician, the, xxxvi, 151, 154–156, 158–159 202
politics, xi, xx, xxxi–xxxii, xxxv–xxxvi, 3, 6, 32, 84, 86, 89, 101–102, 104–105, 113, 144–145, 147, 150–151, 154, 156–160, 162, 167–170, 173–174, 176, 178, 182
practice. *See under* originarity
pragmatism, 85
pragmaticization. *See under* reason; thought
praxis(m), 4, 25, 31–32, 40, 43, 74–76, 83–84, 90–91, 102, 115, 119, 130, 132–133, 149, 157–160, 173
panpolitical, 18, 91, 106, 119, 130, 149
theory and, xxxvi–xxxvii, 4, 43, 81, 84, 86, 89–92, 102, 113, 148–151, 154, 157–159, 201–202 (*see also under* unity)
Pseudo-Dionysius, 28, 163

rationalism, xxv, xxxv, 18, 24, 76, 129, 137–138, 173, 194
reality, historical, 13 34, 40, 83–84, 89–90, 94, 97–98, 116, 128
Realpolitik, 102, 159
reason, xxxiv, xxx–xxxi, xxxviii, 3–4, 95, 97, 143, 150–151, 153, 156,

reason *(continued)*
158–159, 163, 187–190, 194–195, 197, 199–201
human, 81, 159, 169
instrumental (instrumentalization of), xxxi, xxxv, 37, 113, 121, 123
pragmatic, 18, 85, 151
self-correcting, 135, 167–168
technical (technicization of), xxxv, 18, 83–87, 89, 91, 104, 106, 120, 126, 135, 199
without truth, 4, 24–25, 129, 173 (*see also* technicism)
relativism, xviii, xxv, xxviii, xxx–xxxii, xxxvi–xxxvii, 4, 38–39, 40, 50, 58–59, 76, 138–140, 175
religion, vii, xxxi, xxxvi, 3, 6, 26, 74, 104–105, 120, 122, 144, 147, 167–174, 176, 178, 182
revolution, xxv, 5, 42–43, 76, 84, 157, 174 195

Sartre, Jean-Paul, xxii
Scheler, Max, xxiv, 107
Schelling, Friedrich Wilhelm Joseph, 180, xv, xvii, 6, 10, 27–28, 77, 142–145, 163–164
Schopenhauer, Arthur, 183, 186, 203–204
Schwärmerei, 75, 147, 197
scientific method, the, 170–171, 191
scientism, 3, 171, 174
Shaftesbury, 3rd Earl of (Anthony Ashley Cooper), 183, 188, 203–204
situation, 4, 5, 10, 25
definition, xxivn18
historical, xxiv–xxx, xxxv, 4–5, 13–19, 26, 33, 39, 48, 51–53, 73–75, 81–83, 85–87, 89, 91, 93, 95–97, 108–109, 115, 122, 126, 132–137, 146, 150–154, 187–188, 195, 198–201
skepticism, xviii, xxxv 4, 8, 50, 59, 172, 185
social sciences, xxxi, 6, 32–33, 177
solidarity, xiv, xxiv
originary, xxxvi, 5, 15, 22, 38, 47, 86, 132, 154, 196
subjectivism, 49, 62–64, 88, 175
superstructure, 82–84, 109, 150, 195

technicism, 4, 6, 127, 147, 182
technicization. *See under* reason; thought
technics, xxxvii, 85, 91–92, 104, 118, 120, 123, 129, 135, 144, 150–151, 153, 155, 160, 162, 169, 178, 180–181
theology, negative, 23, 28, 145
theory. *See under* praxis(m)
thought
empirical, 32–33
empty, 33, 135, 176
expressive, xxxv, 6, 10, 13, 18, 25, 81–83, 93, 95, 97–100, 104–105, 116–117, 120, 130, 132, 149, 162
historical, 17–20, 26, 54, 88, 96, 104
historicization of, xxxv, 82, 85–87, 104
ideological, 82, 86–87, 89, 93–99, 102, 113–116, 120, 123, 128–130, 133, 138, 146–147, 149, 152–153
instrumental (instrumentalization of), xxxi, xxxiv, xxxviii, 4, 6, 18, 54, 85–86, 88, 91–92, 104–106, 114, 116, 126–128, 135, 151–152, 155, 160, 162, 194, 199
ontological, 17, 86, 89, 96–97, 103, 105–107, 116, 130, 144, 146, 148, 151, 159–161
pragmatic (pragmaticization of), 4, 18, 26, 81, 83–85, 88–89, 93, 96, 103, 105, 116–117, 120–121, 130, 132, 135–136, 147, 149, 153, 155
revelatory, xxxi–xxxii, 6, 10, 13, 15–16, 18–21, 24–26, 81–82, 86, 89, 92–93, 96–98, 100–101, 104–107, 116–117, 127, 129–132,

135, 144, 146–149, 153 (*see also under* truth)
technical (technicization of), 25, 52, 84, 103–105, 113, 123, 160
time
expression of, 15–16, 48–49, 51, 96, 123
falsification of, 95–98
totality, xxiii, xxv, 5, 20, 64–67, 69, 83, 101, 107–108, 129, 131, 140, 143, 175, 180
tradition, xxxiv, xxxvii–xxxviii, 40–42, 44, 97–98 117, 143, 161, 187, 188
transcendence, xi–xiii, xxi, xxix, 8, 44, 63, 85, 88, 139, 145, 152
truth
atemporal, 16, 57–60, 86, 137
ineffability of, xxxiv, 22, 39, 71, 75–76, 100–101, 141–142, 144
inexhaustibility of, 39–40, 63–67, 69, 88–89, 98–101, 103, 106–107, 129, 138–144, 148, 153, 179, 182, 199
interpretation of, xxxii, xxxiv, 16, 39–40, 43, 47, 52, 55–56, 67, 69, 74, 97, 103, 122, 129, 133, 148, 199
listening to, 88, 148, 200
as origin, xxxii, xxxv, xxxvii, 16, 21–22, 63, 75–76, 88, 131, 140, 179, 198, 200
pathway to, 5, 14–15, 39, 48–49, 52–53, 56, 73, 86–87, 91, 97, 129, 130, 132, 135, 198
recovery of, 182
renunciation of, 153, 177–178
revelation of, xxxii–xxxiii, xxxvii, 14–17, 19, 22–23, 43, 48–49, 51–52, 56, 63, 74–75, 91–92, 97, 101, 114, 123, 141, 162
ulteriority of, xxxiii–xxxiv, 19, 22, 24, 37–39, 61, 63, 67, 70–71, 75–76, 88–89, 100, 140–142, 144, 179–180
unicity of, 53–54, 57–59, 70, 73, 138
unobjectifiability of, 20–22, 25, 88, 100

ulteriority. *See under* Being; truth
unity
originary (of theory and praxis), xxxvi, 5, 15, 22, 38, 47, 86, 132, 154, 196
of philosophy (*see under* philosophy)
unsaid, the 18–20, 40, 63, 65–68, 76–77, 96–99

value(s)
Heidegger's critique of, 35–37, 44
historical durability of, 33–36, 40–44
historicity of, 33–35
permanence of, 31–46, 144
speculative, 16–17
Vattimo, Gianni, iii, vii, xi, xxvi, xxxii, xxxvi–xxxvii, 111
Vico, Giambattista, xvii, 97, 117, 134, 162–163, 196–197
violence, 26, 145, 195
virtuality, 60, 63–65, 147
vis veri, 21, 97–98, 183, 197, 204
vis vocabuli, 22, 27
Voltaire (François-Marie Arouet), 110

Weltanschauungen, 8, 84, 114–115
will to power, 93, 169
See also Nietzsche, Friedrich
Wittgenstein, Ludwig, 186, 204
word, the, 16–24, 98–100, 141–143, 181–182, 197
work of art, xiii, xxvi, 22, 59 61, 69, 182